The Transfer of Rights in Securitisations

The Transfer of Rights in Securitisations

A Law and Economics Analysis

Chike J Emedosi

eleven

Published, sold and distributed by Eleven
P.O. Box 85576
2508 CG The Hague
The Netherlands
Tel.: +31 70 33 070 33
Fax: +31 70 33 070 30
e-mail: sales@elevenpub.nl
www.elevenpub.com

Sold and distributed in USA and Canada
Independent Publishers Group
814 N. Franklin Street
Chicago, IL 60610, USA
Order Placement: +1 800 888 4741
Fax: +1 312 337 5985
orders@ipgbook.com
www.ipgbook.com

Eleven is an imprint of Boom (Den Haag).

ISBN 978-90-4730-226-1
ISBN 978-94-0011-461-6 (E-book)

Table of Contents

Preface

Securitisation is a funding mechanism which typically involves the transfer of multiple loan receivables and related security rights. A common feature in the assignment laws of many countries is a requirement that the transfer should be made public in order to be fully effective against third parties. The principle underlying this requirement is that assignments affect third parties, and because of that, they should only arise when they are visible to third parties.

The publicity act traditionally required for transferring loan receivables is that the debtors should be notified of the transfer. Notification to debtors makes the assignment visible in the sense that third parties can ascertain the true "owner" of the loan receivable by enquiring of the relevant debtor. Some transfer methods, such as the English equitable assignment and the Scottish trust, do not require debtor notification or any other true form of publicity for their validity. However, notification may be used to give increased protection against third parties and the debtor. One extreme exception to the publicity principle is an assignment under articles 1321 to 1326 of the French Civil Code. That assignment does not require notification or any publicity for it to be fully effective against third parties. But notification is required for the assignment to be enforceable against the debtor.

Regarding the transfer of security rights, the publicity required usually depends on the type of property and the legal system involved. In some cases, registration in a public register is required. Registration makes the transfer visible in the sense that third parties can ascertain the actual "owner" of the security right by checking the relevant asset register.

These publicity requirements raise a number of issues in securitisation. Given the multiple number of debtors and security rights involve in the transaction, notifying each debtor and registering each security right can be prohibitively costly. The requirement of publicity also makes transfers of future receivables impracticable, as there will be no debtor to notify, or security right to register, at the time of the transaction. Moreover, the transaction parties may prefer to keep the transfer secret for genuine commercial reasons.

Countries are liberalising their assignment laws in a bid to facilitate securitisation in their jurisdictions. Businesses have also devised workarounds that circumvent the publicity requirements when structuring securitisation transactions. These laws and workarounds ("the solutions") differ in their approaches and proprietary effects. The differences, in turn, affect the development of securitisation in various jurisdictions. This book compares the solutions available in a selection of common law, civil law and mixed law systems for transferring loan receivables and related security rights in securitisations, using England, France and Scotland as focus jurisdictions. It aims to determine the solution, or a model solution, that is most efficient for securitisation, using a law and economics approach.

The book is organised into two parts. Part I considers the role securitisation played in the 2007/08 financial crisis, and why securitisation still appeals to businesses and regulators despite the crisis. It contends that securitisation amplified the losses resulting from the crisis, but it was not the primary cause of the crisis. It demonstrates that the credit events that followed the crisis stimulated global efforts to revive the securitisation market. The analysis in this part lays the background for the attempt in Part II to offer solutions that will further the revival effort.

Part II focuses on the comparative analysis. It establishes that the preferred solutions in the focus regimes are the English equitable assignment, the French *bordereau* and the Scottish trust. The assignation by registration approach recently adopted in the Moveable Transactions (Scotland) Act 2023 (hereafter "the registration solution") is also considered in the comparative analysis. It is contended that although the registration solution is the most efficient of the solutions examined, it is not Pareto optimal. This is demonstrated through a novel law and economics approach, which uses a leximetric methodology to measure the transfer solutions against six policy objectives. The book, therefore, proposes a model solution that improves the registration solution and achieves an outcome closest to Pareto optimality. Additionally, it argues that the model solution is transplantable to French law but will require some refinements for it to be transplantable to English law.

Acknowledgements

In writing this book I was assisted by a great many people, only some of whom it is possible to acknowledge here.

First of all, I am grateful to Dr Alisdair MacPherson and Professor John Paterson. The support I received from them in completing the research that became the foundation of this book is invaluable. Indeed, this book would have been much poorer without their suggestions, counsel and unparalleled knowledge.

My gratitude extends to Professor Andrew Steven, Professor Roderick Paisley and the editors of the European International Insolvency Law series at Eleven International Publishing (i.e., Professor Rolef de Weijs and A.M. Verweij), for their insightful comments on the book. Their expertise and thoughtful feedback have helped to improve this book immeasurably. I also wish to thank Dr Tom Burns and Dr Hamish Patrick for their support in the early stages of the research. Dr Burns inspired my interest in the topic, and Dr Patrick provided helpful advice regarding practice.

I must also express my gratitude to the University of Aberdeen and the Scottish Universities Law Institute (SULI) for their generous support in funding the research on which this book is based.

I am thankful to the publishing team at Eleven International Publishing, who expertly steered the publication process. I am particularly grateful to Audrey McMahon and Sanne Hamelink for their unwavering patience and kind assurances. Additionally, I owe special thanks to Rebecca Bryan for her exceptional copy-editing skills. Her keen eye for detail greatly enhanced the clarity and coherence of this book.

It would be remiss of me if I failed to acknowledge the one person whose encouragement and moral support kept me sane and focused throughout this process. To my wife, Chidimma, thank you for your tremendous understanding and patience. This book is dedicated to you.

Part I

1 INTRODUCTION

1.1 Background

The volume of global securitisation issuances declined significantly after the 2007/08 global financial crisis.[1] This was mainly due to lack of demand from investors, occasioned by the perceived role of securitisation in the financial crisis, and the inhibitive regulatory reforms that were introduced after the crisis.[2] The regulatory agenda has since changed from one of inhibition to that of revitalisation,[3] the argument being that a revitalised securitisation market is crucial for financial stability and the growth of economies.[4] This has resulted in various legal and regulatory reforms, at both national and supranational levels, aimed at reviving the market.[5] Recent global challenges, such as climate change and the Covid-19 pandemic, have also added a new impetus to the revival efforts. Securitisation is considered a key funding tool to finance a green energy transition and a recovery from

1 Basel Committee on Banking Supervision and Board of the International Organization of Securities Commissions, *Criteria for Identifying Simple, Transparent and Comparable Securitisations* (Consultative Paper, Bank for International Settlements 2014) 3f. For the historical data report of issuances in Europe and the United States of America see Association for Financial Markets in Europe, 'Securitisation Data Report – Q4 2014' (AFME 2015) 3 <https://www.sifma.org/wp-content/uploads/2017/05/afme-securitisation-data-report-fourth-quarter-2014.pdf> accessed 08 May 2024.

2 Basel Committee on Banking Supervision and Board of the International Organization of Securities Commissions (n 1) 3f. For discussion of some of the reforms introduced in the European Union see Graham Penn and Thomas Papadogiannis, 'Regulating Securitisation in the Aftermath of the Global Financial Crisis: Lessons from Europe' (2021) 36 Journal of International Banking Law and Regulation 225, 236ff.

3 See e.g. Bank of England and European Central Bank, 'The Case for a Better Functioning Securitisation Market in the European Union' (May 2014) <https://www.ecb.europa.eu/pub/pdf/other/ecb-boe_case_better_functioning_securitisation_marketen.pdf> accessed 08 May 2024. See also International Monetary Fund, 'Global Financial Stability Report: Navigating the Financial Challenges Ahead' (IMF 2009) 77.

4 E.g. the European Commission considered securitisation as the bedrock of its ambitious Capital Markets Union and estimated in 2015 that a revived securitisation market could provide more than €120 billion to the economy whilst at the same time enhancing financial stability. See European Commission, 'Action Plan on Building a Capital Markets Union' (Com 468 final, 2015) 4.

5 E.g. the Basel Committee on Banking Supervision published in 2016 an updated standard for the regulatory capital treatment of securitisation exposures, which introduced a preferential capital treatment for "simple, transparent and comparable" securitisations. See Basel Committee on Banking Supervision, *Revisions to the Securitisation Framework: Amended to Include the Alternative Capital Treatment for "Simple, Transparent and Comparable" Securitisations* (Bank for International Settlements 2016) paras 113ff. For an outline of the revitalisation efforts in the EU, England, France and Scotland, see section 3.3.

the Covid-19 crisis.[6] Yet global issuances remain impaired.[7] This is especially true in Europe (including the United Kingdom), where issuances have been steadily declining since the financial crisis, with the total issuance in 2023 declining by almost 21% from 2018 and 47% from the 2007 pre-crisis level.[8]

Securitisation involves the sale of a pool of receivables (typically loans) by an originator to a special purpose vehicle (SPV) for the purpose of transforming the receivables into liquid assets (such as bonds and commercial papers). It is a complex financial technique, and its success depends on whether a particular jurisdiction has the legal infrastructure to enable every aspect of the transaction. It has been noted that any deficiencies in meeting the legal requirements of the transaction can lead to "a complete transactional bar".[9] Various jurisdictions address these requirements differently, with each solution having differing effects on the scope and development of securitisation in the relevant jurisdiction.

A major requirement that arises when structuring securitisation transactions is the need to effect a true sale of the receivables and related security rights. Legal systems generally require a publicity act to be completed before the transfer of property rights can be fully effective (see discussion in chapters 5, 6 and 7). The following has been written about property rights and the need for publicity:

> [b]ecause property rights affect third parties, natural justice requires that such rights should only arise in circumstances where they are apparent to third parties. In other words, property rights should be public.[10]

---

6 See e.g. Organisation for Economic Co-operation and Development, *Mobilising Bond Markets for a Low-Carbon Transition* (OECD 2017) 85ff; Council Regulation (EU) 2021/557 of 31 March 2021 amending Regulation (EU) 2017/2402 laying down a general framework for securitisation and creating a specific framework for simple, transparent and standardised securitisation to help the recovery from the COVID-19 crisis [2021] OJ L116/1.

7 A major exception is the United States of America, where issuances have generally recovered. This is mainly due to the activities of government-sponsored entities like Fannie Mae and Freddie Mac. See Association for Financial Markets in Europe, 'Securitisation Data Report – Q2 2019' (AFME 2019) 6 <https://www.sifma.org/wp-content/uploads/2019/09/Europe-Securitisation-Quarterly-2019-09-23-AFME-SIFMA.pdf> accessed 08 May 2024.

8 Association for Financial Markets in Europe, 'Securitisation Data Report – Q4 2023 & 2023 Full Year' (AFME 2024) 22 <https://www.afme.eu/Portals/0/DispatchFeaturedImages/Securitisation%20Data%20Report%20Q4%202023%20and%202023%20Full%20Year.pdf> accessed 08 May 2024. For the 2007 data see Association for Financial Markets in Europe, 'Securitisation Data Report – Q4 2009' (AFME 2010) 3 <https://www.sifma.org/wp-content/uploads/2017/05/afme-esf-securitisation-data-report-2009-q4.pdf> accessed 08 May 2024.

9 YA Dvorak, 'Transplanting Asset Securitization: Is the Grass Green Enough on the Other Side?' (2001) 38 Houston Law Review 541, 542. See also Philip Wood, *Law and Practice of International Finance* (Sweet & Maxwell 2008) para 28.07.

10 Joanna Benjamin, *Interests in Securities: A Proprietary Law Analysis of the International Securities Markets* (Oxford University Press 2000) 105f.

Although the above quotation relates to the creation of property rights, it is also true for the transfer of property rights. The nature of the publicity required depends on the type of property and the legal system involved. In some jurisdictions, the standard publicity act required for loan receivables is debtor notification. In respect of security rights, registration is typically used.

The difficulty is that a securitisation transaction typically involves multiple loans and related security rights.[11] Notifying each debtor, or registering the transfer of each security right, can be commercially inconvenient. The originator may also wish to keep the sales confidential for genuine commercial reasons. In addition, the requirement of publicity can make transfers of future receivables impracticable since there will be no debtor to notify, or security right to register, at the time of the transaction.

Existing literature has discussed various aspects of these transfer issues in the context of loan receivables.[12] There is, however, scant attention paid to issues involving the related security rights. Yet the value of ensuring the transfer of security rights in securitisations is considerable. For example, in determining the capital requirement of securitisation exposures for banks and other similarly regulated financial institutions, the risk-mitigating effects of security rights attached to receivables are considered.[13] Also, security rights are key factors considered by credit rating agencies in determining the credit quality of securitisation products.[14]

This book addresses this gap by focusing mainly on the transfer of security rights. It examines and compares the legal solutions for transferring security rights in securitisations, using a law and economics approach. It considers the solutions available in a common law system (using English law as a case study), a civil law system (using France) and a mixed legal system (using Scotland), and aims to determine a model solution that is most efficient for securitisations.

This book acknowledges that a security right is inherently tied to the related loan. The purpose of a right in security is to ensure the performance of a loan. There can be no security where there is no underlying obligation.[15] The loan is the principal right, while the right in security is an accessory. This means that a discussion of the property law principle

---

11 E.g. the Elland RMBS 2018 Plc transaction involves 39,000 mortgage loans. See Elland RMBS 2018 Plc (Prospectus, 13 December 2018) <https://www.rns-pdf.londonstockexchange.com/rns/5340K_1-2018-12-14.pdf> accessed 28 May 2024.

12 See e.g. Florian Burnat, 'Titrisation v securitisation: a legal comparison of securitisation in France and the United Kingdom' (2008) 2 Law and Financial Markets Review 143–157; Tom Burns, 'The Transfer of Future Rights in Securitisations: A Comparative Study of the Law in England and Scotland' (2009) 24 Journal of International Banking Law and Regulation 35–43.

13 See e.g. Basel Committee on Banking Supervision, *The Basel Framework* (Bank for International Settlements 2022) para 40.94.

14 See Moody's, 'Rating Methodology: Moody's Global Approach to Rating SME Balance Sheet Securitizations' (Moody's Investors Service, July 2021) 2.

15 William M Gordon and Scott Wortley, *Scottish Land Law*, vol 2 (3rd edn, W Green 2020) para 19.07.

of accessoriness is crucial for this book. In particular, this book explores the extent to which *accessorium sequitur principale* applies in the regimes discussed herein. As a general rule, that principle requires that where the principal right is transferred, any accessory rights are automatically transferred with it.[16] If the principle prevails, the transfer of the debt will be enough to carry the related security right. If it does not prevail and a further step is needed to transfer the security right to the SPV, it makes a stronger case for undertaking research (such as this), which focuses principally on the transfer of security rights. Another implication of the accessory nature of the security right is that the transfer of the security rights cannot be discussed in isolation from the related debt. Hence, frequent references to the transfer of the debt are made in this book.

1.2 Structure

This book is organised into two parts. Part I is the introductory part and comprises chapters 2 and 3. The global financial crisis brought securitisation into the limelight. Two influential reports on the financial crisis, the Financial Crisis Inquiry Report and the Turner Review, firmly place securitisation at the heart of the crisis.[17] Also, the inhibitive regulatory reforms and the subsequent revitalisation efforts are direct consequences of the crisis. It is, therefore, relevant to look back at the crisis and discuss the role securitisation played. It is also relevant to consider why securitisation still appeals to businesses despite the crisis, and why a supposed catalyst of the financial crisis became a key solution to the crisis. Part I focuses on these issues. Chapter 2 discusses the nature and process of securitisation, and its role in the lead-up to the crisis. Chapter 3 considers the economic function and value of securitisation.

The analysis in Part I lays the background for the attempt in Part II to offer solutions that will further the efforts to revive securitisation. Part II focuses on the comparative analysis of the transfer solutions in Scotland, England and France. It comprises chapters 4, 5, 6, 7 and 8. Chapter 4 discusses the research methodology. It concludes that the functional approach, the law and economics approach, and the legal transplant are all relevant for the research. Chapters 5 (Scotland), 6 (England) and 7 (France) identify and discuss various solutions available in the focus regimes for transferring security rights, using a doctrinal

16 Other aspects of the accessory principle relate to: (i) the extent and nature of the security right created; (ii) the discharge of the security right; and (iii) the enforcement of the right. But these aspects are beyond the scope of this research and thus will not be discussed. For discussion of the accessory principle in relation to security over land in Scots law see AJM Steven, 'Accessoriness and Security over Land' (2009) 13 Edinburgh Law Review 387.

17 See e.g. Financial Crisis Inquiry Commission, *Final Report of the National Commission on the Causes of the Financial and Economic Crisis in the United States* (2011) xxiii; JA Turner, *The Turner Review: A Regulatory Response to the Global Banking Crisis* (FSA, March 2009) 41.

approach. Chapter 8 compares these solutions with a view to determining the solution, or a model solution, that is most efficient for securitisation. The analysis in this chapter is based on a novel law and economics approach, which uses a leximetric methodology to measure the transfer solutions against six policy objectives. Both Pareto efficiency and Kaldor–Hicks efficiency are used as criteria for measuring efficiency.

The focus on the transfer of rights means that the primary area of research is property law, particularly the law of assignment (or assignation, as it is called in Scotland) in relation to securitisation.

2 SECURITISATION AND THE 2007/08 GLOBAL FINANCIAL CRISIS

The global financial crisis of 2007/08 has drawn much attention to securitisation and its role during and in the build up to the crisis. In particular, some argue that various misaligned incentives inherent in the securitisation process drove the rapid decline in US mortgage lending standards,[1] itself a factor widely viewed as the primary cause of the financial crisis.[2] This chapter examines the role of securitisation in the global financial crisis. It shows that securitisation amplified the losses resulting from the crisis, but was not itself the primary cause of the crisis. It highlights alternative explanations for why mortgage lending standards may have declined.

2.1 Nature and process of securitisation

2.1.1 *Definition of securitisation*

Professor Schwarcz describes securitisation as:

> [a] category of financing transactions in which companies sell rights to payment under mortgage loans, accounts receivable, lease rentals, or other types of income-producing "financial assets" to a trust or other special-purpose vehicle. The goal is to separate these assets from the risks generally associated with the company. The company then can use these assets to raise funds in the capital markets at a lower cost than if the company, with its associated risks, had borrowed the funds.[3]

This description is helpful not just because of its clarity but also because it further states why a company may want to engage in securitisation. However, securitisation may be

---

1 See e.g. Paul Willen, 'Mandated Risk Retention in Mortgage Securitization: An Economist's View' (2014) 104 American Economic Review 82. See also AJ Levitin, AD Pavlov and SM Wachter, 'Securitization: Cause or Remedy of the Financial Crisis?' (2009) Georgetown Law and Economics Research Paper Series No 1462895 <https://papers.ssrn.com/sol3/papers.cfm?abstract_id=1462895> accessed 06 May 2024.

2 See e.g. Alastair Hudson, *The Law of Finance* (2nd edn, Sweet & Maxwell 2013) paras 44.07ff.

3 SL Schwarcz, 'Securitization and Structured Finance' in *Encyclopedia of Financial Globalization* (Elsevier 2011) 1.

useful for other reasons, aside from low-cost funding. Lenders, for example, use securitisation as a risk management tool.[4] The sale to the special purpose vehicle (SPV) transfers both the rights to payment under the financial assets and the risk of non-payment (i.e. the credit risks) associated with the assets from the lender to the SPV on a non-recourse basis.[5] The credit risk transfer function also means that securitisation is an important tool that banks can use to satisfy their regulatory capital requirements.[6]

2.1.2 *Process of securitisation*

A traditional securitisation process involves a company (commonly referred to as the "originator") identifying some of its income-producing financial assets it wishes to securitise (commonly referred to as "receivables"). The receivables can be short term, such as trade receivables that are payable within 30 days, or long term, such as payments due over a period of years under residential mortgage loans, commercial property mortgages, auto loans, credit card receivables and bank loans.[7] They can also be rights to future receivables, such as income from a commercial mortgage lease commencing at a future date, or income from cinema or airplane tickets yet to be sold.[8]

The originator then separates these receivables from its other assets by transferring them to an SPV in return for a purchase price payable immediately on transfer.[9] This is done in order to insulate the receivables from the risk profile of the originator. To achieve this aim, the transfer must be structured as a true sale, such that the receivables are removed from the originator's bankruptcy estate or patrimony after the transaction.[10]

---

4 See section 3.1.2 for discussion of the benefit of securitisation as a risk management tool.

5 Securitisation is a non-recourse funding in which the SPV takes both the rights of payment and the risk of non-payment. In other words, the company will not be liable to the SPV or the investors in the event of a default on the receivable or the bond. BG Buchanan, *Securitization and the Global Economy: History and Prospects for the Future* (Palgrave Macmillan 2017) 57.

6 See section 3.2.1 for discussion of the regulatory capital requirements.

7 SL Schwarcz, 'The Alchemy of Asset Securitization' (1994) 1 Stanford Journal of Law, Business & Finance 133, 135.

8 Tom Burns, 'The Transfer of Future Rights in Securitisations: A Comparative Study of the Law in England and Scotland' (2009) 24 Journal of International Banking Law and Regulation 35, 37.

9 Hudson (n 2) para 44.10.

10 ibid para 44.15. Securitisation has blossomed into different varieties, many of which do not involve a true sale of receivables. An example of these types of securitisation is the synthetic securitisation. For synthetic securitisations, only the credit risks associated with the receivables are transferred, while the ownership of the receivables remains with the originator. This is typically achieved through the purchase of a credit protection by way of a credit default swap from investors, while the underlying assets (which becomes the "reference entity") remains in the balance sheet of the originator. This contrasts with the traditional true-sale securitisation where both the ownership and credit risks are transferred. This book is focused on traditional (true-sale) securitisations.

The SPV finances the purchase of the receivables by issuing debt securities[11] in the capital market. The maturity of the receivables generally determines the type of debt security issued. For example, a commercial paper issuance may be preferred when the maturity is short term (like trade receivables with maturities ranging up to 270 days).[12] Bonds or notes may be issued where the maturity is long term.[13] These securities represent the right to receive periodical payments from the SPV. The SPV, in turn, fulfils its payment obligations from cash flows generated under the acquired receivables. (The debt securities issued by the SPV will hereafter be referred to as "bonds".)

The bonds are usually issued in multiple tranches with varying yields, credit ratings and maturities to optimise their risk profile.[14] The senior tranche typically has the highest credit rating, the lowest interest rate and a priority right of payment on the securities.[15] The most junior or subordinate tranche has a low or no credit rating and the highest interest rate, will be first to absorb the transaction's credit risks and ranks last on payment.[16] The mezzanine tranche (or intermediate tranche) will usually have a credit rating, with the interest rate and the payment priority rank between the senior and the subordinate tranches. Generally, the senior tranches are sold to investors who are averse to high credit risks; the mezzanine tranches are sold to investors willing to take some credit risks for higher yield, while the originator retains the subordinate tranches.

To ensure that the bonds are highly rated, various credit enhancements are structured into the transaction.[17] Credit enhancement protects investors against incurring losses on their investments when losses occur in the underlying asset pool. It may be provided internally by the originator or externally by a third party.[18] An example of internal credit enhancement is over-collateralisation. This involves the transfer of receivables of a greater face value than the consideration paid by the SPV. The excess value is held to cover payments on the bonds in the event of a default. Other forms of internal credit enhancements often used include the creation of excess spreads – that is, a surplus difference between the interest paid by the debtors and the interest paid out on the bonds. External credit enhancements often used include the purchase of an insurance policy to cover credit losses, standby letters of credit and surety bonds.

11 The term "securities" has multiple legal meanings. For the avoidance of doubt, the term as used in this chapter means debt securities such as bonds, notes and commercial papers, unless the context states otherwise.
12 Commercial papers are short-term debt securities. See Louise Gullifer and Jennifer Payne, *Corporate Finance Law: Principles and Policy* (3rd edn, Hart 2020) 30.
13 Bonds and notes are long-term debt securities – ibid 34.
14 Solomon Deku and Alper Kara, *Securitization: Past, Present and Future* (Palgrave Macmillan 2017) 14.
15 ibid.
16 ibid.
17 Hudson (n 2) para 44.17.
18 Philip Wood, *Law and Practice of International Finance* (Sweet & Maxwell 2008) para 28.38.

The type(s) and amount of enhancements required for any given security to be issued at the desired rating are primarily determined by the credit quality of the receivables and the nature of the bonds being issued. Rating agencies dictate the number of credit enhancements necessary by estimating the losses the asset would suffer under conditions of extreme stress.[19] This estimation is normally based on the historical credit profile of the securitised assets.[20] It has been noted that the highest-rated securities will generally have enhancements at levels several times the highest historical default rates associated with the securitised assets.[21] For instance, a credit card pool with a historical default rate of 3% might require an enhancement cover of a 12% loss rate, i.e. four times the historical default rate. Other essential criteria usually required by rating agencies include legal opinions regarding important commercial and bankruptcy issues – like the degree to which the structure effects a true sale transfer and the bankruptcy remoteness of the SPV.

Another important aspect of securitisation is the servicing of the receivables. In most instances, the originator is preferred to act as a servicing agent and continue collecting the receivables on behalf of the SPV in return for a fee.[22] There are at least four reasons why this is so. The first reason is efficiency. Since the debtors are customers of the originator, the originator will already have payment systems in place, and it will be more efficient to continue with such systems. The second reason is cost. Appointing a different servicer may result in a bank account change, notice of which to the debtors will be necessary. Such notice will be costly given the multiple debtors that are typically involved in securitisation transactions. The third reason relates to customer relationships. Notifying the debtors of the new bank account and servicer may negatively impact the commercial relationship between the originator and the customer/debtor. The originator will want to avoid such eventuality. The fourth reason is that the originator may wish to use the service fees as a form of profit extraction from the transaction.[23]

Any surplus income from the receivables (i.e. profit), after all necessary repayments on the bonds have been made, is extracted from the SPV and paid to the originator using various profit extraction methods. This includes payment of servicing fees or administration fees to the originator, payment of a deferred consideration on the receivables to the originator and payment of a high interest rate on the subordinate (or equity) tranche held

---

19 Standard & Poor's, 'General Criteria: Principles of Credit Ratings' (16 February 2011) 3 <https://www.standardandpoors.com/en_US/delegate/getPDF;jsessionid=5AAFCE21839FDC82DA24C52F4A2587AF?articleId=1903324> accessed 28 May 2024.

20 Where a historic profile is unavailable, a comparison or benchmarking of relative assets with a historic profile may be used.

21 Board of Governors of the Federal Reserve System, 'An Introduction to Asset Securitisation' (The Federal Reserve Board 1989) 14.

22 Deku and Kara (n 14) 11.

23 Philip Wood, *Title Finance, Derivatives, Securitisations, Set-off and Netting* (Sweet & Maxwell 1995) para 5.8; Wood (n 18) para 28.41.

by the originator. These profit extraction methods may apply at different tiers of the payment priorities. For example, the payment of the servicing fees applies near the top tier of payment, while the originator's subordinate tranche (or equity) returns apply after all senior and mezzanine tranches have been fully paid.

An important economic effect of the profit extraction system is that while the originator is able to raise funds on a non-recourse basis through the sale of receivables, the originator will still be able to retain any surplus from the receivables just as if it had granted a security interest over them.[24]

2.2 Origin of securitisation

Modern securitisation was born in the early 1970s as an economic stimulus for the revival of housing markets in the United States of America (US).[25] As part of its initiatives to stabilise the US housing market after the collapse of the market during the Great Depression and, later, the 1960s credit crunch, the US government chartered three entities: the Federal National Mortgage Association (FNMA or Fannie Mae), the Government National Mortgage Association (GNMA or Ginnie Mae) and the Federal Home Loan Mortgage Corporation (FHLMC or Freddie Mac).[26] Fannie Mae was created as a wholly owned government entity in 1938, with the mandate of facilitating a secondary mortgage market by purchasing government-backed residential mortgage loans (i.e. mortgages guaranteed by the Federal Housing Administration (FHA)[27] and the Veterans Administration[28] (VA)).[29]

Fannie Mae funded its mortgage acquisitions mainly by borrowing, and by 1968 its mortgage portfolio had grown to $7.2 billion.[30] The US government reorganised Fannie Mae as a government-sponsored private corporation under the Housing and Urban

24 Wood (n 18) para 28.02.

25 Deku and Kara (n 14) 58f.

26 ibid.

27 The FHA was a federal agency that promoted the government's special housing assistance programme by insuring home mortgages given to low and moderate-income borrowers that were underserved by the private mortgage insurance industry. It was created under the National Housing Act 1934.

28 The VA was a federal agency that helped veterans to acquire home mortgages after World War II under the Servicemen's Readjustment Act 1944.

29 US Government Accountability Office, 'Fannie Mae and Freddie Mac: Analysis of Options for Revising the Housing Enterprises' Long-Term Structures' (GAO-09-782, 2009) 12 <https://www.gao.gov/assets/gao-09-782.pdf> accessed 28 May 2024.

30 Financial Crisis Inquiry Commission, *Final Report of the National Commission on the Causes of the Financial and Economic Crisis in the United States* (2011) 38. References to mortgages in this chapter are to security-backed loans for land rather than to the security right itself, unless the context indicates otherwise. In later chapters, the term is used mainly as the security itself.

Development Act 1968 (the 1968 Act).[31] The 1968 Act also established a new government entity, Ginnie Mae, to take over Fannie Mae's social mortgage programmes and related loan portfolio.[32] With this reorganisation, Fannie Mae was authorised to buy a broader range of mortgages, while Ginnie Mae was authorised to guarantee government-backed mortgages at the secondary market level.[33] Another significant change that the 1968 Act initiated was the introduction of a new financing device: securitisation.[34] Section 804(a) stated that:

> [t]o provide a greater degree of liquidity to the mortgage investment market and an additional means of financing its operations under this section, [Fannie Mae] is authorized to set aside any mortgages held by it under this section, and, upon approval of the Secretary of the Treasury, to issue and sell securities based upon the mortgages so set aside. Securities issued under this subsection may be in the form of debt obligations or trust certificates of beneficial interest, or both.

Section 804(b) had a similar provision for Ginnie Mae:

> [Ginnie Mae] is authorized, upon such terms and conditions as it may deem appropriate, to guarantee the timely payment of principal of and interest on such trust certificates or other securities as shall (1) be issued by [Fannie Mae], or by any other issuer approved for the purposes of this subsection by [Ginnie Mae], and (2) be based on and backed by a trust or pool composed of [FHA-backed mortgages and VA-backed mortgages].

On 19 February 1970, Ginnie Mae, in association with Fannie Mae, created and issued the first pass-through mortgage-backed securities (MBS) known as Ginnie Maes.[35] These securities were backed by a pool of home mortgages insured by the FHA and the VA. The security holders received interest and principal payments which Ginnie Mae guaranteed. Ginnie Mae, in turn, had the full credit backing of the US government.[36]

---

31 Housing and Urban Development Act 1968, s 801. It has been suggested that this move was to remove the burgeoning debts of Fannie Mae from the federal budget. See US Government Accountability Office (n 29) 13.

32 Housing and Urban Development Act 1968, s 801.

33 BG Buchanan, 'Back to the Future: 900 Years of Securitization' (2014) 15 The Journal of Risk Finance 316, 328.

34 Section 804 of the 1968 Act, the section providing for the new financing device, was titled "Mortgage-Backed Securities".

35 Buchanan (n 5) 49.

36 US Government Accountability Office (n 29) 13.

The process of the MBS involved a mortgage lender placing a pool of mortgages with similar terms and interest rates in a trust, with certificates of ownership being sold to investors. This effectively removed the mortgage loans from the lender's balance sheet, and the principal and interest payments received from the underlying mortgage loans were passed through to the certificate holders.[37]

The Emergency Home Finance Act 1970 chartered the third entity, Freddie Mac, to purchase long-term home loans from thrifts and help stabilise the industry.[38] Additional pass-through securities were later issued by Freddie Mac and Fannie Mae in 1971 and 1981 respectively, with the first private pass-through security being issued by Bank of America in 1977.[39]

Most of the pass-through securities were long-term fixed-rate loans based on the equal treatment of all the security holders. This made the securities vulnerable to changes in interest rates and prepayment risks.[40] Investors were particularly affected as the interest rate and prepayment risks made the maturity of the pass-through securities unknown and the expected cash flows unstable. In response to this barrier, two investment banks, Salomon Brothers and First Boston, developed the first collateralised mortgage obligations (CMOs) for Freddie Mac in 1983.[41] These CMOs were multi-class securities backed by pools of Freddie Mac-acquired mortgages and structured into a series of different maturity tranches.[42] The maturity periods could range from 1–3, 3–10, 10–15 and 15–25 years, with the priority of payments emulating a waterfall in descending order of seniority. Yet the mechanism did not entirely address the interest rate and prepayment risks. It only meant that security classes with longer maturities now had greater interest rates and prepayment risks.

Other types of asset-backed securities, i.e. non-mortgage-backed securities with asset pools, such as credit card receivables, auto loans and equipment leases, were developed, with the first asset-backed security (ABS) being issued in 1985.[43] Private labelled MBS issuance extended abroad, with the first European MBS being issued in the UK in 1987.[44]

37 Natalya Vinokurova, 'How Mortgage-Backed Securities Became Bonds: The Emergence, Evolution, and Acceptance of Mortgage-Backed Securities in the United States, 1960–1987' (2018) 19 Enterprise & Society 610, 628f.

38 US Government Accountability Office (n 29) 14.

39 US Securities and Exchange, 'Enhancing Disclosure in the Mortgage-Backed Securities Markets' (www.sec.gov, January 2003) s II(c) <https://www.sec.gov/news/studies/mortgagebacked.htm> accessed 28 May 2024.

40 Deku and Kara (n 14) 60.

41 ibid.

42 See Buchanan (n 5) 73.

43 ibid 77.

44 ibid 73.

2.3 The global financial crisis

To discuss the role of securitisation in the global financial crisis, it is important to put the crisis in context. The crisis can be considered to have evolved in a series of successive stages. These stages are briefly discussed below.

2.3.1 *The subprime mortgage crisis*

The crisis began when major global financial institutions that had invested substantially in US subprime home mortgages reported significant losses in spring 2007.[45] This resulted from the sharp decline in US housing prices and the consequent rise in default rates.

Following the Dotcom crisis in the early 2000s,[46] the Chairman of the US Federal Reserve Board (the Fed), Alan Greenspan, reduced interest rates from about 6.5% to 1% to keep the US economy strong.[47] This coincided with the then evolving policy of increased home ownership in the US, initiated by Bill Clinton's administration in the 1990s.[48] These accommodating monetary and housing policies went on to trigger housing and credit bubbles in the US.

The growing demand from several international and local investors (including the government-sponsored entities or GSEs) for mortgage-backed securities and the belief that house prices would increase indefinitely pressed mortgage lenders to reach deeper into low-income borrowers by offering different types of new mortgage products, which even at the time ought to have been understood as toxic. The Financial Crisis Inquiry

---

45 A subprime mortgage is a type of loan awarded to borrowers who have poor credit histories and are more likely to default than prime borrowers. Instances of a poor credit history may include payment delinquencies, charge-offs and bankruptcies. In contrast, an Alt-A mortgage is backed by a borrower with a better credit history than a subprime borrower, but the mortgage does not qualify as a prime mortgage because it is characterised with either low or no documentation, a higher loan-to-value ratio or a poor debt-to-income ratio.

46 The Dotcom bubble started after the US Federal Reserve Board (the "Fed") dropped the interest rate in 1998. The drop in interest rate coincided with a period of rapid growth in stock prices in the internet industry, which was due to extreme growth in usage and adaptation of the internet at the time. These factors spurred many investors to speculate and invest in any internet-based company, at any valuation, leading to a stock market bubble. At the peak of the bubble, a start-up internet-based company could become a public company and raise a considerable amount of capital through an initial public offer. The Fed's increase in interest rates on 21 March 2000 and the growing loss of investor confidence in the internet industry occasioned the stock market downturn in 2002. By the end of the downturn, most publicly traded internet companies folded, resulting in high layoffs and the collapse of the US job market.

47 Alan Greenspan, 'Federal Reserve Board's Semi-Annual Monetary Policy Report to the Congress' (The Federal Reserve Board 2002) <https://www.federalreserve.gov/boarddocs/hh/2002/february/testimony.htm> accessed 28 May 2024.

48 See e.g. US Department of Housing and Urban Development, 'The National Homeownership Strategy: Partners in the American Dream' (US Department of Housing and Urban Development, May 1995) <http://www.globalurban.org/National_Homeownership_Strategy.pdf> accessed 28 May 2024.

Commission (FCIC) identified some of these new products as: "I-O (interest-only), low-doc, no-doc, or ninja (no income, no job, no assets) loans; 2-28s and 3-27s; liar loans; piggyback second mortgages; payment-option or pick-a-pay adjustable-rate mortgages."[49]

These products – especially the hybrid adjustable-rate mortgages (ARMs), such as 2-28s and 3-27s, and payment-option ARMs – enabled low-income borrowers to pay discounted interest rates in the initial years of the mortgages (typically called the "teaser" period). These discounted rates would later reset and increase substantially after the "teaser" period, leaving borrowers with few options: they could either refinance into another ARM or, since they were not likely to be able to afford the new higher payments, sell the mortgaged homes and repay their loans. If the preceding options were unattainable, the borrowers would be forced to default. But with rising house prices, borrowers and mortgage lenders had no cause to worry about repayment risk since borrowers could always refinance with another lower interest rate ARM.[50] Remarkably, in what may seem to have been an endorsement of the practice, Greenspan noted in 2004 that "[m]any homeowners might have saved tens of thousands of dollars had they held adjustable-rate mortgages rather than fixed-rate mortgages".[51]

It turned out that an overwhelmingly growing number of the new mortgages were subprime mortgages and Alt-A mortgages (both, hereafter, referred to as "subprime mortgages"). By 2008, a total of 27 million subprime mortgages had been sold, representing half of all mortgages outstanding in the US, with the GSEs, FHA and other government agencies either holding or guaranteeing 19.2 million of these.[52] Private financial institutions and investors held the remaining 7.8 million subprime mortgages.[53] As will be seen below, the securitisation technology that is the particular focus of this book funded and transferred a substantial part of these 27 million subprime mortgages from "Main Street" lenders in the US to "Wall Street" investors around the globe.[54]

Housing prices began to drop towards the end of 2006, just as ARM interest rates started to reset higher (after the teaser period). The falling housing prices also meant borrowers could not refinance or sell for their loan repayment. Therefore, borrowers with unaffordable home mortgage loans defaulted and had their homes repossessed. But the

49 The FCIC Final Report (n 30) 6.

50 Christopher Mayer, Karen Pence and Shane M Sherlund, 'The Rise in Mortgage Defaults' (2009) 23 Journal of Economic Perspectives 27, 45.

51 Alan Greenspan, 'Understanding Household Debt Obligations' (The Federal Reserve Board 2004) <https://www.federalreserve.gov/boarddocs/speeches/2004/20040223/> accessed 28 May 2024.

52 The FCIC Final Report (n 30) 456; Edward Pinto, 'Memorandum: Sizing Total Federal Government and Federal Agency Contributions to Subprime and Alt-A Loans in U.S. First Mortgage Market as of 6.30.08' (Financial Crisis Inquiry Commission, November 2010) 4.

53 Pinto (n 52) 4.

54 For further discussion of the cause of the subprime crisis see CJ Emedosi, 'The 2007/2008 Global Financial Crisis: A Further Reassessment of the Originate-to-Distribute Narrative' (2020) 35 Banking and Finance Law Review 279.

falling home prices also meant that banks were holding huge asset losses in their balance sheets.

2.3.2 *The interbank credit crisis*

Concerns had arisen with reports of significant losses in the US subprime mortgage market in the autumn of 2007. Citigroup and Merrill Lynch reported a total of $23.8 billion and $24.7 billion losses, respectively, by the end of the year.[55] Other large financial institutions such as Morgan Stanley, Bear Stearns and Bank of America were also forced to report billions more in mortgage-related losses.[56] Consequently, global credit contraction began. Banks were unwilling to lend to each other because they feared they would not be paid back.[57] Banks also felt the need to "hoard" as much cash as they could to enable them to meet their day-to-day liquidity needs. This led to a sharp rise in the London Inter-Bank Offered Rate (LIBOR).[58] The credit tightening was of particular concern because most financial institutions' business models were highly dependent on wholesale funding (i.e. interbank funding). On 15 September 2007, it was revealed that Northern Rock (by some measurements the largest mortgage lender in Britain, and the first major casualty of the credit crisis) had asked for emergency support from the Bank of England. This would later trigger the first run on a major UK bank for over 100 years.[59] Northern Rock was eventually nationalised on 17 February 2008 after its failed bid to recapitalise.[60]

2.3.3 *The solvency crisis*

The credit crisis had spread to other parts of the financial system by the end of summer 2008. Major blue-chip companies (like General Electric) were unable to raise funds from the corporate commercial paper market to service their business operations. The GSEs were placed into conservatorship on 7 September 2008 after reporting huge losses.[61] American International Group, the biggest insurance group in the world at the time, was also rescued on 16 September 2008 through an initial liquidity support from the US

55 The FCIC Final Report (n 30) 256.
56 ibid.
57 ibid 252.
58 ibid.
59 See George Walker, 'Sub-Prime Loans, Inter-Bank Markets and Financial Support' (2008) 29 Company Lawyer 22.
60 George Walker, 'Credit Crisis-Regulatory and Financial Systems Reform' (2007) 22 Butterworths Journal of International Banking & Financial Law 567, 569.
61 The FCIC Final Report (n 30) 309f.

government in return for a stake in the company.[62] The US authorities, however, decided not to rescue the troubled Lehman Brothers.[63] Lehman was forced into bankruptcy on 15 September 2008; this would later be identified as the event that triggered the subsequent economic turmoil.[64]

2.4 The role of securitisation in the global financial crisis

By 2002, securitisation had already become the leading method of financing subprime originations. Table 2.1 below reflects the important role played by securitisation in financing subprime originations. At least 80% of subprime mortgage originations from 2005 to 2006 were securitised.

Table 2.1 Mortgage originations and subprime MBSs

	Total Mortgage Originations ($B)	Subprime Mortgage Originations ($B)	Subprime Share in Total Originations	Subprime MBSs ($B)	Total Subprime Securitised
2001	2,215	190	8.6%	95	50.4%
2002	2,885	231	8.0%	121	52.7%
2003	3,945	335	8.5%	202	60.5%
2004	2,920	540	18.5%	401	74.3%
2005	3,120	625	20.0%	507	81.2%
2006	2,980	600	20.1%	483	80.5%

Source: Inside Mortgage Finance, 'The 2007 Mortgage Market Statistical Annual Key Data' (2006).

New forms of securitisation, such as collateralised debt obligations (CDOs), CDOs-squared, synthetic CDOs and hybrid CDOs, created additional complexity and obscured the true quality of the underlying subprime mortgage pool. These structures were used as channels for transferring subprime mortgages (and their associated risks) originating from neighbourhoods across the US to investors around the globe. Securitisation amplified the crisis through these complex and obscure structures by: (i) adopting credit enhancement systems that made the US housing market intrinsically dependent on rising

62 ibid 350.
63 ibid 338f.
64 ibid 343.

house prices and refinancing; (ii) multiplying the effect of the losses suffered during the crisis; and (iii) facilitating over-reliance on credit rating agencies and their flawed mathematical models. These are explained below. The prevalent argument that securitisation created conditions for misaligned incentives in the financial system, which resulted in the weakening of due diligence among market players in the securitisation process, is also discussed.

2.4.1 *Creation of complex financial products*

2.4.1.1 Subprime residential mortgage-backed securities

Subprime residential mortgage-backed securities (RMBS) were backed by subprime mortgages. The added credit risk inherent in subprime RMBS[65] made their structure more complex than traditional securitisations (such as prime RMBS). While traditional securitisations used a basic senior/subordinate tranche structure, subprime RMBS, in addition to the senior/subordinate tranche structure, employed other layers of flexible credit enhancements (CE) that came from excess spread (ES) and over-collateralisation (OC).[66]

The problem with the ES/OC subprime RMBS structure (the ES/OC structure) was that it was based on the defining features of subprime mortgages. As mentioned earlier, subprime mortgages were designed to incentivise or force prepayments through refinancing after the teaser periods, as house prices were expected to keep rising. With this in mind, subprime RMBS were in turn designed to have a thin tranche structure, and low subordination level, from inception. The structure expected that since borrowers would prepay by refinancing, the deal would shrink and the CE would build up as amortisation occurred over time.[67] The dynamics of the model above made the subprime RMBS structure intrinsically dependent on rising house prices, making the market more susceptible to the consequences that ensued in the wake of the housing bust.[68] As will be

65 Subprime RMBS are residential mortgage-backed securities with a majority of subprime residential mortgage loans in their collateral pool.

66 See earlier discussion in section 2.1.2.

67 Unlike standard securitisations which have a fixed tranche thickness (this is because the structure had, from inception, built-up and allocated the total amount of CE that will always be present for each tranche), the flexible ES/OC feature in subprime RMBS meant that the CE will be built up over time in the transaction to reach a target level of over-collateralisation (OC target). This was done by using the excess spreads to accelerate the amortisation of principal on senior tranches through the process of "turboing". Once the OC target has been met (usually within three years), and subject to certain performance targets, the prepaid principal would step down by amortising subordinate tranches.

68 See generally Gary Gorton, 'Slapped by the Panic of 2007' (The Federal Reserve Bank of Kansas City, Jackson Hole Conference 2008) <https://www.parisschoolofeconomics.eu/docs/guesnerie-roger/gorton.08.04.08.pdf> accessed 28 May 2024.

seen below, many of the thin subordinate tranches in these subprime RMBS were re-securitised into CDOs.

2.4.1.2 CDOs

This chapter has so far described the nature and structure of a traditional securitisation in that MBS and ABS are securities issued against a pool of mortgage loans (i.e. MBS) or non-mortgage loans (i.e. ABS) from which the cash flows are used to repay investors. CDOs, or collateralised debt obligations, are distinct from MBS and ABS in that the underlying asset pool in a CDO arrangement is generally made up of transferable financial instruments (such as bonds, swaps, notes, MBS and ABS) rather than a more illiquid asset pool (such as trade receivables, credit card loans, auto loans and mortgage loans) to which the traditional securitisation structures apply.

Private issuers enhanced the marketability of their RMBS through the tranching system.[69] This system made it possible for approximately 75% of these RMBS to be rated AAA or AA (called "senior tranches"), thereby matching the GSEs' AAA-rated securities. However, while most of these senior AAA tranches were highly liquid on the capital market, the subordinate or subprime tranches (mainly BBB-rated tranches) were difficult to sell despite their relatively high yields. To address this issue, private issuers created a second-level securitisation by collecting these subprime tranches that had become difficult to sell from many RMBS and repackaged them into new CDOs. These CDOs would then have approximately 75% of their tranches rated AAA even though they formerly consisted of subprime RMBS tranches.

Wall Street security firms and the rating agencies justified these AAA ratings on the basis that the repackaging of many BBB-rated RMBS from different regions of the country would create additional diversification benefits, significant enough to make the possibility of simultaneous losses on all the securities very unlikely.[70] They believed that as long as losses were limited, only the subordinate class of the CDO would absorb the losses while the senior class investors would continue to be paid.[71] This assumption and the models on which the CDOs were based would later prove to be wrong as the performance of the underlying mortgage-backed securities turned out to be highly correlated across all regions.

---

69 The earlier agency tranche structure – i.e. the CMO developed for Freddie Mac in 1983 – was designed to address prepayment and interest rate risks, and not credit risks. This was because agency securities were considered free from credit risk since they had explicit or implicit government backing. The tranche structures that were introduced into CDOs were designed to address credit risk. This was because CDOs were led by private issuers and had no government backing.

70 The FCIC Final Report (n 30) 127.

71 ibid.

By 2004, as house prices continued to rise nationally, CDO issuers became dominant buyers of subprime tranches of the RMBS.[72] Table 2.2 below highlights the result of a UBS (United Bank of Switzerland) investigation into the number of residential mortgage deals (by mortgage loan type) that served as collateral for 420 CDOs structured between 2003 and 2007. As shown in Table 2.2, the exercise revealed that 3,113 (out of the total 4,008 residential mortgage deals) were subprime and Alt-A RMBS. This high demand for subprime RMBS tranches by CDOs issuers further fuelled an increase in the origination of subprime mortgages.

Table 2.2 Residential mortgage deals in 420 ABS CDOs

	Subprime	Alt-A	Seconds	Prime	Total
2003	215	63	7	144	429
2004	371	252	25	188	836
2005	488	452	62	209	1,211
2006	522	487	69	142	1,220
2007	150	113	21	28	312
Total	**1,746**	**1,367**	**184**	**711**	**4,008**

Source: UBS, 'Mortgage and ABS CDO Losses', 13 December 2007.

The success in transforming a large portion of subprime RMBS tranches into AAA-rated tranches through the CDO technology made CDO deals attractive to originators. To further exploit this rating arbitrage, originators created another market for subprime tranches of CDOs (mainly BBB rated) by recycling the tranches into another CDO. This next-level CDO was called a CDO-squared. The CDO-squared would, in turn, issue bonds with approximately 75% of their tranches rated AAA.

2.4.1.3 Synthetic CDOs

In addition to the above complex structured finance products, another subset of CDOs called synthetic CDOs prevailed. Generally, there are two types of CDOs: true sale CDOs (or ABS CDOs) and synthetic CDOs. In a true sale CDO deal, the pool of financial assets was removed from the originator's balance sheet and sold to the SPV in return for cash generated from investors. A synthetic CDO deal, on the other hand, only involved the transfer of the credit risks associated with the financial assets (reference assets), while the

72 It has been argued that CDO issuers were buying almost all of the BBB-rated tranches. See Laurie S Goodman, *Subprime Mortgage Credit Derivatives* (John Wiley & Sons 2011) 315.

assets remained on the originator's balance sheet.[73] The discussion, so far, has been based on true sale CDOs. A synthetic CDO is different in that it does not contain any actual tranche of RMBS nor directly place the RMBS tranches into CDOs as collateral. Instead, it simply "references" the RMBS or CDO tranches through credit default swaps.[74] In other words, in place of actual mortgage assets, synthetic CDOs contained credit default swaps (CDS or swaps).

A CDS is a contract that allows a corporate or sovereign bond buyer to transfer credit risks associated with the bond to a swap seller (typically an insurance company). The buyer of the swap (the "protection buyer") makes periodic payments to the swap seller (the "protection seller") throughout the contract. In return, the protection seller agrees to compensate the protection buyer for any loss resulting from a credit default on the reference asset, i.e. the underlying bond.[75]

In the context of synthetic CDOs, the CDS would have RMBS, CDO and/or ABS tranches as reference assets. The CDO originator is the protection buyer, while the investors are the protection sellers. Under the CDS contract, the protection buyer (i.e. the originator) agrees to pay cash flows in the form of premiums to the protection sellers over an agreed period. In return, the protection seller agrees to pay the buyer an amount of loss created by the failure of, or a relevant credit event on, the reference RMBS, CDO or ABS tranches. The applicable credit event may include a default in interest or principal payments or a reduction in the value of the reference assets.

During the crisis, most of these CDS were referenced to CDO, ABS and RMBS tranches. These tranches were, in turn, backed mainly by subprime mortgages. For example, American insurance giant American International Group (AIG) sold $76 billion worth of CDS to holders of CDO, ABS and MBS tranches and guaranteed payments in the event of default in the referenced securities.[76] The problem arose when market players transformed these swaps from being protection instruments into being speculation instruments by introducing a "pay as you go" CDS (also called "naked CDS" or "shorts"). This new breed of CDS created markets for parties with no connection with the underlying subprime assets to place bets against the housing market. The swaps were subsequently packaged as synthetic CDOs and sold to investors.

The image below reflects the structure of Goldman Sachs's first major synthetic CDO, Abacus 2004-1, which was worth $2 billion.[77] The CDO contained swaps that referenced RMBS, CDO and ABS tranches. As the sole "short" investor (i.e. an investor betting against the referenced asset), Goldman Sachs bought swap protection on the referenced securities

73 The FCIC Final Report (n 30) 142.
74 ibid.
75 See generally Hudson (n 2) paras 40.49ff; Gullifer and Payne (n 12) 258ff.
76 The FCIC Final Report (n 30) xxiv.
77 ibid 143.

from the CDO. The CDO, in turn, issued securities to "long" investors (i.e. investors betting that the referenced assets will perform well). Investors in synthetic CDOs were either funded or unfunded. Funded investors invested cash up front, while unfunded investors did not.

The unfunded investors, which included AIG, received annual premiums from the CDO in return for the promise to pay the CDO the sum of $1.8 billion should the referenced assets fail.[78] The funded investors received scheduled principal and interest from the CDO in return for the promise to pay the CDO $195 million should the reference assets fail.[79]

78 ibid.
79 ibid.

Figure 2.1 Goldman Sachs's Abacus 2004-1 Synthetic CDO

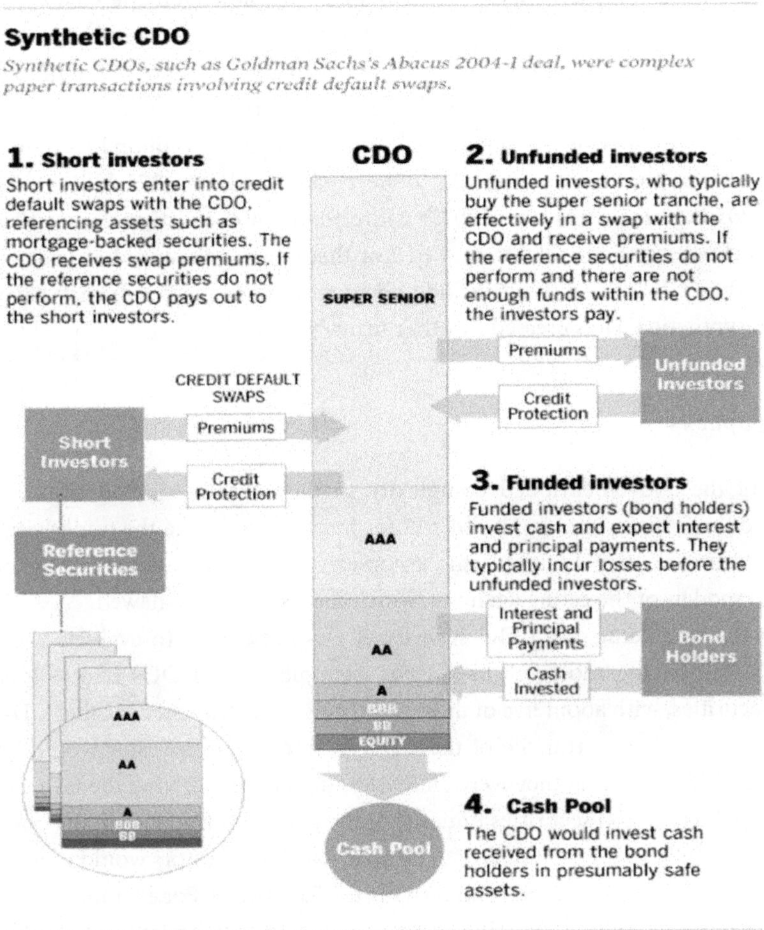

Source: FCIC <http://fcic-static.law.stanford.edu/cdn_media/fcic-reports/fcic_final_report_full.pdf>.

2.4.2 *Amplification of losses*

The proliferation of synthetic CDOs, occasioned by the advent of the "pay as you go" CDS, amplified the losses incurred from the housing market collapse by encouraging multiple bets on the same bonds. This occurred, for example, in the CDS that referenced $12 million worth of bonds in an M9 tranche (BBB rated) of Citigroup's MBS deal, CMLTI 2006-NC2.[80] Several synthetic CDOs contained CDS in which the M9 tranche was

80 ibid 145.

referenced. The bet was that for as long as the M9 bonds did not fail, short investors would continue to make regular payments (i.e. premiums) into the CDO. The CDO would in turn pay to long investors. If the bond failed, the long investors would pay the short investors to the extent of their loss. The FCIC noted that more than $50 million was at stake in such bets in early 2007.[81] Thus, what would have amounted to a $12 million loss on the failure of the M9 bonds could potentially amount to a $50 million loss or more.

The FCIC found that Goldman Sachs alone created and sold $73 billion worth of synthetic CDOs between 2004 and 2007.[82] More than 3,400 mortgage securities were referenced in those synthetic CDOs, and 610 of them were referenced at least twice.[83] According to the FCIC, this did not include how many times the bonds may have been referenced in synthetic CDOs created by other firms.[84]

2.4.3 *Opacity*

As a result of the abovementioned complexity in their intermediation chain, CDOs contributed to the crisis by making it difficult for investors to locate the underlying risks attached to securities they bought. This complexity forced investors to rely on the mathematical models of the rating agencies, which themselves were flawed.

To assess the true value of a CDO security, it was imperative to evaluate the credit quality of the underlying mortgage loans. For example, most CDOs had at least 100 underlying securities, with about five of those securities being tranches of other CDOs. To assess the performance of a tranche of the CDO of interest, an investor would have to assess the 95 RMBS (assuming they were all RMBS) directly underlying the CDO, as well as five additional sets of 100 securities underlying the five CDO tranches in the pool. This means that nearly 595 RMBS would have to be assessed. The investors would then have to assess thousands of mortgages directly underlying the 595 RMBS. For example, Citigroup's CMLTI 2006-NC2 had up to 4,499 subprime mortgages directly underlying it.[85] Using an average of 4,000 underlying mortgages, investors would have 2,380,000 (i.e. 4,000 x 595) mortgages to deal with.

Besides the above difficulty, most of the CDO deals had underlying asset pools that a CDO collateral manager actively managed. This created significant flexibility in the asset pool but also made CDO securities more difficult to assess.[86] The fluidity of the asset pool

81 ibid.
82 ibid xxiv.
83 ibid xxv.
84 ibid.
85 ibid 71.
86 CDOs could either have a fixed underlying asset pool or a dynamic asset pool where the CDO collateral manager could buy and sell assets into the CDO in line with agreed procedures.

meant that it would be difficult for an investor to determine which mortgage was in the pool without the guidance of the CDO collateral manager.

2.4.4 *The originate-to-distribute narrative*

Traditionally, banks originated loans and held them through maturity.[87] This model of lending was known as the originate-to-hold model. Under this model, banks did not sell loans to third parties, and deposits mainly funded loans. Over time, banks replaced the traditional originate-to-hold lending model with an originate-to-distribute model (or OTD model).[88] In the originate-to-distribute model, banks originated loans and sold them to investors.

The practice of the OTD model increased in the US after the establishment of the three government-sponsored entities (Ginnie Mae, Fannie Mae and Freddie Mac) and the subsequent issuance of the first pass-through mortgage-backed securities in 1970.[89] The OTD model of lending had its advantages. It expanded banks' sources of funding and reduced their dependence on deposits. But the model was criticised for lowering banks' incentives to screen borrowers and ensure their creditworthiness.[90] Since banks knew they would not have to live with the credit consequences of the loans they originated, they had little incentive to originate high-quality loans. This criticism led some to cite securitisation as the primary cause of the mortgage subprime crisis.[91] They argued that the misaligned incentives inherent in the model led to the accumulation of the unprecedented number of subprime mortgages that triggered the crisis (hereafter referred to as the "OTD narrative").

But alternative explanations of why the mortgage screening standards were weakened have been given.[92] The mortgage subprime crisis was more serious than the OTD model itself could cause, and the crisis would not have occurred but for the role played by the US government's housing policies in the period up leading to the crisis.[93] For example, blaming the originate-to-distribute model for the fallen mortgage screening standards does not explain why standards were not similarly lowered in the origination of other non-mortgage financial assets which were securitised and performed well during the

87 Vitaly M Bord and João AC Santos, 'The Rise of the Originate-to-Distribute Model and the Role of Banks in Financial Intermediation' (2012) FRBNY Economic Policy Review 21, 21.

88 ibid.

89 For discussion of the establishment of the GSEs and their mandates, see Emedosi (n 54) 288ff.

90 See e.g. Benjamin J Keys and others, 'Did Securitization Lead to Lax Screening? Evidence from Subprime Loans' (2010) 125 Quarterly Journal of Economics 307.

91 See e.g. US Treasury, 'Financial Regulatory Reform: A New Foundation' (The Department of the Treasury, June 2009) 44; Willen (n 1) 82; Levitin, Pavlov and Wachter (n 1).

92 See Peter J Wallison, *Bad History, Worse Policy: How a False Narrative about the Financial Crisis Led to the Dodd-Frank Act* (AIE 2013) 22ff; Emedosi (n 54).

93 Emedosi (n 54).

crisis. Benmelech and others examined the performance of loans purchased by collateralised loan obligations (CLOs)[94] between 1997 and 2007 and compared them to similar loans that were not securitised.[95] They found no consistent evidence that securitised loans were riskier than comparable non-securitised loans. They also found that CLOs performed no worse than comparable unsecuritised loans originated by the same bank – even loans originated by the bank that acted as the CLO underwriter performed equally well as the rest of the CLO portfolio.[96]

Also, the OTD narrative does not explain why mortgage originators (like New Century, Ameriquest, Countrywide Financial and Option One) suffered substantial losses as a result of the direct risks they faced through mortgage warehousing. Security issuers (like Citibank, UBS, Lehman Brothers, etc.) also suffered significant losses through RMBS tranche warehousing.

Furthermore, most of the RMBS and CDO issuers invested in the equity tranches of the RMBS and CDOs – the riskiest tranche. For example, the FCIC found that Citigroup had a total of $55 billion worth of subprime-related exposures by November 2007.[97] These subprime exposures included retained CDO tranches and payment guarantees provided by Citibank (a subsidiary of Citigroup) to their CDO investors in the form of liquidity puts.[98] Specifically, in July 2003, Citigroup issued a $1.5 billion CDO named Grenadier Funding. This CDO included a $1.3 billion tranche that was backed by a liquidity put from Citibank, which would be triggered should the CDO tranche fail.[99] The foregoing suggests that most of the originators and issuers had enough incentives to ensure that the RMBS and CDOs performed successfully and the OTD model was not the primary reason why mortgage screening standards were weakened in the lead-up to the crisis.

2.5 CONCLUSION

Securitisation has been cited as the main culprit in the blame game that ensued after the global financial crisis. In particular, critics have held its originate-to-distribute model responsible for the steep decline in mortgage screening standards during the crisis. This stained reputation has resulted in a significant drop in the issuance of securitisation since the crisis. The perceived shortcoming has also occasioned a vigorous response from regulators and policymakers globally.

94 CLOs are ABS backed by pools of corporate loans.
95 Efraim Benmelech, Jennifer Dlugosz and Victoria Ivashina, 'Securitization without Adverse Selection: The Case of CLOs' (2012) 106 Journal of Financial Economics 91.
96 ibid.
97 The FCIC Final Report (n 30) 260.
98 A contract allowing a party to compel another party to buy an asset under certain credit events.
99 The FCIC Final Report (n 30) 138.

This chapter helps shed more light on the role of securitisation in the global financial crisis. It shows that securitisation played a leading role in amplifying the effect and losses of the financial crisis through the creation of complex financial products and opacity. However, contrary to the dominant argument that the OTD model of securitisation caused the decline in mortgage lending standards in the lead-up to the crisis, this chapter indicates that the deterioration in mortgage lending standards was more serious than the originate-to-distribute model alone could effect.

3 SECURITISATION: ECONOMIC FUNCTION AND VALUE

Despite its role in the 2007/08 global financial crisis (GFC), securitisation is still regarded as an essential source of funding. The European Central Bank (ECB) and the Bank of England jointly published two papers in 2014, acknowledging the fall of securitisation in the European Union (EU) after the GFC and advocating for its rehabilitation.[1] The International Monetary Fund (IMF), for its part, noted in its 2009 Global Financial Stability Report that the need for a revived securitisation was "critical" to limit the effect of the GFC.[2] Countries and regional authorities have also initiated extensive legal and regulatory reforms in a bid to revive securitisation in their jurisdictions since the GFC.[3]

The predictable question resulting from the above turn of events can be framed in three ways. First, why was a supposed catalyst of the financial crisis regarded as a key solution to the crisis? Secondly, why does securitisation still appeal to businesses (including financial and non-financial institutions) despite the losses it occasioned during the financial crisis? And lastly, how does securitisation benefit an economy? This chapter considers these questions. The chapter also considers how the post-crisis regulatory and credit events motivated the need for a revitalised securitisation market. The analysis of the chapter proceeds in three sections. Section 3.1 broadly explains the aims and benefits of securitisation as a funding tool, risk management tool, and investment tool for businesses. Section 3.2 analyses the regulatory and credit events that followed the GFC and how they stimulated the need for a revitalised securitisation market. By way of conclusion, the last section highlights some of the key regulatory and legal measures that have been taken for the revival of securitisation, focusing mainly on the EU, England, Scotland and France.

The utility of this chapter to the overall research is to establish the motivation for the competitive drive between national authorities (particularly since the GFC) to formulate attractive and efficient domestic legal solutions that would enable the growth of securitisation in their jurisdictions. This will, in turn, set an appropriate basis for the

---

1 See European Central Bank and Bank of England, 'The Impaired EU Securitisation Market: Causes, Roadblocks and How to Deal with Them' (April 2014) <https://www.ecb.europa.eu/pub/pdf/other/ecb-boe_impaired_eu_securitisation_marketen.pdf> accessed 28 May 2024; Bank of England and European Central Bank, 'The Case for a Better Functioning Securitisation Market in the European Union' (May 2014) <https://www.ecb.europa.eu/pub/pdf/other/ecb-boe_case_better_functioning_securitisation_marketen.pdf> accessed 28 May 2024.

2 International Monetary Fund, 'Global Financial Stability Report: Navigating the Financial Challenges Ahead' (IMF 2009) 77.

3 See section 3.3.

subsequent comparative analysis of the solutions available in England, Scotland and France (the focus regimes) for the transfer of security rights in securitisations.

3.1 Financial value of securitisation

The need for, and importance of, finance for businesses and economies cannot be overemphasised. Expressing this importance in 1858, William Gladstone – later British Prime Minister – described finance as "the stomach of the Country, from which all the other organs take their tone."[4] Gladstone's analysis of the importance of finance is all the more true for businesses, as the usual barrier to a company's growth is the lack of access to finance.[5]

The two main sources of finance for a company are equity and debt.[6] Each source has its attendant costs for the company. For each equity granted, the company owner must be willing to cede some control of the company and pay high returns to investors in the form of dividends. Debt financing, for its part, has costs arising from both the demand and the supply sides. From the demand side, the credit rating that determines the potential cost of debt (i.e. the interest rate) is mainly determined based on the company's general riskiness. The company must be willing to accept certain restrictive covenants in the debt agreement (e.g. negative pledges) and/or commit its assets as collateral for the debt financing. From the supply side, banks[7] (the leading suppliers of corporate loans) deal with at least two limitations. First, banks largely depend on short-term deposits from retail customers to fund long-term loans, a discrepancy known as maturity mismatch.[8] Secondly, banks are required to maintain a minimum capital ratio against risk-weighted loans in their balance sheets in case of potential losses on the loans.[9] This situation significantly limits banks' lending capacity, as the capital that could have been used for other purposes to generate income for the bank as well as provide credit to the larger economy will be tied down to meet capital requirements.

---

4 John Cannon and Robert Crowcroft (eds), *The Oxford Companion to British History* (2nd edn, Oxford University Press 2015) 404.

5 Ross Brown and Neil Lee, *Funding Issues Confronting High Growth SMEs in the UK* (ICAS 2014).

6 For discussion of the basic sources of company finance see Louise Gullifer and Jennifer Payne, *Corporate Finance Law: Principles and Policy* (3rd edn, Hart 2020) ch 2.

7 The term "bank" as it will be used in this chapter refers to a commercial bank that accepts deposits, provides loans, and offers other financial or investment services to the public. This applies unless otherwise indicated by the context.

8 For discussion see John Armour and others, *Principles of Financial Regulation* (1st edn, Oxford University Press 2016) ch 13.

9 For further discussion see Ross Cranston and others, *Principles of Banking Law* (3rd edn, Oxford University Press 2017) 40ff. The minimum capital requirement is discussed in more detail at section 3.2.1.

Securitisation is a valuable finance technique that provides an all-round solution to the above debt finance issues, such that all market participants will benefit from it. For the issuing company, securitisation helps to reduce funding costs through financial disintermediation and asset segregation, diversify funding sources and reduce dependence on bank loans, and manage corporate risks. For regulated financial institutions like banks, securitisation helps to expand sources of funding and liquidity, release the capital that would otherwise have been held against balance sheet loans, and diversify risks in the financial system. For investors, securitisation can be an efficient means of diversifying and managing investors' risk-return profile since securitisation products are designed to address specific investor preferences on risks and returns. These benefits of securitisation are discussed in the following sections in terms of securitisation as a funding tool, a risk management tool, and an investment tool.

3.1.1 *Securitisation as a funding tool*

Existing theory suggests two reasons why securitisation may reduce the cost of funding for corporations. These are namely the rating arbitrage justification and the financial disintermediation justification. These theories are discussed in sections 3.1.1.1 and 3.1.1.2.

3.1.1.1 The rating arbitrage justification

As noted earlier, companies primarily finance their business activities through equity and debt financing (that is, on-balance sheet financing). It was also noted that these sources of financing have their attendant costs, with the equity providers seeking to be paid dividends as a reward for their investments, while the debt providers seek interest payments. An important determinant of cost of funding is the credit risks associated with the company. The lower the probability of the company fully meeting its financial obligations as they fall due, the higher the cost of funding. Suppose that a car manufacturing company, ABC, with a triple-B credit rating wishes to raise funds of $100 million by issuing bonds. The interest rate (i.e. the cost of funding) the company is expected to pay will be measured against the corporation's triple-B credit rating, which is the benchmark treasury yield (or the central bank risk-free interest rate) plus the prevailing yield spread for triple-B issuers in the bond market.[10] The interest rate will also be measured against the company's credit rating even if the company uses a portfolio of its high-rated car loans as collateral for the bond issue. The reason for this is that in the event that the company is unable to meet its

10 See Emily Beau and others, 'Bank Funding Costs: What Are They, What Determines Them and Why Do They Matter?' (2014) 4 Bank of England Quarterly Bulletin 10.

debts as they fall due, the company creditors will have full recourse to all the company's assets (including those used as collateral for the bond issue) during insolvency proceedings.

Suppose instead that ABC creates a special purpose vehicle (SPV) and sells the car loans to the SPV on a true sale arrangement.[11] This means that if the SPV issues a bond backed by the car loans, the bond's credit rating will be determined based on the performance of the car loans and the credit enhancements arranged for the bond issue. The bonds will no longer be based on ABC's triple-B rating and can be structured to have better ratings.[12] The reason for this is that ABC's creditors cannot lay claim to the car loans sold to the SPV in the event of ABC's insolvency since the loan receivables are now legally owned by the SPV (and are no longer part of ABC's estate). ABC can then work with the rating agencies to obtain the desired rating for each bond class through credit enhancement mechanisms.

A practical example can be seen in Ford Motor Company's asset-backed securitisation deal, FCAOT 2016-C, in 2016. Ford had a Baa2[13] credit rating from Moody's[14] and needed to raise $1.3 billion to fund its business operations. Instead of issuing on-balance sheet notes that would have been priced at 1.73% (based on Ford's Baa2 rating), Ford raised up to 95% (i.e. the portion of the issued notes with Class A ratings) of the $1.3 billion at a reduced average cost of 0.904% based on the A ratings generated by FCAOT 2016-C notes.[15] Accordingly, Ford saved up to 82.6 basis points it would have paid on interest rates had it issued on-balance sheet notes.

The rating arbitrage justification presupposes the existence of two fundamentals for securitisation to be attractive to companies. First, the size of the company matters. An empirical study has shown that securitisation users are several times larger than the average publicly traded company and have more receivables on their balance sheets.[16] This is because a securitisation transaction usually involves substantial transaction costs and requires an ample receivables portfolio to make it commercially viable.

---

11 For discussion of a true sale securitisation see section 2.1. See also Gullifer and Payne (n 6) 481ff.

12 See generally Frank J Fabozzi and Vinod Kothari, *Introduction to Securitization* (John Wiley & Sons 2008) 14.

13 This is the equivalent of BBB as used by the other two major credit rating agencies, Fitch and Standard & Poor's.

14 Moody's, 'Rating Action: Moody's Upgrades Ford and Ford Credit Long-Term Ratings to Baa2 from Baa3; Outlook Is Stable' (2016) <https://www.moodys.com/research/Moodys-upgrades-Ford-and-Ford-Credit-long-term-ratings-to--PR_343854> accessed 28 May 2024.

15 Ford, 'Ford Credit Auto Owner Trust 2016-C Prospectus' (2016) 1 <https://www.ford.com/finance/content/dam/ford-credit/us/asset-backed-securitization/us/public-retail-securitization/ford-credit-auto-owner-trusts/prospectuses/ot.2016-C.pros.pros.pdf> accessed 28 May 2024.

16 Michael Lemmon and others, 'Securitization and Capital Structure in Nonfinancial Firms: An Empirical Investigation: Securitization and Capital Structure in Nonfinancial Firms' (2014) 69 The Journal of Finance 1787.

Second, the receivables should have a higher credit quality than the corporation itself. For example, Church & Dwight, a major US manufacturer of household products, had no credit rating from a major rating agency when it began its asset-backed commercial paper (ABCP) programme[17] in 2003. The company obtained a B1 rating from Moody's by the end of 2003, and over time the rating grew to a Baa2 long-term rating and a P-1 short-term rating[18] in 2011. The company disclosed in its 2012 SEC Form 10-K that it had ended its ABCP programme in 2011 because its P-1 credit rating could then issue an on-balance sheet commercial paper security that had a lower interest rate (due to its high credit rating) than the ABCP programme.[19]

3.1.1.2 Financial disintermediation justification for non-banking corporations

John Reed, a former chairman of Citicorp, described securitisation as "the substitution of more efficient public capital markets for less efficient, higher cost, financial intermediaries in the funding of debt instruments."[20] To perform their intermediation role, banks raise funds from individual investors and on-lend to corporations – in other words, they act as both borrowers and lenders of funds. As borrowers of funds, banks rely mainly on borrowing from retail deposits and short-term wholesale funding markets to raise funds for their lending businesses. The borrowed funds (especially short-term wholesale funds) usually come at a cost for the bank, which is the interest rates the bank has to pay the lender as compensation for the credit default risk. As lenders of funds, banks determine the interest rates to be offered to their customers by adding the cost of funding (i.e. the interest rates paid on their borrowed funds), the borrower's credit risk premium, any operating costs the bank incurs, and a mark-up over and above these costs.[21] In other words, the bank passes the cost of its borrowed funding to the corporate borrower plus a profit mark-up charge. The mark-up charge is necessary to keep the bank profitable. By providing credit directly through investors in the capital market, securitisation is said to help the originator avoid this profit mark-up that banks and other financial intermediaries would otherwise charge.

17 An ABCP is a short-term debt security that is issued by an SPV or a conduit.

18 P-1 rating is the highest short-term rating that indicates that an issuer (typically a commercial paper issuer) has superior ability to repay short-term debt obligations.

19 Church & Dwight Co Inc, '2011 Annual Report to the Securities and Exchange Commission' (SEC 2012) 2 <http://investor.churchdwight.com/node/25441/html> accessed 28 May 2024.

20 Leon T Kendall, 'Securitization: A New Era in American Finance' in Michael J Fishman and Leon T Kendall (eds), *A Primer on Securitization* (The MIT Press 1996) 2.

21 See generally Richard Button, Silvia Pezzini and Neil Rossiter, 'Understanding the Price of New Lending to Households' (2010) 3 Bank of England Quarterly Bulletin 172.

3.1.1.3 Further justifications

While relying on Kronman and Jackson's theory of monitoring costs, Schwarcz has further explained why capital markets are willing to fund securitisation transactions at a lower rate than traditional secured lending.[22] The theory of monitoring costs is based on the need for creditors to monitor and ensure that a borrowing company does not engage in activities that will devalue its assets.[23] Since interest rates on loans are determined when the loan is made, a borrower may be incentivised to take actions that increase the loan's riskiness after the loan is made. Kronman and Jackson argue that creditors incur costs by monitoring the borrower to curtail this risk of borrower misbehaviour.[24]

They further argue that a secured creditor will incur lower monitoring costs than an unsecured creditor since the secured creditor only needs to monitor the borrower's actions toward the collateral backing its loan. In contrast, the unsecured creditor will have to monitor the borrower's general assets.[25] Based on the foregoing, Schwarcz argues that if secured lending reduces monitoring costs for protected creditors, securitisation carries the idea further by substantially eliminating monitoring costs for capital market investors.[26] He reasons that since securitisation involves a true sale of the originator's assets to the SPV, a bankruptcy of the originator would not affect the assets sold to the SPV. Consequently, monitoring the actions of the originator will not be necessary. Schwarcz concludes that securitisation truly reduces funding costs, and it is not a zero-sum game.[27]

There are questions about the impact of securitisation on the originating company's valuation. The securitisation process transfers valuable assets of the originating company to an SPV, which creates low-risk debt that has a priority claim on the transferred assets. Does the low interest rate associated with securitisation reduce the originating company's weighted average cost of capital? This question is motivated by the Modigliani and Miller theorem on company valuation. The theorem states that in a perfect universe, where there are no taxes, bankruptcy costs or market frictions, a company's value will be unaffected by how it is financed (whether it is by debt or equity).[28] Modigliani and Miller later advanced the theorem to consider the economic advantage of an interest tax shield (as interest payments on debts are tax-deductible), making debt financing more attractive. In this

---

22 SL Schwarcz, 'The Alchemy of Asset Securitization' (1994) 1 Stanford Journal of Law, Business & Finance 133, 150.

23 Thomas H Jackson and Anthony T Kronman, 'Secured Financing and Priorities among Creditors' (1979) 88 The Yale Law Journal 1143, 1149.

24 ibid 1149.

25 ibid 1153. For discussion of some of the contractual provisions in a loan agreement which help the lender to monitor the activities of the borrower see Gullifer and Payne (n 6) 204ff. These provisions include restrictive obligations, information undertakings and financial covenants.

26 Schwarcz, 'The Alchemy of Asset Securitization' (n 22) 151.

27 ibid.

28 See Franco Modigliani and Merton Miller, 'The Cost of Capital, Corporation Finance and the Theory of Investment' (1958) 48 The American Economic Review 261.

regard, they concluded that a company's optimal finance structure would be one in which it is 100% debt financed.[29]

Critics have questioned this theory over time by recognising market imperfections that explain its limitations. A prominent explanation given was the effect of bankruptcy costs on the valuation of an over-leveraged company. It was argued that the more debt financing employed, the higher the probability of financial distress and eventual bankruptcy of the company. Consequently, the increased cost of financial distress reduces some of the value gained from the interest tax shield. It was concluded that the optimum is reached when the value of the interest tax shield offsets the value of expected bankruptcy costs.[30]

This brings the focus back to the initial question: does securitisation increase a company's value? In Modigliani and Miller's perfect market model, securitisation would not be needed since it would offer no advantage over other less costly alternatives (i.e. equity and debt financing). However, imperfections (such as bankruptcy costs, transaction costs, market segmentation, tax, risk-pricing differences, asymmetric information, etc.) are rife in today's financial market. The existence of these market imperfections explains how securitisation can create value for the originating company since securitisation seeks to mitigate some costs related to market imperfections through its arbitrage features. Accordingly, by raising finance through an SPV that is designed to be bankruptcy-remote both from the originating company and in itself, securitisation is said to mitigate the effect of bankruptcy costs on the originating company's value and exploit the difference in risk pricing in financial markets to the company's advantage.[31]

Also, the existence of market segmentation and differences in risk-reward appetites of capital market investors is said to explain the economic value of the securitisation tranche system.[32] For example, pension funds investors are typically low risk-takers and would prefer AAA-rated bonds; asset or fund managers would typically want riskier but high-yielding bonds and so would prefer BBB-rated bonds; while mutual funds and hedge funds are typically high-yield credit investors that would prefer to invest in CCC-rated (or subordinated) bonds. Exploiting these market frictions by creating investor-tailored tranche structures enables the company to market the securities efficiently.

Furthermore, Lemmon and others have shown empirically that securitisation creates value to the originating company. Their study of the impact of securitisation announcements

29 Franco Modigliani and Merton Miller, 'Corporate Income Taxes and the Cost of Capital: A Correction' (1963) 53 The American Economic Review 433.

30 See Alan Kraus and Robert H Litzenberger, 'A State-Preference Model of Optimal Financial Leverage' (1973) 28 The Journal of Finance 911; James H Scott, 'A Theory of Optimal Capital Structure' (1976) 7 The Bell Journal of Economics 33.

31 Lemmon and others (n 16) 1795.

32 Fabozzi and Kothari (n 12) 279.

on equity and bond prices of 231 sample originating companies found that the combined price results show that investors view the news as positive and bid up the value of the average stock by about 1%.[33] They concluded that securitisation creates real value to the originating company.[34]

3.1.2 *Securitisation as a risk management tool*

All organisations have to control a certain amount of risk associated with their kind of business to either eliminate the risk or minimise its impact. This measure is even more important in the case of banks as they are traditionally prone to financial and systemic risks. For example, in providing its primary function as a financial intermediary,[35] a bank will always have to deal with the maturity mismatch (or cash-flow mismatch) between its main source of funding (i.e. retail deposits and short-term wholesale funds) and its use of funds (i.e. loans). Banks fund themselves principally through deposits and short-term wholesale funds.[36] For example, in deposit funds, a bank enters into a debt obligation with the depositor where the bank becomes the debtor and the depositor the creditor.

The terms of the debt obligation will typically require the bank to repay the deposit either on demand or at a specific future time (usually between one and twelve months). The bank then transforms a pool of these short-duration deposits into long-term loans by on-lending the deposits to third-party corporate or household borrowers on a medium- or long-term basis (usually between three and seven years). This traditional banking business model and the maturity transformation make banks inherently vulnerable to liquidity and credit risks.

The liquidity risk is that the bank will not have enough liquidity or funds to repay depositors' withdrawal requests or other obligations when they fall due since the bank has transformed the underlying short-duration deposits into long-term loans. Also, since granting credit to the economy is one of the main functions of a bank, the credit risk entails that there is a risk that third-party borrowers will default in repaying what they owe to the bank. The financial crisis strongly showed the systemic consequences that can arise if these risks are not well managed.

Securitisation is a key risk management tool that can hedge against these financial risks, for the benefit of both banks and the financial system in general. First, by serving as a means of turning the otherwise illiquid loans into liquid asset-backed securities (ABSs), securitisation enables the bank to obtain funding either through the issuance of the ABSs

---

33 Lemmon and others (n 16) 1811.

34 ibid 1814.

35 Securities and insurance firms are the two other main providers of financial intermediation services.

36 Beau and others (n 10) 3.

to investors in the capital market or by retaining the ABSs and using them as collateral for short-term wholesale funding needs. This reduces the likelihood of the bank becoming liquidity-constrained and further expands the bank's ability to grant new credit to the real economy.

Secondly, since true-sale securitisation entails an outright transfer of the loan receivables and their associated credit risks to investors, it is a valuable tool for banks to mitigate the impact of credit risks on their balance sheets. This is also important for financial stability since the credit risks, which would otherwise have been concentrated in the banking system, are now diversified into other non-banking sectors that may be less leveraged, less interconnected and less dependent on unstable short-term funding.

The events leading to the financial crisis have raised questions on the efficacy of securitisation as a risk management tool. Its utility for credit risk management has particularly come under severe scrutiny. A large part of the credit risks that were thought to have been removed by securitisation remained in the banking system in the form of retained ABS tranches and off-balance sheet credit support for the ABSs issued.

For instance, banks often retained and hedged large parts of their senior tranche collateralised debt obligations (CDOs) that were unmarketable by buying credit protection from monoline insurance companies (a practice that became known as "negative basis trade", as the coupons earned on the CDOs were higher than the insurance premium required). This allowed banks to remove the CDOs from their trading books and understate the true risk they held, while they still reported expected profits from the negative basis trade as realised profits. The credit protection would later become worthless after the 2008 monoline insurance market crisis, with banks left to bear the credit losses on the CDOs.[37] An instance of the off-balance sheet credit support played out in the Citigroup's $1.5 billion CDO named Grenadier Funding, where a $1.3 billion tranche was guaranteed by Citibank.[38] This meant that, despite the credit risk transfer effected by securitisation, Citibank retained about 87% of the credit risk.

However, these flaws exposed by the financial crisis do not invalidate the positive impact a well-functioning securitisation market can have on the financial system in terms of credit and liquidity risk management. Appropriate regulation that ensures that credit risks are truly removed from the banking system can curb the flaws. For example, the recent EU significant risk transfer (SRT) regime requires competent national authorities

37 For discussion of the large increase in retained super-senior tranches of CDOs in Citigroup and Merrill Lynch see the Financial Crisis Inquiry Commission, *Final Report of the National Commission on the Causes of the Financial and Economic Crisis in the United States* (2011) 196 and 257. See also Markus K Brunnermeier, 'Deciphering the Liquidity and Credit Crunch 2007–2008' (2009) 23 Journal of Economic Perspectives 77, 80.

38 The FCIC Final Report (n 37) 138. See also Charles W Calomiris, 'The Subprime Turmoil: What's Old, What's New, and What's Next' (2009) 15 The Journal of Structured Finance 6, 15.

and firms to ensure that the regulatory capital relief claimed as a result of securitisation adequately reflects the economic substance of the entire securitisation transaction and is commensurate to the retained risks.[39] This regulatory measure ensures all residual risks are identified, accounted for and included in the originating bank's regulatory capital calculation. This will disincentivise banks from engaging in negative basis trade and providing off-balance sheet credit support that has the effect of retaining the transferred risk with the originating banks.

3.1.3 *Securitisation as an investment tool*

Liquid assets are typically easier to invest in than illiquid assets. This is even truer for institutional investors (such as pension funds, insurance companies, mutual funds and hedge funds) who would usually prefer easy and low-cost exit access for their investments. Assets like mortgage loans, corporate or personal loans, auto loans, book debts, and other trade receivables are far less liquid, making investments in these asset classes difficult. By transforming these assets into tradable securities, securitisation broadens the investment opportunities in these asset classes for interested investors who would otherwise not have been able to access the market due to liquidity, operational and geographical limitations. This is because, as tradeable securities, the assets can now be easily bought and sold on recognised stock exchanges around the world, with minimal costs.

Furthermore, the flexibility of securitisation can enable investors to diversify their investments more efficiently in terms of their maturities, risks, yields, geographical location and underlying asset class. For example, through its tranche and credit enhancement structures, securitisation can be used to tailor cash flows and risk exposures to meet investors' specific maturity needs and risk and yield preferences. This is especially important for investors restricted to investing only in investment-grade and long-term, or short-term, securities. Securitisation also broadens the pool of high-quality securities with attractive yields relative to government bonds or Treasury bills.

3.2 Securitisation as an instrument for economic growth after the GFC

This section attempts to answer the question previously cited in the introductory part of this chapter: why was the supposed cause of the financial crisis seen as the solution to the crisis? The answer intends to further explain the economic importance of securitisation

39 Council Regulation (EU) 2017/2401 of 12 December 2017 amending Regulation (EU) No 575/2013 on prudential requirements for credit institutions and investment firms [2017] OJ L347/1, arts 243 and 244.

and why the current global debate is about reviving and strengthening the securitisation market. The rest of this section briefly analyses the post-crisis capital and liquidity reforms initiated by the Basel Committee on Banking Supervision (BCBS)[40] and how they impacted banks' ability to grant new credit for the economy (the credit-impact analysis). The aim is to demonstrate how the regulatory and credit events that followed the GFC, and the eventual economic fallout, motivated the need for a revitalised securitisation market. Since this research is primarily focused on three European jurisdictions (i.e. England, France and Scotland), the credit-impact analysis in this section will pay special attention to Europe.

3.2.1 *Basel III framework*

After the GFC, banks and other financial institutions were forced to shrink their balance sheets in a bid to strengthen their capital and liquidity positions as they anticipated imminent regulatory reforms. In December 2010, the BCBS issued one of its long-awaited post-crisis banking reform frameworks which imposed higher capital requirements, and introduced new liquidity and leverage standards for banks in a bid to make banks more resilient to financial shocks.[41] This initial post-crisis BCBS banking reform framework was later labelled Basel III.[42]

A brief description of Basel III's significance may be useful to put its effect on banks' credit conditions in context. Before the GFC, banks' total minimum regulatory capital ratio was 8% (Basel II).[43] Basel II defined capital in two tiers: Tier 1 capital – comprising a bank's own funds like paid-up common shares and retained earnings (also known as disclosed reserves) and other qualifying innovative capital instruments; and Tier 2 capital – comprising a bank's supplementary funds like undisclosed reserves, hybrid (equity/debt) capital instruments and subordinated debt. Basel II required that the minimum percentage of Tier 1 capital to the total capital (i.e. Tier 1 plus Tier 2 capital) must be 50%.[44] The framework further required that 25% of the 50% Tier 1 capital must be funded with the bank's own funds (i.e. paid-up common shares and retained earnings).

40 The main global standard setter for the prudential regulation of banks.

41 Basel Committee on Banking Supervision, *Basel III: A Global Regulatory Framework for More Resilient Banks and Banking Systems* (Bank for International Settlements 2011).

42 An updated version of the BCBS rule was published in June 2011, with the current updated version (now labelled Basel IV) published in December 2017. See Basel Committee on Banking Supervision, *Finalising Post-Crisis Reforms* (Bank for International Settlements 2017).

43 Basel Committee on Banking Supervision, *International Convergence of Capital Measurement and Capital Standards: A Revised Framework* (Comprehensive version, Bank for International Settlements 2006) paras 5 and 40. The minimum capital is calculated as: capital / risk-weighted assets x 100%.

44 ibid 49(iii).

For example, suppose that bank ABC's total risk-weighted assets[45] were $100 million. For bank ABC to meet the Basel II minimum capital requirement, the bank would not only be required to have a total minimum capital of $8 million. It would also need to fund at least $4 million of the $8 million capital with Tier 1 capital. The bank ABC would then be required to fund at least $2 million of the $4 million Tier 1 capital with paid-up common shares and retained earnings. No minimum standard was set for liquidity and leverage ratios under Basel II.

After the GFC, Basel III formally subdivided Tier 1 capital into Common Equity Tier 1 (CET 1) and Additional Tier 1 capital.[46] CET 1 mainly consisted of paid-up common shares and retained earnings, while Additional Tier 1 consisted of qualifying Tier 1 instruments that were not included in the CET 1.[47] Basel III also increased the total minimum capital ratio from 8% to 10.5%.[48] On the composition of the 10.5% minimum capital, Basel III increased the CET 1 capital from 2% to 7%. The Additional Tier 1 capital was reduced from 2% to 1.5%. The Tier 2 capital was reduced from 4% to 2%.

Furthermore, the CET 1 minimum capital required could increase to 9.5% in periods of excess credit growth (i.e. an additional 2.5% countercyclical buffer), bringing the total possible minimum capital to 13% (i.e. 9.5% CET 1 plus 1.5% Additional Tier 1 plus 2% Tier 2 capital).[49] Using the example above, bank ABC will (under the Basel III framework) be required to have a total minimum capital of $13 million capital (with at least $9.5 million to be funded by CET 1 capital) against the $100 million risk-weighted assets during credit boom periods. In other words, the bank will need to raise $9.5 million of its own funds (as against the former $2 million under Basel II) to meet Basel III capital requirements. Hence, Basel III did not only seek to increase the regulatory capital level, it also sought to improve the quality of the regulatory capital by focusing more on the bank's own funds. The intention was to enhance banks' capacity to absorb losses as a going concern.

Basel III also introduced a non-risk-based 3% minimum leverage ratio requirement to complement the risk-based capital requirement.[50] The leverage ratio was calculated as a bank's total Tier 1 capital divided by its total exposure (on-balance and off-balance sheet

45 Risk-weighted assets are assets of a bank, weighted (i.e. adjusted by a percentage factor) according to their respective risk level. They are calculated by multiplying each of the bank's assets (such as cash, loans, security investments, etc.) by their respective risk weights. The idea of risk-weighted assets is meant to discourage banks from holding risky loans or security assets since a riskier asset will attract a higher risk weight. For further discussion see Cranston and others (n 9) 40ff.

46 *Basel III: A Global Regulatory Framework* (n 41) para 49.

47 ibid 52ff.

48 ibid annex 1.

49 ibid 142ff.

50 ibid 151ff.

exposure), expressed as a percentage.[51] This was intended to address the high leverage level of banks during the GFC. For example, the Financial Crisis Inquiry Commission (FCIC) found that major investment banks were operating a leverage ratio as high as 40:1 (i.e. about 2.5% if expressed in percentage) by the end of 2007.[52] This meant that for every $40 in assets, the investment banks only contributed $1 of their own capital and borrowed the remaining $39, indicating a very low level of loss absorbency.

Another important feature of Basel III was the introduction of minimum standards for banks' Liquidity[53] Coverage Ratio (LCR) and Net Stable Funding Ratio (NSFR).[54] The new LCR standard required that the ratio of a bank's high-quality liquid assets (numerator) to its total net cash outflow (denominator) over the next 30-day stressed period was more than or equal to 100%.[55] The NSFR, on the other hand, required that the ratio of a bank's total available stable funding (the numerator)[56] to its total required stable funding (the denominator)[57] was more than or equal to 100%.[58] These new standards corrected banks' cash-flow mismatches in two ways. First, the LCR strengthened banks' resilience in meeting their short-term (i.e. 30-day) obligations as they fell due. Second, the NSFR created incentives for banks to fund their activities with long-term funding (i.e. equity and debt instruments with more than one-year maturity periods).

To minimise the impact of Basel III on banks, the framework was made subject to transition periods.[59] However, as will be demonstrated in the next section, Basel III induced banks to cut down on their lending activities, which inevitably weighed on the financing of the real economy. The situation was more severe in the EU. The European Banking Authority (EBA) imposed a stricter Core Tier 1 capital level of 9% on 65 major EU banks, which would also apply during credit downturns (Basel III's Tier 1 level was 7%). It also required full compliance with the 9% threshold by the end of June 2012 (while

51 ibid 153ff.

52 The FCIC Final Report (n 37) 65.

53 Liquidity represents available cash or assets that can easily be sold for cash, which is needed to meet liabilities as they may come due.

54 *Basel III: A Global Regulatory Framework* (n 41) paras 40ff.

55 Basel Committee on Banking Supervision, *Basel III: The Liquidity Coverage Ratio and Liquidity Risk Monitoring Tools* (Bank for International Settlements 2013) paras 22f.

56 A bank's total available stable funding is the share of the bank's capital (e.g. equity instruments) and liabilities (e.g. debt instruments) with a maturity of more than one year.

57 A bank's total required stable funding is the amount of stable funding the bank is required to hold considering the residual maturities and the liquidity nature of its assets as well as those of its off-balance sheet exposures.

58 Basel Committee on Banking Supervision, *Basel III: The Net Stable Funding Ratio* (Bank for International Settlements 2014) para 9.

59 For the capital and leverage measures see *Basel III: A Global Regulatory Framework* (n 41) paras 94f and annex 4. For the LCR measures see *Basel III: The Liquidity Coverage Ratio* (n 55) para 10. For the NSFR measures see *Basel III: The Net Stable Funding Ratio* (n 58) para 8.

the transition of Basel III was meant to be fully complied with by January 2019).[60] Furthermore, the EBA's capital requirement was largely unexpected – it was published barely four months after the 2011 EU-wide stress test that informed the EBA's 9% capital requirement.[61]

3.2.2 *Credit-impact analysis of Basel III and the motivation for the revival of securitisation*

The significant changes introduced by Basel III, particularly the EBA, would undoubtedly inflict substantial costs on banking operations in the euro area in terms of higher capital and liquidity costs. To increase its capital ratio, a bank would have to either raise its Tier 1 and Tier 2 capital levels (the numerator of the capital ratio) or reduce its risk-weighted assets (the denominator of the capital ratio) – which would also include cutting down on lending.[62] A capital increase approach (i.e. issuing more common shares, cutting down dividend payments, and/or issuing more qualifying Tier 2 capital instruments) would have little or no impact on the broader economy. However, an asset reduction approach (particularly in terms of cutting down loan supply) could adversely affect the broader economy – especially an EU bank-based economy that was struggling to recover from the financial crisis.

It is important to note that neither Basel III nor the EBA prescribed any formal approach for the capital exercise. The EBA only recommended that banks should first consider the capital increase approach, while resort to the shedding of credit supply should be kept to a minimum.[63] According to the EBA's 2012 final report on the capital exercise implementation, the banks increased their capital to a total of €115.7 billion (with €83.2 billion raised through the capital increase approach, and the remaining €32.5 billion was derived from measures taken to reduce risk-weighted assets).[64]

---

60 European Banking Authority, 'Recommendation on the Creation and Supervisory Oversight of Temporary Capital Buffers to Restore Market Confidence' (EBA BS No 173, 2011) 5.

61 Before the formal announcement of the EBA's 9% capital requirement, the Financial Times reported that the 9% requirement was "well beyond the current expectations of banks and analysts". See Patrick Jenkins, Ralph Atkins and Peter Spiegel, 'Europe's Banks Face 9% Capital Rule' *Financial Times* (London, 11 October 2011).

62 In its survey on how banks responded to the introduction of the 1988 capital requirement (Basel I), the BCBS concluded that "bank capital pressures during cyclical downturns in the US and Japan may have limited bank lending in those periods and contributed to the economic weakness in some macroeconomic sectors". See Patricia Jackson and others, 'Capital Requirement and Bank Behaviour: The Impact of the Basel Accord' (Bank for International Settlements, April 1999) 2.

63 European Banking Authority (n 60) 5.

64 European Banking Authority, 'Final Report on the Implementation of Capital Plans Following the EBA's 2011 Recommendation on the Creation of Temporary Capital Buffers to Restore Market Confidence' (EBA BS No 188, 2012) 7.

The EBA further reported that one of the measures taken to reduce the risk-weighted assets involved a reduction in risk-weighted assets of €42.9 billion arising from cuts on lending.[65] The EBA concluded that the capital exercise did not lead directly to a significant reduction of lending into the real economy since the reduced €42.9 billion risk-weighted assets were 0.87% of total risk-weighted assets as of September 2011.[66]

Other studies have shown that the reduction in credit supply arising because of the capital exercise did have a negative effect on the economy. For example, in their study on the scale of the reduction in credit supply and how it affected the EU economy, Reint Gropp and others found that the capital exercise banks raised their capital ratios mainly by reducing credit supply to retail and corporate clients.[67] They also found that firms who were more dependent on the capital exercise banks experienced a reduction in total assets, sales and investment growth after the EBA capital exercise, suggesting that the capital exercise had a real adverse effect.[68]

Mésonnier and Monks, in their study, confirmed that the capital exercise did have a macroeconomic impact on credit supply. They suggested that the scale of the effect was reduced mainly due to the accommodative monetary policies provided by the European Central Bank (ECB) to support lending over the same period.[69] Such monetary subsidies included the reduction of the Eurozone interest rates to a record low of 0.75%[70] and the ECB's long-term refinancing operations (LTROs) – a three-year cheap loan scheme for European banks initiated to support bank lending in the euro area.[71]

In his speech at an ECB conference in December 2012, Benoît Cœuré (a member of the Executive Board of the ECB), while acknowledging the deterioration in the ability of small and medium-sized businesses in the euro area to access bank finance after the financial crisis, noted that the "rejection rates and rates on granted loans increased, and so did the share of firms citing access to finance as their dominant concern."[72] He further noted that "on average, loans extended to non-financial corporations and households have

65 ibid 11.

66 ibid.

67 Reint Gropp and others, 'Banks Response to Higher Capital Requirements: Evidence from a Quasi-Natural Experiment' (2019) 32 The Review of Financial Studies 266, 287.

68 ibid 294.

69 Jean-Stéphane Mésonnier and Allen Monks, 'Did the EBA Capital Exercise Cause a Credit Crunch in the Euro Area?' (2015) 11 International Journal of Central Banking 75, 107.

70 James Wilson, 'ECB Cuts Interest Rates to Historic Low' *Financial Times* (London, 5 July 2012).

71 European Central Bank, 'ECB Announces Measures to Support Bank Lending and Money Market Activity' (8 December 2011) <https://www.ecb.europa.eu/press/pr/date/2011/html/pr111208_1.en.html> accessed 21 January 2024.

72 Benoît Cœuré, 'SME Financing: A Euro Area Perspective' (13 December 2012) <https://www.ecb.europa.eu/press/key/date/2012/html/sp121213.en.html> accessed 21 January 2024.

declined more than during previous crises, mainly because bank funding shocks have been larger than in the past."[73]

With the banks still re-adjusting their balance sheets to meet the EBA capital ratio and the succeeding Capital Requirements Directive IV (CRD IV),[74] their ability to finance the real economy was impaired. The funding problem was further deepened due to the over-reliance of the European economy on bank lending, much more so than other leading economies. For instance, in 2013, the total amount of assets held by banks to GDP ratio was found to be 334% in the EU compared to 115% in the US – just a little over one-third of the European banking sector.[75] On the other hand, the EU capital market was underdeveloped and small compared to the US capital market.[76] This over-reliance on bank lending led the European Commission in September 2015 to announce its plan to build a Capital Markets Union (CMU) that would provide alternative sources of funds for businesses and the wider economy. At the heart of the CMU plan was the revival of securitisation in the EU. The Commission noted that securitisation would generate additional funding of more than €100 billion to the EU economy if it could be revived to its pre-crisis level.[77]

There are clear reasons why the revival of a well-functioning securitisation market became attractive to EU policymakers (and their counterparts in other jurisdictions) during the post-crisis regulatory exercise. Securitisation can increase the availability of funding and reduce the cost of funding for the real economy. For example, to address their regulatory capital needs, banks can obtain low-cost financing by issuing ABSs (backed by either personal loans, corporate loans or SME loans) to investors in the capital market. The funds realised from the ABSs issuance can subsequently be used by banks to provide new loans to the real economy at a low-cost rate, improve banks' regulatory capital level, and/or meet their day-to-day liquidity needs. Furthermore, banks can strengthen their liquidity position by retaining the ABSs as high-quality liquid assets (the numerator of the LCR) and using them as collateral for short-term financing needs.

---

73 ibid.

74 CRD IV was an EU legislative package intended to implement Basel III in the EU. It consisted of Council Directive 2013/36/EU of 26 June 2013 on access to the activity of credit institutions and the prudential supervision of credit institutions and investment firms [2013] OJ L176/338, and Council Regulation (EU) 575/2013 of 26 June 2013 on prudential requirements for credit institutions and investment firms and amending Regulation (EU) No 648/2012 (Text with EEA relevance) [2013] OJ L176/1.

75 Sam Langfield and Marco Pagano, 'Bank Bias in Europe: Effects on Systemic Risk and Growth' (2016) 31 Economic Policy 51, 54. In 2012, it was calculated as 255% in the EU compared to 60% in the US. See European Savings and Retail Banking Group, 'Financial Systems in Europe and the United States: Structural Differences Where Banks Remain the Main Source of Finance for Companies' (ESBG May 2016) 5.

76 The total EU stock market capitalisation amounted to $10.4 trillion in 2012 compared to $18.7 trillion in the US. See Association for Financial Markets in Europe, 'The Economic Benefits of High Quality Securitisation to the EU Economy' (AFME 2013) 7.

77 European Commission, 'Action Plan on Building a Capital Markets Union' (Com 468 final, 2015) 4.

Securitisation can also act as an efficient tool for transferring banks' risk-weighted loan assets. Since a true-sale securitisation entails an outright transfer of the loan receivables (and their associated credit risks) to investors, securitisation serves as a useful tool for banks to keep their risk-weighted loan assets (the denominator of the regulatory capital ratio) at a minimal level, while still being able to profitably raise funds from the loan sale and grant new credit for the economy. Also, since securitisation helps banks to keep their loan assets at a minimal level, it can, in turn, reduce banks' total required stable funding (the denominator of NSFR), putting banks in a better position to achieve the Basel III 100% NSFR requirement.

Therefore, securitisation was seen as a useful funding tool that would improve banks' capital and liquidity positions and increase capital markets' participation in creating credit for the wider economy.

3.3 Conclusion

While the stigma attached to securitisation during the GFC and the consequent aggressive regulatory reforms[78] applied to securitisation products led to a steep decline of the global securitisation market, the regulatory and credit events that emerged after the financial crisis brought to the fore the economic benefits of a well-functioning securitisation market. There are clear reasons why authorities and market players are desirous of a revitalised securitisation market after the GFC.

First, a well-functioning market for securitisation can potentially improve banks' regulatory capital adequacy ratio, enhance banks' liquidity position, open up an alternative and stable source of funding for banks and other non-banking institutions, and diversify credit risks across sectors and asset classes – all of which are crucial for the growth and stability of financial systems as well as the real economy. Secondly, authorities have acknowledged that the crisis's poor performance of securitisation products was largely limited to the US subprime RMBS market. The EBA, for example, noted in a 2015 report that the EU securitisation market performed very well "with almost zero losses before, during and after the crisis."[79] The EBA advised that the harsh and all-inclusive regulatory approach applied to EU securitisations after the financial crisis "may no longer be appropriate".[80]

Accordingly, the campaign for a revitalised securitisation market called for legal and regulatory solutions that would strike the right balance between the need to minimise the

78 See e.g. Marke Raines, 'UK Regulation of Term Securitization Following a Hard Brexit' (2018) 13 Capital Markets Law Journal 534.

79 European Banking Authority, 'EBA Report on Qualifying Securitisation' (EBA, 2015) 47.

80 ibid 7.

potential risks associated with securitisation and the need to maximise its benefits. European authorities (at both national and EU levels) have been at the heart of this campaign. At the regional level, the EU has adopted the BCBS's recommended regulatory framework, differentiating between "simple, transparent and comparable" securitisation products (that do not need harsh regulatory treatment) and those identified as complex and opaque.[81] This regulatory compromise aims to promote simple and transparent securitisation structures by applying favourable capital and regulatory treatment to them.

At the national level, authorities are also reforming their domestic legal framework (since the crisis) to enable all aspects of the securitisation transaction and consequently facilitate securitisation market development in their jurisdictions. The focus regimes (i.e. England, Scotland and France) have been active in this regard. For example, the securitisation-specific provisions of the French Monetary and Financial Code (MFC) – the main legislation governing securitisation in France – have twice been updated (in 2008 and 2017) since the financial crisis (see section 7.1 for discussion of some of the updates). The October 2017 update (which entered into force on 3 January 2018) attempts to enhance the ability of non-bank private investors to acquire loan-backed securities by creating a new financing entity to complement the existing securitisation entities.[82] This update aims at diminishing the effect of the French banking monopoly rule (which prohibits persons other than French-licensed or EU-passported banks, or French securitisation entities, from granting loans or acquiring non-matured debt receivables) on the growth of securitisation in France.[83]

The UK government, for its part, has been capitalising on the flexible nature of the common law system in England (through case law and judicial precedent), and its recognition of equitable title and trust structures, to advance the course of securitisation in England. For example, in determining the characterisation of securitisation as a true sale, the English courts have demonstrated their willingness to uphold the structure of

81 The relevant EU regulatory framework includes: Council Regulation (EU) 2017/2402 of 12 December 2017 laying down a general framework for securitisation and creating a specific framework for simple, transparent and standardised securitisation, and amending Directives 2009/65/EC, 2009/138/EC and 2011/61/EU and Regulations (EC) No 1060/2009 and (EU) No 648/2012 [2017] OJ L347/35, arts 18ff; Council Regulation (EU) 2021/557 of 31 March 2021 amending Regulation (EU) 2017/2402 laying down a general framework for securitisation and creating a specific framework for simple, transparent and standardised securitisation to help the recovery from the COVID-19 crisis [2021] OJ L116/1; and Council Regulation (EU) 2017/2401 of 12 December 2017 amending Regulation (EU) No 575/2013 on prudential requirements for credit institutions and investment firms [2017] OJ L347/1, arts 260, 262 and 264.

82 Ordinance No 20171432 (amending the French MFC provisions on alternative investment funds and banking transaction prohibitions to nonbanking entities). For discussion see chapter 7.

83 Hubert Blanc-Jouvan, 'Direct Lending: A Matured Market?' (February 2018) 12–14 <https://webstorage.paulhastings.com/Documents/Default%20Library/spotlight_credit_funds_magazine_midres.pdf> accessed 28 May 2024.

securitisation as set up by parties and not be quick to re-characterise it.[84] The introduction of the Business Contract Terms (Assignment of Receivables) Regulations 2018 is another example of the efforts made to facilitate securitisations under English law. The Regulations nullify contractual terms which prohibit or restrict the assignment of receivables.[85]

The old-fashioned and restrictive nature of the existing Scots law on assignation[86] and pledge is well documented.[87] This aspect of Scots law has severely disabled securitisation transactions in Scotland and led to capital flight as Scottish businesses would rather structure their securitisation transactions under English law (or other favourable regimes) in order to avoid the inefficiencies and complications associated with Scots law.[88] While Scotland may appear to be behind its peers in reforming the law to produce a better functioning securitisation market, the newly introduced Moveable Transactions (Scotland) Act 2023 would usher in favourable reforms if and when it becomes fully effective.[89] The Act would introduce, among others, a new regime under which registration would be an alternative to intimation[90] (in the case of assignation of claims) and delivery (in the case of pledge). These reforms are expected to facilitate the development of the securitisation market in Scotland.

84 *MBNA Europe Bank Limited v The Commissioners of HM Revenue and Customs* [2006] EWHC 2326 (Ch), per Briggs J at [90f].

85 Business Contract Terms (Assignment of Receivables) Regulations 2018 (SI 2018/1254), reg 2. The Regulations, however, do not cover (i) receivables that are owed to large enterprises or special purpose vehicle, and (ii) various types of contracts, including contracts concerning interest in land, certain derivatives contracts and contracts in connection to prescribed financial services. See regs 3 and 4 of the Regulations. For further discussion see section 6.2.4.2.

86 Assignment is called assignation in Scotland.

87 See e.g. Tom Burns, 'The Transfer of Future Rights in Securitisations: A Comparative Study of the Law in England and Scotland' (2009) 24 Journal of International Banking Law and Regulation 35. See also RG Anderson and JWA Biemans, 'Reform of Assignation in Security: Lessons from the Netherlands' (2012) 16 Edinburgh Law Review 24; Jonathan Hardman, 'Some Legal Determinants of External Finance in Scotland: A Response to Lord Hodge' (2017) 21 Edinburgh Law Review 30. See chapter 5 for discussion of these difficulties.

88 See e.g. Scottish Law Commission, *Business and Regulatory Impact Assessment: Draft Moveable Transactions (Scotland) Bill 2017* (Scot Law Com No 249, 2017) 8f.

89 For a background discussion of these reforms see Scottish Law Commission, *Discussion Paper on Moveable Transactions* (DP 151, 2011); Scottish Law Commission, *Report on Moveable Transactions* (Scot Law Com No 249, 2017).

90 Notice is called intimation in Scotland.

Part II

4 METHODOLOGY FOR ANALYSIS OF TRANSFER SOLUTIONS

This chapter proceeds as follows. Section 4.1 discusses the nature of a functional approach to comparative law and its relevance to this study. Section 4.2 examines the law and economics approach and its relevance to this study. It finds that the efficiency norm of the approach will be useful in determining the most desirable solution. The nature and relevance of the legal transplant theory are discussed in section 4.3.

4.1 The functional approach

4.1.1 An overview of the approach

The functional approach to comparative law requires that the function of a rule should be the common denominator for comparative research. Its foundational framework was traced to Ernst Rabel,[1] who suggested that "the social purpose of the rules and the service of the concepts to this purpose" should stand at the centre of comparative studies.[2] Professor Rabel, however, did not provide a detailed methodology for the approach.[3] Professors Konrad Zweigert and Hein Kötz later presented a modernised explanation of the functional approach and provided more forceful methodological guidance in their book, *Introduction to Comparative Law*.[4] The book is described as a "famous and highly influential" work on the functional method.[5] As a result, the discussion of the functional

1 See Julie De Coninck, 'The Functional Method of Comparative Law: Quo Vadis?' (2010) 74 Rabels Zeitschrift 318, 321; Jaakko Husa, 'Metamorphosis of Functionalism – or Back to Basics?' (2011) 18 Maastricht Journal of European and Comparative Law 548, 549f.

2 Ernst Rabel, 'Some Major Problems of Applied Comparative Law, Especially in the Conflict of Law (Summary)' in Association of American Law Schools (ed), *Summarized Proceedings of the Institute in the Teaching of International and Comparative Law* ([Publisher not identified] New York 1948) 111.

3 See Ralf Michaels, 'The Functional Method of Comparative Law' in Mathias Reimann and Reinhard Zimmermann (eds), *The Oxford Handbook of Comparative Law* (2nd edn, Oxford University Press 2019) 346, 367 (noting that Rabel's suggestion was "almost in passing" and "he was not interested in expansive methodological debate").

4 Konrad Zweigert and Hein Kötz, *Introduction to Comparative Law* (3rd edn, Oxford University Press 1998), see especially ch 3.

5 Jaakko Husa, 'Farewell to Functionalism or Methodological Tolerance?' (2003) 67 Rabels Zeitschrift 419, 422. See also Michele Graziadei, 'The Functionalist Heritage' in Pierre Legrand and Roderick Munday (eds), *Comparative Legal Studies: Traditions and Transitions* (1st edn, Cambridge University Press 2003)

approach in this chapter begins with the approach as expounded by Konrad Zweigert and Hein Kötz.

Zweigert and Kötz argue that "[t]he basic methodological principle of all comparative law is that of functionality."[6] Their functional comparative approach is based on three fundamental theses. The first thesis is that the law is primarily a mechanism to solve common practical problems.[7] This claim establishes the need for comparisons to always begin with the definition of the problem the law is designed to address. They argue that the problem definition exercise must be done in purely functional terms – i.e. without any reference to the legal rules or concepts of a particular legal system.[8] Thus, for example, instead of investigating how other legal systems regulate the arrestment of funds held by a debtor in a bank, the comparatist is required to try to find out how other legal systems have sought to prevent a bank from transferring to the debtor the funds it holds in the debtor's name.

The second thesis is that the problems the law is designed to address are similar across different legal systems. According to the two scholars, "[i]f law is seen functionally as a regulator of social facts, the legal problems of all countries are similar. Every legal system … is open to the same questions and subject to the same standards, even in countries of different social structures or different stages of development."[9] The essence of the first and second theses is to show that different legal systems are comparable since the problem the law addresses is universal.

The third thesis claims that the legal system of every society solves the problems "by quite different means though very often with similar results".[10] For Zweigert and Kötz, societies are not only faced with similar problems, but they also tend to resolve these problems in a similar way. They termed this thesis the *praesumptio similitudinis*, or the presumption of similarity. They claim that the presumption of similarity should operate as the yardstick for testing the accuracy of comparative results:

> [T]he comparatist can rest content if his researches … lead to the conclusion that the systems he has compared reach the same or similar practical results, but if he finds that there are great differences or indeed diametrically opposite results, he should be warned and go back to check again whether the terms in

100, 102 (noting that the book arguably "contains the best current account of the essential features of the functional approach").

6 Zweigert and Kötz (n 4) 34. This statement was criticised as being a postulation of "methodological monopoly" and an "implicit lack of methodological tolerance". See respectively Michaels (n 3) 343 and Husa (n 5) 426.

7 Zweigert and Kötz (n 4) 34f.

8 ibid 34.

9 ibid 44.

10 ibid 34 and 39.

> which he posed his original question were indeed purely functional, and whether he has spread the net of his researches quite wide enough.[11]

The above premises form the basis of their *tertium comparationis* theory of functionalism. Only rules that perform the same function (or solve the same social problem) can be usefully compared.[12]

According to Zweigert and Kötz, the functional method can be embarked on in three stages. The first stage begins with the definition of a specific practical problem, which must be done in purely functional terms.[13] The next stage is to give an objective description of how each legal system has solved the problem being investigated. At this stage, the comparatist is free to present the legal solution of a particular jurisdiction "on its own terms", with relevant references to statutory rules, court decisions, and laws in their systematic contexts.[14] The comparatist's search for a solution at this stage is not limited to the statutory and legal rules of the relevant jurisdiction. He is also expected to resort to other extra-legal sources (such as standard-form contracts, legal writing and general business practices) if the solution to the problem being investigated cannot be found in black-letter laws.[15]

The third stage requires the comparatist to compare and evaluate the solutions identified in stage two from a purely functional perspective.[16] In other words, the solutions identified must be isolated from their doctrinal and conceptual contexts and be seen in the light of the social problem they are created to address before comparison and evaluation can take place.

4.1.2 *Limitations of the approach*

Despite the methodological guide the functional method provides, the method has been criticised for being "too limited in its application by its premises and operational problems."[17] Its *praesumptio similitudinis* theory has been regarded as "highly

11 ibid 40.
12 ibid 34.
13 ibid.
14 ibid 43.
15 ibid 43f.
16 ibid 44.
17 Oliver Brand, 'Conceptual Comparisons: Towards a Coherent Methodology of Comparative Legal Studies' (2007) 32 Brooklyn Journal of International Law 405, 420.

questionable"[18] and "doubtful".[19] It has been argued that social problems are already shaped by culture, religion, languages and legal traditions, even before they become legal problems. And "[a] legal system can only confront the problems as they present themselves, and the actual problems differ dramatically from one society to the next."[20] This limitation inflicts significant operational restrictions on the methodology. If the foundational premise is defective, the functionalist ability to evaluate and determine which solutions are better will be limited. This is because a legal solution that effectively mitigates a problem in one society might not be appropriate for another society if the problem being solved in the former is different from that in the latter.

The functional method has also been criticised for providing the comparatist with limited comparative and evaluative tools, as comparatists are required to isolate the solutions being compared from their conceptual and doctrinal contexts before evaluation can take place. Professor Ralf Michaels argues that it is impossible to separate the function of law from its doctrinal context and still measure the residual functional component against a model function.[21] In this sense, he concluded that "better-law theory is not compatible with functionalist comparative law."[22]

The *tertium comparationis* theory has also been criticised for being restrictive since it limits comparables to those with the same function. This has the effect of excluding possible comparisons which, though not functionally equivalent, may be usefully compared for a particular purpose. Professor Esin Örücü gave an example of how English statutes and German statutes that relate to entirely different subject matters may be usefully compared if the purpose of the comparison is to establish how such documents are prepared and how detailed they are in order to develop an understanding of such a law.[23]

Finally, functionalism is criticised for not providing legal comparatists with a concrete method to follow. Professor Ralf Michaels notes that:

> "the functional method" is a triple misnomer. First, there is not one functional method, but many. Second, not all allegedly functional methods are "functional" at all. Third, some projects claiming adherence to it do not even follow any recognizable "method".[24]

---

18 Richard Hyland, 'Comparative Law' in Dennis Patterson (ed), *A Companion to Philosophy of Law and Legal Theory* (1st edn, Blackwell 1996) 189.

19 James Q Whitman, 'The Neo-Romantic Turn' in Pierre Legrand and RJC Munday (eds), *Comparative Legal Studies: Traditions and Transitions* (Cambridge University Press 2003) 312, 313.

20 Richard Hyland, *Gifts: A Study in Comparative Law* (Oxford University Press 2009) 69ff.

21 Michaels (n 3) 380.

22 ibid.

23 Esin Örücü, *The Enigma of Comparative Law* (Springer Netherlands 2004) 20.

24 Michaels (n 3) 347.

4.1.3 *Relevance of the approach*

The functional approach is relevant to this research despite the above limitations. While agreeing that different doctrinal structures may create different problems and that solutions to practical problems may not be isolable from their doctrinal legal framework, it is contended that the transnational and transactional nature of securitisation will eventually overcome these limitations.[25] Moreover, being a part of private law that is essential for economic growth, it is usual to find that developed economies (like the focus regimes) are normally faced with the same legal issues associated with securitisation, and they tend to address these issues (maybe through different means) very often with similar results.

The functional approach is relevant for identifying the solutions for transferring security rights in the focus regimes. These solutions will be described purely as they are (and not as they ought to be) and on their own terms. Relevant references to statutory rules, court decisions, business practices and laws in their systematic context will be made. Accordingly, the solutions identified in the three focus regimes are reported separately in chapters 5, 6 and 7 of this book. Due to the limited evaluation and comparative tool of the functional method, the method will be complemented with the law and economics approach for the evaluation and comparative exercise undertaken in chapter 8.

4.2 The law and economics approach

4.2.1 *An overview of the approach*

While explaining the aim of his article on social cost,[26] Professor Ronald Coase noted that two different parts co-exist in the field of law and economics.[27] He stated that one part studies the "influence of the legal system on the working of the economic system."[28] Thus, this approach is aimed at economists, and the focus is on economic problems.[29] He noted that his article on social cost adopts this approach by using "the concept of transaction costs to demonstrate the way in which the legal system could affect the working of the

25 Functionalists have since taken a more cautious approach and admitted that the functional method is only appropriate when comparing legal systems with similar societal backgrounds and where the subject matter under consideration is not subject to "strong moral and religious influence". See Hyland (n 20) 69.

26 Ronald Coase, 'The Problem of Social Cost' (1960) 3 The Journal of Law & Economics 1.

27 Ronald Coase, 'Law and Economics and A. W. Brian Simpson' (1996) 25 The Journal of Legal Studies 103.

28 ibid 104.

29 This approach has been termed the "old" law and economics approach. See Richard A Posner, *Economic Analysis of Law* (7th edn, Aspen Publishers 2007) 23.

economic system."[30] The other part, according to Coase, entails the use of economic theories to analyse legal rules and institutions.[31] This approach is often called the economic analysis of law or the "new" law and economics. It is focused on legal problems and aimed at lawyers. The importance of this distinction is that it explains the analytical scope of the present research, which focuses on the economic analysis of law.

The foundation of the economic analysis of law approach can be traced to the eighteenth and early nineteenth centuries with the works of Smith,[32] Bentham,[33] Pigou[34] and Beccaria.[35] However, Coase's article on social cost,[36] Calabresi's article on the law of torts[37] and Posner's book on economic analysis of law[38] have been recognised as marking the beginning of the new law and economics movement as an independent and specialised field of study.[39]

4.2.1.1 Coase

Coase's analysis of the externality problem in his article "The Problem of Social Cost" can be divided into two parts. The first part analyses the problem of social cost from a hypothetical-world point of view, where transaction costs are assumed to be zero.[40] The second part analyses the problem from a real-world point of view, where transaction costs are indeed positive.[41] He developed what became known as the Coase theorem in the first part. That theorem states that in a world of no transaction costs and where property rights are well defined and tradable, (i) parties to an externality will negotiate their way to achieve an efficient solution[42] and (ii) the efficient solution reached will be the same regardless of how the law defines property rights.[43] The first limb of the theorem is known as the "efficiency hypothesis". The second limb is called the "invariance hypothesis", which

30 Ronald Coase, 'The Nature of the Firm: Influence' (1988) 4 The Journal of Law, Economics, and Organization 33, 35.
31 Coase, 'Law and Economics and A. W. Brian Simpson' (n 27) 103.
32 Adam Smith, *An Inquiry into the Nature and Causes of the Wealth of Nations* (W Strahan and T Cadell, 1776).
33 Jeremy Bentham, *An Introduction to the Principles of Morals and Legislation* (John Bowring ed, W Tait 1843).
34 Arthur C Pigou, *The Economics of Welfare* (4th edn, Macmillan 1932).
35 Cesare Beccaria, *On Crimes and Punishments* (Henry Paolucci translation, Bobbs Merrill 1963).
36 Coase, 'The Problem of Social Cost' (n 26) 1.
37 Guido Calabresi, 'Some Thoughts on Risk Distribution and the Law of Torts' (1961) 70 The Yale Law Journal 499.
38 Posner, *Economic Analysis of Law* (n 29).
39 Werner Z Hirsch and Evan Osborne, 'Law and Economics – Valuable but Controversial' (1992) 17 Law & Social Inquiry 521.
40 Coase, 'The Problem of Social Cost' (n 26) 2–15.
41 ibid 15ff.
42 ibid 2ff.
43 ibid 6ff.

implies that government rules are irrelevant for the efficient allocation of resources provided there are no transaction costs, and property rights are well defined and can be modified by market transactions.

While the Coase theorem seems to have received more attention from literature, the article's main thesis is in the second part,[44] where Coase (inadvertently) laid the foundations of the economic analysis of law. The following two subsections briefly describe the two parts of the article.

a) The Coase theorem (no transaction cost)

Professor Coase's social cost article seeks to resolve the economic problem of a negative externality. A negative externality occurs when the voluntary exchange of market agents imposes an uncompensated cost on a non-market agent or an unrelated third party. According to economists, an unaddressed externality event (in a perfect and unregulated market system) leads to an inefficient market equilibrium and, therefore, market failure, since the equilibrium price does not accurately reflect the product's true cost.[45] The equilibrium price only reflects the marginal "private" cost and not the marginal "social" cost occasioned by the externality.

Before Coase, economists largely followed the proposition of Professor Pigou, who argued that externalities could be internalised by making businesses fully liable for the damage they cause to others.[46] Thus, if ABC Ltd in the course of doing its manufacturing business pollutes the groundwater and inflicts damage of £100 yearly on farmer Mike, Pigou argued that this externality could be corrected by either restricting the harmful activities of ABC Ltd or imposing a yearly tax of £100 on it.[47] This traditional approach only sees the firm as the culprit that should be restrained.

The Coase theorem was introduced to disprove Pigou's approach. Coase criticised the approach, arguing that the problem is reciprocal: to avoid harm to the farmer will inflict harm on the firm.[48] He further argued that the main question to be determined is: should ABC Ltd be allowed to harm farmer Mike or should farmer Mike be allowed to harm ABC Ltd?[49] He asserted that the solution that ensures the greatest net social benefit will produce a more efficient outcome.[50] Thus, using the hypothetical case above, Coase's solution to the problem will depend on whether ABC Ltd's income from its manufacturing business is

44 See ibid 19 (noting that the aim of the article is "to indicate what the economic approach to the [externality] problem should be [where transaction cost is positive]").

45 Thomas Helbling, 'Externalities: Prices Do Not Capture All Costs' (IMF December 2018).

46 Pigou (n 34) 127ff.

47 ibid.

48 Coase, 'The Problem of Social Cost' (n 26) 2.

49 ibid.

50 ibid.

more than farmer Mike's £100 loss. Also, the solution will depend on who amongst ABC Ltd and farmer Mike is the cheapest cost avoider. For example, if the harm to farmer Mike can be avoided by moving the farm to adjacent land at a cost less than £100, moving the farm to adjacent land would produce a more efficient outcome.

In addition to its non-reciprocal treatment of externality, Pigou's approach also implied that the externality problem can only be properly dealt with through direct government regulation.[51] Coase rejected this view.[52] He argued that there are circumstances where market solutions to the externality problem produce better results than direct government intervention. According to Coase, where transaction costs[53] are non-existent and the rights of the various parties are well defined by law, parties will contract their way to an efficient outcome (i.e. market solution) without the need for government intervention.[54] Thus, using the hypothetical case above, suppose that ABC Ltd gains a yearly net income of £100 from its manufacturing business, and it will cost £70 yearly to install a machine that will eliminate the pollution. Suppose also that farmer Mike earns a yearly net income of £50 from the farm.

Table 4.1 Illustration of Coase's efficiency and invariance hypotheses

	ABC Ltd earns £100 yearly **Farmer Mike earns £50 yearly** **A yearly cost of £70 to prevent pollution**
Farmer Mike has the legal right	It will be cheaper for ABC Ltd to negotiate and pay farmer Mike slightly above £50 yearly for permission to pollute. That way, the externality problem is solved. A Pareto efficient outcome is reached: ABC Ltd is better off since paying farmer Mike is cheaper than installing a pollution control machine, and farmer Mike is better off since he will earn more than his yearly income. The concept of Pareto efficiency is discussed in more detail in section 4.2.2.2.
What if ABC Ltd has the legal right?	The same efficient outcome will be achieved. ABC Ltd will continue to pollute. This is because it will not be worthwhile for farmer Mike to pay ABC Ltd the £70 yearly that is needed to prevent the pollution, since he only makes £50.

The thrust of this illustration is that the same efficient outcome (i.e. allowing ABC Ltd to pollute) will be reached regardless of the initial rights established by law.

Coase argued that a market solution would continue to produce the most efficient and desirable outcome, provided that the increase in the value of production resulting from

51 Pigou (n 34) 127ff.

52 Coase, 'The Problem of Social Cost' (n 26) 2.

53 "Zero transaction costs" in this context broadly means the absence of any impediments to, or costs of, negotiation.

54 Coase, 'The Problem of Social Cost' (n 26) 42ff.

the market solution is greater than the transaction cost involved in bringing about the market solution.[55] But where the transaction cost of bringing about the market solution is greater than the resulting value of production, making a market solution impossible, he noted that the initial allocation of legal rights does matter in this circumstance,[56] in which case the alternative solution will lie with the government.[57]

b) Positive transaction cost

Coase himself admitted that a world without a transaction cost is "a very unrealistic assumption".[58] He noted that:

> [i]n order to carry out a market transaction it is necessary to discover who it is that one wishes to deal with, to inform people that one wishes to deal and on what terms, to conduct negotiations leading up to a bargain, to draw up the contract, to undertake the inspection needed to make sure that the terms of the contract are being observed, and so on. These operations are often extremely costly, sufficiently costly at any rate to prevent many transactions that would be carried out in a world in which the pricing system worked without cost.[59]

So, transaction cost is positive and should be factored into the economic analysis. On this, and the relevance of legal rules in the determination of market efficiency, Coase noted that:

> [o]nce the costs of carrying out market transactions are taken into account it is clear that such a rearrangement of rights will only be undertaken when the increase in the value of production consequent upon the rearrangement is greater than the costs which would be involved in bringing it about. When it is less, the granting of an injunction (or the knowledge that it would be granted) or the liability to pay damages may result in an activity being discontinued (or may prevent its being started) which would be undertaken if market transactions were costless. In these conditions the initial delimitation of legal rights does have an effect on the efficiency with which the economic system operates. One arrangement of rights may bring about a greater value of production than any other. But unless this is the arrangement of rights

55 ibid 15f.
56 ibid 16.
57 ibid 17.
58 ibid 15.
59 ibid.

> established by the legal system, the costs of reaching the same result by altering and combining rights through the market may be so great that this optimal arrangement of rights, and the greater value of production which it would bring, may never be achieved.[60]

In other words, where the transaction costs are high enough to prevent or discontinue market solutions, legal rules directly influence market (in)efficiency. Coase went on to recommend how legal rules should approach the externality problem where transaction costs are prohibitive:

> While most economists seem to be under a misapprehension concerning the character of the situation with which they are dealing, it is also the case that the activities which they would like to see stopped or curtailed may well be socially justified. … What has to be decided is whether the gain from preventing the harm is greater than the loss which would be suffered elsewhere as a result of stopping the action which produces the harm.[61]

The thrust of Coase's argument is that the problem is not externality but high transaction costs.[62] If transaction costs are high, government actions or rules will affect efficiency. And since transaction costs exist in the real world, governments and courts should understand the economic implications of their actions. The solution is not simply one of restraining those responsible for the externality. Instead, the solution is one of adopting frameworks that minimise transaction costs and assign liability to the cheapest cost avoider party.[63]

4.2.1.2 Calabresi

Professor Calabresi's article on liability rules and risk distribution[64] (published the same year as Coase's article on social cost) and a later book on the costs of accidents[65] laid the foundations of economic analysis of liability rules in tort law.[66] Being a legal scholar, Calabresi was only interested in using economic theory to analyse and answer the legal question of who should be liable for injuries in tort law. He rejected the prevailing fault system or negligence regime of tort law and argued for a mixed system that is based on

60 ibid 16.

61 ibid 27.

62 In other words, the only thing making economic efficiency dependent on legal rules is high transaction costs and not externality.

63 Coase, 'The Problem of Social Cost' (n 26) 18 and 27.

64 Calabresi, 'Some Thoughts on Risk Distribution and the Law of Torts' (n 37).

65 Guido Calabresi, *The Costs of Accidents: A Legal and Economic Analysis* (Yale University Press 1970).

66 Roger Van den Bergh, 'Introduction: The Impact of Guido Calabresi on Law and Economics Scholarship' (2008) 1 Erasmus Law Review 1, 2.

strict liability for harmful activities.[67] Calabresi argued (just as Coase did) that the principal goal of tort law should be to minimise the sum of the costs of accidents and the costs of avoiding accidents by placing liability on the party who is the cheapest cost avoider.[68] This implies that Calabresi also recognises the reciprocal dimension of torts.[69]

Calabresi provided a guiding principle for determining the cheapest cost avoider among parties involved. He defined this as the party who is in a better position to cause the cost to be reflected in the price of the product derived from the harmful activity, regardless of whether the party is at fault or not.[70] His argument, which is similar to Coase's invariance and efficiency thesis, was that in a free and competitive market economy, the cost would always find its way into prices, regardless of which party is initially liable (i.e. a competitive market would always achieve an efficient outcome regardless of legal rules).[71] He gave an example of an injured employee, noting that it makes no difference whether the employee or the employer suffers the cost of the injury. If the employee suffered the cost, the employee would insure and demand higher wages to pay the insurance cost. Alternatively, if the employer suffered the cost, the employer would lower wages. Calabresi argued that "[e]ither way … the cost would find its way into wages and into prices."[72]

Calabresi, however, differed from Coase on the factors that make a market solution unattainable. While Coase emphasised high transaction costs as the major obstacle to a market solution, Calabresi focused on monopoly and individual rational differences.[73] Both authors seem to agree that an externality is not necessarily the problem. Rather, Coase's transaction costs and Calabresi's monopoly and individual rational differences are the problems that justify government (or state) intervention.

An essential difference in the approach taken by Coase and Calabresi is how they relate efficiency to the concept of justice (or fairness). For Coase, the dominant normative goal of legal rules is efficiency. The consideration of other normative factors like justice is excluded.[74] Calabresi on his part believes legal rules must have two principal goals: justice and efficiency. He argues that efficiency and justice determine the choice of liability rules, and where there is a conflict between the two values, "fairness becomes a final test which any system of accident law must pass."[75] He sees justice as the predominant goal.[76] The

67 Calabresi, *The Costs of Accidents: A Legal and Economic Analysis* (n 65) 311ff.

68 ibid 276, 285 and 316.

69 See also Calabresi, 'Some Thoughts on Risk Distribution and the Law of Torts' (n 37) 506.

70 ibid 505.

71 ibid 506.

72 ibid.

73 ibid 506f.

74 James Hackney, 'Guido Calabresi and the Construction of Contemporary American Legal Theory' (2014) 77 Law and Contemporary Problems 45, 50.

75 Calabresi, *The Costs of Accidents: A Legal and Economic Analysis* (n 65) 24.

76 Guido Calabresi, 'An Exchange: About Law and Economics: A Letter to Ronald Dworkin' (1980) 8 Hofstra Law Review 553, 58 (noting that justice should be a veto in the pursuit of efficiency).

professional background of both scholars may have informed the difference in their approach: Coase was an economist, while Calabresi is a legal scholar.

Calabresi's regard for justice explains his consideration of the problem of individual rational differences. While Coase's transaction cost theory presupposes an all-knowing and all-rational economic world, Calabresi recognises that such a world does not exist.[77] He argues that there are some differences in the capabilities of individuals to calculate risks and make rational decisions for themselves.[78] He notes that "one of the two actors may, in practice, be far better able than the other to evaluate the expected accident risk, that is, the expected accident costs."[79]

Calabresi's regard for justice also explains his approach in determining the cheapest cost avoider, which takes parties' bargaining powers and rationality differences into consideration (thus incorporating fairness into the analysis). For example, Calabresi's resource-allocation and loss-distribution theory implies that: (i) cost of injuries would be borne by the activities that cause them, regardless of fault;[80] and (ii) reflecting the cost in the price spreads the cost widely to consumers (rather than placing the cost on an individual party).[81] His subsequent approach in determining the cheapest cost avoider in his later publications expresses a similar bias towards fairness. For example, his 1965 article identifies the cheapest cost avoider as "the better informed party"[82] and his 1972 article (with Hirschoff) identifies the party who "is in the best position to make the cost-benefit analysis between accident costs and accident avoidance costs, and to act on that decision once it is made"[83] as the cheapest cost avoider.

4.2.1.3 Posner's wealth maximisation concept

Professor Posner's economic analysis of law builds on Coase's invariance and efficiency thesis. Coase's argument that the initial allocation of legal rights influences economic activities if transaction costs are high[84] implies a need for a guiding principle on how states should allocate legal rights to promote efficiency. Posner therefore proposes that states should, in that circumstance, aim to maximise the wealth of the society by giving rights to those parties who would have secured them had market solutions been possible.[85] In other

77 Calabresi, 'Some Thoughts on Risk Distribution and the Law of Torts' (n 37) 506.
78 ibid 506.
79 Guido Calabresi, 'The Decision for Accidents: An Approach to Nonfault Allocation of Costs' (1965) 78 Harvard Law Review 713, 726.
80 Calabresi, 'Some Thoughts on Risk Distribution and the Law of Torts' (n 37) 505.
81 ibid 517.
82 Calabresi, 'The Decision for Accidents' (n 79) 729.
83 Guido Calabresi and Jon T Hirschoff, 'Toward a Test for Strict Liability in Torts' (1972) 81 The Yale Law Journal 1055, 1060.
84 Coase, 'The Problem of Social Cost' (n 26) 16.
85 Posner, *Economic Analysis of Law* (n 29) 15.

words, he suggests that states (particularly courts) should "mimic" what the market solution would have been had it been possible.

Thus, using the hypothetical case above, where ABC Ltd earns a yearly net income of £100 and farmer Mike earns £50, suppose that the transaction cost is high enough to make a market solution impossible. Posner proposes that the state should allocate the right to ABC Ltd – being the party who would have purchased the right if originally owned by farmer Mike or would not sell it if it was the original owner of the right in Coase's costless world.

Posner's wealth maximisation theory rests on two fundamental assumptions of microeconomics: (i) that resources are scarce in relation to human wants; and (ii) that people are rational maximisers of their individual satisfaction or utility.[86] To Posner, efficiency is the sole standard for all proposed legal solutions.[87] He defines efficiency as the "allocation of resources in which value is maximized".[88] He states that the economic value of a thing is how much one is willing and able to pay for it or the least amount one will accept to part with it.[89] He measures efficiency in terms of willingness to pay.

4.2.2 *Basic concepts and models*

What does the foregoing analysis have to do with the present research? First, it shows that legal rules affect efficiency. This shows the need to carry out research that analyses the efficiency of laws. Second, the analysis introduces the reader to some interesting economic concepts (such as efficiency, justice, transaction costs, externalities and market solutions), which are all relevant to the present research. This section discusses these concepts and their utility to this research in more detail. The methodological limitations of the economic analysis of the law approach and how these limitations will be addressed in this research are also discussed. Before commencing these discussions, it is essential to first explain the two distinct methods of economic analysis of law: positive analysis and normative analysis.[90]

86 ibid 3f.
87 Richard A Posner, 'Book Review (Reviewing Guido Calabresi, The Cost of Accidents: A Legal and Economic Analysis (1970))' (1970) 37 University of Chicago Law Review 636, 638 (arguing that the value of "justice" is unimportant in practice). This argument supports Coase's approach.
88 Posner, *Economic Analysis of Law* (n 29) 11.
89 ibid 10.
90 ibid 24.

4.2.2.1 Positive and normative economic analysis of law

The positive economic analysis of law aims at explaining existing legal rules and their outcomes.[91] Conversely, the normative analysis of the law aims at evaluating alternative legal solutions and determining which of the solutions is most desirable.[92] Taking the goal of reviving securitisation in the European Union (EU) as an example, positive analysis will explain the existing legal framework for securitisation and how it has either inhibited or revived securitisation issuances in the EU using facts and figures. Normative analysis will show that the legal framework adopted to attain the revival goal is inefficient and that the EU could achieve a better result, at a lower cost, by using an alternative framework.

The normative approach will be used to answer the main question which the present research aims to answer: "which of the focus regimes' solutions is most desirable for securitisation transactions?"[93]

4.2.2.2 Normative analysis: the efficiency criterion

This research raises an important question about the evaluation standard to be used for determining the most desirable solution. The leading metric for most economic analysis of law literature is "efficiency".[94] However, mentioning "efficiency" without more does not give an adequate answer to the evaluation question. This is because the normative claim of efficiency – that law ought to be efficient – itself raises further questions. Precisely how will the efficiency norm be measured? Will it have a justice content? If yes, will justice play a dominant role?

According to Schäfer and Ott, efficiency means that "given the resources initially available and their allocation, the members of a society have achieved the highest possible level of utility."[95] Different criteria have been adopted in measuring when the "highest possible level of utility" in a society has been achieved. In economic analysis of law, the two leading efficiency criteria are the Pareto criterion and the Kaldor-Hicks criterion.[96]

According to the Pareto criterion, a state of affairs is Pareto superior if a move from position X to position Y makes at least one person better off and no one worse off.[97] Thus,

---

91 Richard Posner, 'Some Uses and Abuses of Economics in Law' (1979) 46 The University of Chicago Law Review 281, 285 (describing positive economic analysis of law as "the use of economic analysis to explain what is or has been or to predict what will be").

92 Posner, *Economic Analysis of Law* (n 29) 34.

93 For discussion of the normative analysis see chapter 8.

94 Eli M Salzberger, 'The Economic Analysis of Law – The Dominant Methodology for Legal Research?!' (2007) University of Haifa Faculty of Law Legal Studies Research Paper No. 1044382, 219 <http://www.ssrn.com/abstract=1044382> accessed 28 May 2024.

95 Hans-Bernd Schäfer and Claus Ott, *The Economic Analysis of Civil Law* (Edward Elgar 2004) 8.

96 Jules L Coleman, 'Economics and the Law: A Critical Review of the Foundations of the Economic Approach to Law' (1984) 94 Ethics 649, 650f.

97 Vilfredo Pareto, *Manual of Political Economy* (AS Schwier and AN Page eds, August M Kelley Publishers 1971) 17–15, 105–106 (establishing the Pareto criterion).

using securitisation as an example, suppose a bank wishes to raise capital to fund a new loan valued at £2.5 billion. The bank sells a portfolio of its mortgages worth £2 billion to a special purpose vehicle (SPV) at a discounted price of £1.8 billion for the capital raise. The sale means that the bank (i.e. the originator) loses £2 billion worth of illiquid mortgages but gains £1.8 billion worth of liquid cash, which it can immediately use to fund the new loan. This makes the bank better off since it values the new loan (i.e. £2.5 billion) more than the £2 billion mortgages. The investors are also better off since they lose £1.8 billion and gain £2 billion. And since all parties to the transaction are better off, the allocation of resources brought about by the sale is Pareto superior to the allocation of resources before the sale. Where all possible Pareto changes have occurred (i.e. no further Pareto change is possible), such a state of affairs becomes Pareto efficient or Pareto optimal.

The Pareto criterion has been criticised for being too limited in its applicability to real-life situations. Calabresi argued that "any given society is always or will always immediately arrive at a Pareto optimal point", and policymakers are confronted with making laws that will necessarily make someone worse off.[98] Indeed, going by Coase's invariance and efficiency thesis, if further Pareto changes were possible in a market system, they would have occurred through market solutions.

The importance of legal rules in the real world implies that negative externalities exist and cannot be addressed through market solutions because of prohibitive transaction costs. Take securitisation, for example: third parties like the originator's unsecured creditors, the obligors, and existing and future business partners of the originator are most likely to be affected by a securitisation transaction. Thus, if an unsecured creditor believes that securitisation will reduce the unencumbered assets of the originator (which would have been available to them in the event of the originator's default) and therefore make them worse off, the transaction will be inefficient and undesirable according to the Pareto criterion. This shows that the applicability of the criterion as the standard for measuring efficiency may be limited.

The notion of the Kaldor-Hicks criterion – otherwise called "wealth maximisation"[99] – was introduced to address the limitation of the Pareto criterion.[100] The Kaldor-Hicks efficiency criterion argues that a move from position X to position Y is efficient if the winners from the change could compensate the losers from the change and still be better off. Thus, in a securitisation transaction, if the aggregate benefit to the securitisation parties (i.e. the originator and the investors) exceeds any net harm to third parties (like the

98 Guido Calabresi, 'The Pointlessness of Pareto: Carrying Coase Further' (1991) 100 The Yale Law Journal 1211.

99 Posner, *Economic Analysis of Law* (n 29) 13.

100 Nicholas Kaldor, 'Welfare Propositions of Economics and Interpersonal Comparisons of Utility' (1939) 49 The Economic Journal 549; JR Hicks, 'The Foundations of Welfare Economics' (1939) 49 The Economic Journal 696.

originator's unsecured creditors and the obligors to the securitisation transaction), the transaction will be efficient. Posner describes Kaldor-Hicks efficiency as the dominant standard for measuring efficiency in law and economics.[101]

Kaldor-Hicks improvement is sometimes called "potential Pareto improvement" since no one will be worse off after the change if the winner(s) actually compensates the loser(s). However, Kaldor-Hicks efficiency is only concerned with whether the winner *can* adequately compensate the loser and still be better off, not whether the loser *has* actually been compensated.[102] This effect may be better explained when compared to Coase's invariance and efficiency thesis and Posner's wealth maximisation. Coase's invariance and efficiency theses explain how market agents will always contract their way to a Pareto efficient outcome (regardless of legal rules) in a world of zero transaction costs.[103] Conversely, Kaldor-Hicks efficiency is concerned with how legal rules should allocate rights when transaction costs make market solutions impossible.[104] It prescribes that where market solutions are impossible because of high transaction costs, the law should assign the legal right to the party who would have ended up with it if a market solution were possible.[105]

Going back to the earlier pollution hypothesis, suppose that ABC Ltd would lose £115 if it could not manufacture and farmer Mike would lose £100 if ABC Ltd could manufacture. Further, suppose that a market solution is impossible because of a high transaction cost. The Kaldor-Hicks criterion requires, in such circumstances, that the law or courts should assign the legal right to ABC Ltd – being the party who would have purchased the right if originally owned by farmer Mike, or would not sell if it was the original owner of the right, in Coase's costless world. The problem with the Kaldor-Hicks efficiency solution can immediately be seen from the scenario: it leads to a "winner-takes-all" outcome. ABC Ltd will have £115 but farmer Mike will get nothing for losing what he values. Thus, the Kaldor-Hicks criterion is criticised for being unfair and disadvantageous to the poor,[106] as it measures efficiency based on willingness and ability to pay.

The Kaldor-Hicks criterion has also been criticised for being contradictory.[107] Scitovsky argues that the Kaldor-Hicks efficiency criterion may justify a move from position X to position Y and at the same time justify a move from position Y to position X. He uses

101 Posner, *Economic Analysis of Law* (n 29) 13.

102 ibid.

103 Coase, 'The Problem of Social Cost' (n 26) 42ff.

104 Jules Coleman, 'The Normative Basis of the Economic Analysis of Law' (1982) 34 Stanford Law Review 1105, 1108.

105 ibid.

106 CT Wonnell, 'Efficiency and Conservatism' (2001) 80 Nebraska Law Review 643, 660.

107 T de Scitovszky, 'A Note on Welfare Propositions in Economics' (1941) 9 The Review of Economic Studies 77, 88.

mathematical evidence and the example of import duties to illustrate his point.[108] A move from a "no duty" status to a "positive duty" status may be shown to be efficient under the Kaldor-Hicks criterion since the state gets more money. Yet the same Kaldor-Hicks test may be used to justify a move from a "positive duty" status to a "no duty" status, which favours businesses. This contradiction is called the "Scitovsky Paradox".

The above limitations associated with both Pareto efficiency and Kaldor-Hicks efficiency will be addressed in this research by adopting both criteria as standards for measuring efficiency, with Pareto efficiency being the dominant criterion. In other words, if a move achieves a Pareto improvement, the move will be considered as most desirable even if an alternative move achieves a Kaldor-Hicks improvement. However, where a Pareto move is impossible, the Kaldor-Hicks criterion will be used as the standard for measuring efficiency. Sections 4.2.3 and 8.2.1 explain how this will work.

4.2.3 *Pareto efficiency and Kaldor-Hicks efficiency: application and research scope*

Some argue that legal systems function as competitive markets for the supply of different solutions to a specific legal problem.[109] This is truer with securitisations and the competitive efforts of nations to revitalise securitisation markets in their different jurisdictions. Through their laws and practices, states have strived to provide attractive solutions to address the transfer issue posed by securitisation. To attract securitisations into their markets, states try to ensure that receivables are easily transferable. But these efforts will normally conflict with the property law principle of publicity, which protects third parties that may be affected by the transfer.[110] The publicity requirements of notification and registration aim to protect potential third parties (like future creditors) who may be misled into believing that the transferred receivables and related security rights are part of the originator's assets if the transfer was not publicised.[111] The requirement for notification protects the obligors from unknown creditors, so that they are always aware of who they are indebted to.[112]

But these publicity requirements impose high transaction costs on both the originator and the investors. The transaction costs are often too high for market solutions to absorb given the multiple number of obligors involved. For example, negotiating with all the

108 ibid.

109 See e.g. Anthony Ogus, 'Competition Between National Legal Systems: A Contribution of Economic Analysis to Comparative Law' (1999) 48 International and Comparative Law Quarterly 405.

110 For discussion of the publicity principle see section 8.1.

111 See section 8.1.

112 See Eleanor Cashin-Ritaine, *Contractual Assignments of Claims for Sums of Money in Franco-German Civil and Commercial Relations* (LGDJ 2001) 408f.

obligors involved in a mortgage-backed securitisation transaction involves a very high cost, as that will mean dealing with thousands of obligors. This high transaction cost, and its prohibitive nature, has made government (or state) intervention necessary. There is, therefore, a need for some trading off. The relevant question is: how much of the publicity values should be sacrificed in pursuing an enabling framework for transferring rights in securitisation transactions?[113]

The focus regimes have tried to address this question, albeit in different ways. Notable legal solutions adopted so far in the focus regimes include the English equitable assignment,[114] the French *bordereau*,[115] and the Scottish trust and the registration solution adopted under the Moveable Transactions (Scotland) Act 2023[116] (the focus solutions). This research analyses and compares these solutions, using both Pareto and Kaldor-Hicks as criteria for measuring efficiency. To help with an in-depth and valuable analysis, some assumptions and exclusions are necessary.

First, the Scottish assignation will be considered as the current state of affairs (or the status quo) for transferring receivables and related security rights. The choice of the Scottish assignation as the status quo is mainly because of its strict adherence to the publicity principle compared with the English and French standard assignment laws.[117] The choice is also informed by the fact that the publicity requirement is the major difficulty the focus solutions are designed to address.[118] It will also be assumed that the focus solutions are the alternative states of affairs the status quo could be moved to. The aim is to analyse the improvement made by each alternative state of affairs and the extent such improvement achieves a Pareto efficient outcome or a Kaldor-Hicks efficient outcome. An improvement that achieves a Pareto efficient outcome will be considered the superior outcome, while an improvement that achieves a Kaldor-Hicks efficient outcome will be considered the weaker outcome.

Second, it will be assumed that the third parties that are negatively affected by the transfer are the obligors and potential assignees and creditors of the originator. These are the most likely third parties that would be negatively affected by the transfer.[119]

113 See chapter 8 for discussion.
114 See chapter 6 for discussion.
115 See chapter 7 for discussion.
116 See chapter 5 for discussion.
117 See section 8.1.2 for discussion.
118 See section 8.2 for discussion.
119 In theory, an externality analysis generally applies to all third parties and is not restricted to a particular class. However, researching such a wide range of parties will be impracticable. It is essential to limit this research to the obligors and the potential assignees/creditors of the originator (the focus third parties) for a close-ended analysis to be achieved. Third parties that will mainly be affected by the transfer are those commercially interested in the relevant rights. These will typically include the focus third parties. Section 8.2.1 identifies other third parties that may be commercially interested (i.e. the originator's

4.3 Legal transplant

4.3.1 *An overview of the concept*

Professor Alan Watson defined legal transplant as "the moving of a rule or a system of law from one country to another, or from one people to another".[120] Watson argued that the transplanting of laws is easy and "extremely common".[121] Even customary law could be borrowed.[122] He claimed that the nomadic character of rules makes the idea of a close relationship between law and society a fallacy.[123] Borrowing is the most common mode of legal development.[124] Therefore, he argued, the proper focus of comparative law as an academic discipline should be the study of the relationships between legal systems, especially where such relationships result from borrowing.[125]

Watson's legal transplant theory also has its critics. One of the strongest opponents of the theory is Pierre Legrand. Professor Legrand rejects the theory and argues that it is insensitive to systems' cultural and social differences.[126] He notes that a law or rule is "an accretion of cultural elements"[127] and can only be understood when considered in the context of cultural viewpoints from which it originates.[128] If rules cannot be detached from their cultural contexts without losing their original meaning, rules cannot travel. And since rules cannot travel, legal transplants are impossible, he argues.[129]

A more moderate view taken by other scholars acknowledges the practice of legal borrowing but suggests that the borrowed law undergoes some transformation in the receiving jurisdiction.[130] Professor Gunther Teubner uses his concept of "legal irritants" in relation to the transplant of the continental principle of good faith into British contract

---

unsecured creditors and the SPV's creditors/assignees) and discusses why they are not considered in the present research.

120 Alan Watson, *Legal Transplants: An Approach to Comparative Law* (2nd edn, University of Georgia Press 1993) 21.

121 ibid 95 and 107.

122 ibid 114.

123 ibid 108.

124 ibid 21.

125 ibid 117.

126 Pierre Legrand, 'The Impossibility of "Legal Transplants"' (1997) 4 Maastricht Journal of European and Comparative Law 111.

127 ibid 116.

128 Legrand noted that this cultural element of the rule is an effective part of "the ruleness of the rule" – ibid 116f.

129 ibid 114.

130 See e.g. Gunther Teubner, 'Legal Irritants: Good Faith in British Law or How Unifying Law Ends Up in New Divergencies' (2003) 61 The Modern Law Review 11; Esin Örücü, 'Law as Transposition' (2002) 51 International and Comparative Law Quarterly 205.

law by the European Consumer Protection Directive 1994.[131] He argues that the term "legal transplant" is a misleading metaphor and that the concept of "legal irritants" better expresses the result of direct legal transfers.[132] For Teubner, a direct legal transfer does not amount to transforming an alien rule into a familiar rule, as transplantation suggests. Instead, "it works as a fundamental irritation which triggers a whole series of new and unexpected events" in the receiving jurisdiction.[133] He argues that "[l]egal irritants cannot be domesticated. … Rather they will unleash an evolutionary dynamic in which the external rule's meaning will be reconstructed and the internal context will undergo fundamental change."[134]

Professor Esin Örücü uses the concept of "legal transposition" to show that legal transfers undergo "tuning and fitting" in order to make the borrowed law compatible with the culture and needs of the receiving jurisdiction.[135] According to Örücü, a successful legal transposition will require internal "tuning" (that is, tuning by the receiving jurisdiction) at all levels, including judicial consideration of the borrowed law and legal education.[136]

4.3.2 Relevance and application to this research

It is difficult not to admit that legal borrowings are possible. Jurisdictions indeed borrow laws and ideas from one another. An obvious example is the reception of Roman law in most parts of Western Europe. Scotland, for example, is a beneficiary of Roman law, and some aspects of Scots private law, such as the law of pledge, are still substantially based on Roman law.[137] Other instances of legal borrowing include the comprehensive transplant of the French Civil Code into the Ethiopian Civil Code of 1960 and Turkey's adoption of the Swiss and German codes after the establishment of the Turkish Republic in 1922.[138] Moreover, the legislation establishing law reform commissions in some jurisdictions

131 Teubner (n 130).
132 ibid.
133 ibid 12.
134 ibid.
135 Örücü (n 130) 207.
136 ibid 208.
137 For discussion of the reception of Roman law in Scotland see William Gordon, 'Roman Law in Scotland' in R Evans-Jones, *The Civil Law Tradition in Scotland* [The Stair Society, supplementary series, vol 2] (Stair Society 1995) 13.
138 See respectively René David, 'A Civil Code for Ethiopia: Considerations on the Codification of the Civil Law in African Countries' (1962–1963) 37 Tulane Law Review 187 and Mathias Siems, *Comparative Law* (2nd edn, Cambridge University Press 2018) 253.

presupposes and encourages legal borrowings.[139] The preceding discussion makes Legrand's argument (that transplants are impossible) less forceful.

This research considers Örücü's view (that legal borrowings are possible but subject to internal modifications) more practical. Indeed, Watson acknowledged the possibility of the borrowed law undergoing modifications in the receiving jurisdiction. Responding to Legrand's criticism, he acknowledged that a transplanted rule may not operate the same way it does in its origin system and that the significance of this consequence is one of the main themes of his legal transplant theory.[140] He believed that the donor system does not control the final result of the borrowing process. Instead, the recipient system has the final say on the mode of application of the borrowed law.[141] He noted that the critical point "is not the identity of interpretation but the fact that identity of rule does lead to much greater similarity between the two systems."[142]

Based on the foregoing, this research will assess the transferability of the "best solution" to the focus regimes. Consideration will be given to whether the solution is compatible with the receiving regime, and necessary adjustments will be suggested.

4.4 Conclusion

This chapter demonstrates that the three comparative law approaches (i.e. the functional approach, the economic analysis of law approach and legal transplant) are relevant to this research. The functional approach will be used to identify the transfer solutions available in the focus regimes. The law and economics approach will be used to compare and evaluate the solutions identified in order to determine the best solution. The research will also assess the practicability of transferring the "best solution" to the relevant focus regimes.

---

139 E.g. under s 3(1)(b) of the Law Commissions Act 1965 English and Scottish law commissioners are required "to obtain such information as to the legal systems of other countries as appears to the Commissioners likely to facilitate the performance of any of their functions". For an equivalent provision in Northern Ireland see the Justice (NI) Act 2002, s 51(2)(f).

140 Alan Watson, 'Legal Transplants and European Private Law' (2000) 4 Electronic Journal of Comparative Law para VII.

141 George Mousourakis, 'Legal Transplants and Legal Development: A Jurisprudential and Comparative Law Approach' (2013) 54 Acta Juridica Hungarica 219, 233.

142 Watson (n 140) para VI.

5 TRANSFER OF RIGHTS UNDER SCOTS LAW

This chapter begins the solution identification exercise by examining the solutions available in Scotland. The aim is to identify the preferred transfer solution and show why it is so preferred.

Security rights are part of property law,[1] and so is their transfer.[2] Therefore, the creation and transfer of security rights in Scotland are subject to the general principles of the Scottish law of property. Two such principles that will keep emerging in the issues discussed in this chapter are the publicity principle and the principle of unitary ownership. The former is a rigid common law principle which requires real rights to be constituted and transferred publicly. The latter requires that a thing is only susceptible to a single title at any one time.[3] The consequence of the principles' application being that ownership[4] of security rights in a securitisation should only pass to the special purpose vehicle (SPV) when the required public act is completed. Such is the significance of the publicity

1 Security rights (excluding cautionary securities and uncrystallised floating charges) are real rights. Real rights are rights held directly over a thing. In contrast, personal rights are rights held against a person or group of persons. Real rights are enforceable against anyone who interferes with the rights held in the relevant property. Examples of real rights are ownership rights, security rights, servitudes and proper liferents. An ownership right is the "main" real right from which the other real rights flow. Hence these other real rights are regarded as "subordinate" real rights. Personal rights, on the other hand, are enforceable against persons liable by virtue of obligations arising from e.g. contract, delict or unjustified enrichment. While the creation and transfer of real rights are matters of property law, the creation of personal rights is a matter of the law of obligations and the transfer is a matter of property law. See generally KGC Reid, *The Law of Property in Scotland* (Butterworths 1996) paras 4f; GL Gretton and AJM Steven, *Property, Trusts and Succession* (4th edn, Bloomsbury Professional Scotland 2021) paras 2.1ff.

2 Professors Gretton and Steven note that "[m]uch of property law is about the transfer of rights from one person to another": Gretton and Steven, *Property, Trusts and Succession* (n 1) para 1.29.

3 This does not preclude two or more persons from co-owning or sharing the title, as in the case of common or joint ownership, provided they are owning under a single title. Reid, *The Law of Property* (n 1) paras 536 and 603. Also, the single title rule only relates to the right of ownership, and not real rights in general. Therefore, while only one person can own a thing, it does not preclude two or more different real rights to exist in a thing. Thus, a house can be owned by A (and A alone), but leased and possessed by B, with C and D having security rights over the same house. See Reid, *The Law of Property* (n 1) 6; Gretton and Steven, *Property, Trusts and Succession* (n 1) paras 2.11ff.

4 The question of whether security rights (or incorporeal property generally) can be owned or not is a matter of debate. For discussion of the argument that rights are held not owned see e.g. GL Gretton, 'Ownership and its Objects' (2007) 71 Rabels Zeitschrift 802. Cf Reid, *The Law of Property* (n 1) 16. See also RG Anderson, *Assignation* (Edinburgh Legal Education Trust 2008) para 1.09. This book does not hold a strong view on this issue and the terminology used here depends upon the context.

principle.[5] As a result of the foregoing, to gainfully discuss the solutions available in Scotland for the transfer of security rights, it is necessary to dedicate a section of this chapter to discussion of the nature of security rights in Scots law and the impact the publicity principle has in their constitution. As will be seen below, the publicity required for transferring a security right generally depends on the publicity used in constituting it.

Accordingly, this chapter is divided into four sections. The first section discusses the Scottish law of security rights generally. It demonstrates the dominance of the publicity principle, the difficulties arising from this dominance and the efforts made so far to mitigate these difficulties.[6] Section 5.2 discusses the accessoriness of security rights. It demonstrates that the transfer of rights to debt does not always mean that the related security rights will automatically pass under Scots law. This establishes the importance of treating the transfer of security rights separately from the transfer of rights to debt in securitisation transactions in Scotland. Section 5.3 discusses the two main solutions available for transferring security rights in securitisations. These solutions are assignation and trust. The assignation by registration solution newly introduced by the Moveable Transactions (Scotland) Act 2023 (hereafter "the registration solution") is also considered in section 5.3. This chapter concludes in section 5.4 that the ability of the trust to separate ownership rights from beneficiary rights without invoking the publicity principle makes it the preferred method of transferring security rights under *current* Scots law (i.e. excluding the registration solution, as its operative provisions are not yet in force).

5.1 SECURITY RIGHTS IN SCOTS LAW: NATURE AND CONSTITUTION

5.1.1 *Definition and types of security rights*

A security right has been defined as "any right which a creditor may hold for ensuring payment, or for satisfaction of his debt, distinct from, and in addition to, his right of action and execution against the debtor under the latter's personal obligation."[7] Security rights

5 Although the principle is also present in English law, the fact that an equitable ownership right can be created without complying with the principle makes it less significant. For a comparison, see David L Carey Miller and Malcolm M Combe, 'The Boundaries of Property Rights in Scots Law: Report to the XVIIth Congress of Comparative Law' (2006) 10 Electronic Journal of Comparative Law 1, 3.

6 Though a strict adherence to the publicity principle is unfavourable to commerce in some respects (particularly in commercial transactions, like securitisations, that involve bulk sales), the principle has its value. Hence the need to strike the right balance between the need for publicity and the need for commerce. These issues are discussed in more detail in chapter 8.

7 W Gloag and J Irvine, *Law of Rights in Security, Heritable and Moveable: Including Cautionary Obligations* (W Green 1897) 1.

can be personal or real.[8] A personal security right (also called "cautionary security") is the Scottish equivalent of the English suretyship.[9] It arises where a third party (the cautioner) undertakes to pay a debt owed by a debtor (the principal obligant) in the event that the debtor defaults.[10] Thus, where the creditor cannot obtain payment of a debt from the debtor, a cautionary security entitles the creditor to call on the cautioner to pay the outstanding debt. The security is "personal" because it can only be enforced against the cautioner. On the other hand, a real security is a "right held by a creditor in property in security of a debt".[11] The right is "real" because it gives the holder a direct right in the security property, which is enforceable against any person who interferes with the right.[12]

Usually, the underlying rights in security used in backing securitisations are rights held in property. For example, mortgage-backed securities (MBS) involve security rights held on land. The same also applies to commercial mortgage-backed securities (CMBS). Some asset-backed securities (ABS) typically involve security rights in property.[13] Collateralised debt obligations (CDOs) are also good examples: they usually include debts that are backed by security rights held in property.[14] It is for this reason that the rest of this chapter will focus on real security rights.

5.1.2 *Types and constitution of real security rights*

The actual method by which a real security right can be constituted varies according to the nature of the property in which the right is held.[15] Property can be classified in two

8 There are various other ways security rights can be classified in Scots law, e.g. fixed and floating securities, heritable (or immoveable) and moveable securities, proper and improper securities, possessory and non-possessory securities, express, tacit and judicial securities, and notification and non-notification securities. For more details on these classes of security rights see Scottish Law Commission (SLC), *Discussion Paper on Moveable Transactions* (DP 151, 2011) paras 5.11ff.

9 It was observed in *Aitken's Trustees v Bank of Scotland* 1944 SC 270, at 279, that the general principles of caution in Scotland and surety in England are "nearly the same".

10 GJ Bell, *Principles of the Law of Scotland* (10th edn, T&T Clark 1899) para 245.

11 Reid, *The Law of Property* (n 1) para 5.

12 ibid para 3.

13 E.g. auto loan ABS typically comprise security rights held in automobiles.

14 E.g. collateralised loan obligations (a type of CDO) typically comprise corporate loans secured by assets of the borrowing company.

15 For floating charges, the ability to even grant the security will depend on the nature of the debtor, who must be an incorporated company, a limited liability partnership, a society registered under the Co-operative and Community Benefit Societies Act 2014, a building society, a European economic interest grouping or a UK economic interest grouping. See, respectively, Companies Act 1985, s 462(1); Limited Liability Partnerships (Scotland) Regulations 2001 (SSI 2001/128), reg 3; Co-operative and Community Benefit Societies Act 2014, s 62; Financial Services (Banking Reform) Act 2013 (Commencement (No 8) and Consequential Provisions) Order 2015 (SI 2015/428), art 4 and Sch 1; European Economic Interest Grouping Regulations 1989 (SI 1989/638), reg 18 and Sch 4 (as amended by the European Economic Interest Grouping (Amendment) (EU Exit) Regulations 2018 (SI 2018/1299)).

different ways in Scots law: it can either be moveable or heritable, or corporeal or incorporeal. The implication of this is that a property can be (i) corporeal moveable property, (ii) incorporeal moveable property, (iii) corporeal heritable property, or (iv) incorporeal heritable property.[16]

Corporeal moveable property has a physical presence and can easily move itself or can be easily moved.[17] Incorporeal moveable property, on the other hand, does not have a physical presence and is incapable of physical possession.[18] Therefore, cars, books and other physical goods are all corporeal moveable property, while rights arising under a contract,[19] delict, unjustified enrichment, trust, intellectual property rights and insurance policies are examples of incorporeal moveable property.

Heritable property generally means land and rights pertaining to land.[20] Corporeal heritable property consists of land and the right of ownership in land.[21] Incorporeal heritable property, on the other hand, consists of all other rights connected with land.[22] Therefore, subordinate real rights (like proper liferents (or *usufructs*), praedial servitudes, leases and standard securities) and certain personal rights (like contractual rights to acquire land) are all examples of incorporeal heritable property.

---

16 Reid, *The Law of Property* (n 1) paras 11ff; Gretton and Steven, *Property, Trusts and Succession* (n 1) paras 1.21ff.

17 A McDouall, Lord Bankton, *An Institute of the Law of Scotland in Civil Rights: With Observations upon the Agreement or Diversity between them and the Laws of England* (1751–53, reprinted by Stair Society, vols 41–42, 1993–95) I, iii, 36.

18 Gretton and Steven, *Property, Trusts and Succession* (n 1) para 1.24.

19 Gretton and Steven suggest that not all contractual rights are moveable. They cite an example of a contractual right to acquire land as incorporeal heritable property, and not incorporeal moveable property. See ibid.

20 Gretton and Steven, *Property, Trusts and Succession* (n 1) para 1.21. The use of "heritable" (instead of "immoveable") reflects the distinction that existed between moveable and heritable property under the old Scots law of succession. Traditionally, heritable property (i.e. land and its accessories) could only be inherited by the heir-at-law, who was normally the first son, while moveable property was inheritable by other successors of the deceased estate and was administered and distributed by an executor. Under the modern law, such distinction no longer exists in relation to the devolution of an intestate estate. See Succession (Scotland) Act 1964, s 1. The distinction is however preserved in matters relating to the distribution of the surviving spouse's prior and legal rights, and succession to titles, coats of arms and honours. See again Succession (Scotland) Act 1964, ss 9(3), 10(2) and 37(1)(a). A replacement of the word "heritable" with "immoveable" was suggested by the SLC in its 1976 consultative memorandum. See generally Scottish Law Commission, *Corporeal Moveables: Some Problems of Classification* (Consultative Memorandum 26, 1976) paras 31f.

21 Land, as used here, includes buildings and any other property physically attached to the land.

22 Gretton and Steven, *Property, Trusts and Succession* (n 1) para 1.24.

5.1.2.1 Security over corporeal moveable property: nature and difficulties

a) Pledge

As a general rule under Scottish common law, a real right over corporeal moveable property can only be constituted when possession of the property has been delivered.[23] While this possessory rule has been relaxed in respect of contracts of sale by virtue of sections 17 and 18 of the Sale of Goods Act 1979,[24] the rule remains valid for constituting security rights over corporeal moveables.[25] As a result, the main form of voluntary security over corporeal moveables in Scots law requires the delivery of possession to the creditor.[26] This form of security is called pledge (or possessory pledge).[27] The Moveable Transactions (Scotland) Act 2023 introduces a new form of pledge, known as "statutory pledge", which requires only registration for its validity.[28] However, since the operative parts of the Act are not yet in force, the following discussion focuses mainly on possessory pledge.

Pledge differs from lien because it arises voluntarily (i.e. expressly) by contract, while lien is a tacit security (i.e. it arises by operation of law).[29] Another tacit security available in Scots law over corporeal moveable property is the landlord's hypothec. This is a non-possessory security, which gives a landlord a right in security over goods belonging to the tenant and located within a leased premises.[30] Since securitisations are typically involved

---

23 J Erskine of Carnock, *An Institute of the Law of Scotland* (Edinburgh Legal Education Trust 1773) II, i, 19f; J Dalrymple, Viscount Stair, *The Institutions of the Law of Scotland* (DM Walker ed, Edinburgh University Press 1981) II, i, 11; Bell, *Principles* (n 10) para 1300.

24 These sections allow ownership of corporeal moveables to pass when parties intend for it to pass in a contract of sale; and there are general default rules that apply when the intention is not expressed. These provisions are substantially the same as those under the original Sale of Goods Act 1893, ss 17 and 18.

25 Section 62(4) of the Sale of Goods Act 1979 disapplies the provisions of the Act concerning contracts of sale from a transaction in the form of a contract of sale but designed to operate as a security. Bell, *Principles* (n 10) para 1364; Gloag and Irvine, *Security* (n 7) 188f. On whether a transfer of ownership rights in a corporeal moveable (without delivery of possession) for security purposes can give rise to a competent security, Lord Deas held that "it is perfectly settled beyond all question in our law and practice that such an assignation if not followed by possession confers no security whatever." See *Clark v West Calder Oil Co* (1882) 9 R (CSIH) 1017.

26 Other forms of voluntary security over corporeal moveables that do not require delivery to the creditor include floating charges, ship mortgages, aircraft mortgages and agricultural charges. These are discussed in section 5.1.2.1(b).

27 For discussion of the forms of delivery required see AJM Steven, *Pledge and Lien* (Edinburgh Legal Education Trust 2008) paras 6.07ff. See the paragraph below for discussion of the validity of other forms of delivery besides actual delivery.

28 Section 48(2) of the Act. The new form of pledge can be created over all corporeal moveables (except an aircraft and a ship). In terms of incorporeal moveables, it can only be created over intellectual property (including an application for, or licence over, intellectual property). Other types of incorporeal moveables may be added later through statutory instruments. See s 47 of the Act.

29 See Steven, *Pledge and Lien* (n 27) para 9.01.

30 See Gloag and Irvine, *Security* (n 7) 430. The application of the landlord's hypothec is now limited to commercial leases, and its principal enforcement mechanism (i.e. sequestration for rent) has been abolished. See Bankruptcy and Diligence etc. Act (Scotland) 2007, s 208(1) and (3). For a comprehensive

with security rights that are acquired expressly or voluntarily, the analysis in this section is only concerned with voluntary securities.

A pledge is a proper security. It only grants the pledgee (the creditor) a subordinate real right over the pledged asset, while the pledger (the debtor) retains title (i.e. ownership).[31] By contrast, in an improper security (or *fiducia cum creditore* security) title is transferred to the creditor for security purposes. The debtor, on the other hand, will have a personal right against the creditor to acquire title once the debt is fully paid.[32] An example of improper security is assignation in security, which is discussed in section 5.1.2.2.

The requirement to deliver possession in a pledge is rooted in the publicity principle, which requires real rights to be created publicly. The reason is that real rights affect third parties (and not merely the parties to the agreement that brought the real right into existence) and therefore require for their constitution not just the private act of agreement between the parties but also an external act to put such third parties on notice of their existence.[33] So, if A wishes to create a security right in a corporeal moveable for B, the publicity act required of A and B for the security to be valid is to put B in possession of the security property. Possession makes B's right over the property discoverable by third parties who will be potentially affected by the right.

However, the possessory rule limits the usefulness of pledge in many commercial cases. It makes it difficult for a debtor to create security rights over corporeal moveables they use to run their day-to-day business. The creditor, on the other hand, may not have the necessary storage facilities to hold possession. This difficulty is exacerbated by the rule in *Hamilton v Western Bank*,[34] which suggests that actual physical delivery is a prerequisite for constituting a pledge. This essentially casts doubt on the validity of other forms of delivery (i.e. constructive and symbolic delivery) which could have been more practicable, especially for goods stored in a warehouse belonging to a third party or goods aboard a

discussion of the landlord's hypothec under Scots law see Andrew Sweeney, *The Landlord's Hypothec* (Edinburgh Legal Education Trust 2021).

31 The implication of acquiring a proper security right is that: (i) the security provider could grant more than one security right over the same asset; (ii) the provider could transfer their ownership rights in the encumbered asset to a third party subject to the security right; (iii) the provider would remain entitled to the income or fruits derived from the encumbered asset; and (iv) if the debt is satisfied, the security would automatically extinguish (without the need for conveyance) once the debt is fully paid back. SLC, *Discussion Paper on Moveable Transactions* (n 8) paras 5.11f.

32 For improper security, (i) the security provider would not be able to grant another security right or transfer another ownership right in the security property since they have already ceded title to the creditor – they can, however, grant a security right over their personal rights against the secured creditor; (ii) the creditor would be entitled to the income or fruits derived from the security owner – although this would typically be credited to the debt or be paid to the security provider; and (iii) where the debt is later paid off, the security property must be reassigned to the debtor. See generally SLC, *Discussion Paper on Moveable Transactions* (n 8) paras 5.13ff.

33 Gloag and Irvine, *Security* (n 7) 8.

34 (1856) 19 D (CSIH) 152.

ship. It has been argued that the *Hamilton* rule was implicitly overturned following the court's recognition of the pledge of bills of lading (which represents an indirect possession of the goods being shipped) in *North Western Bank Limited v John Poynter Son & Macdonalds*.[35] However, the rule has not been expressly overruled. To clarify the law on the validity of other forms of delivery, the Moveable Transactions (Scotland) Act 2023 would repeal the rule in *Hamilton* when it becomes fully effective.[36]

It should be noted that a sale contract can be used to create a security right under common law. However, this will still require the debtor (or a third party) to transfer the security property *ex facie* absolutely and give up possession to the creditor.[37] The party granting the security will, in turn, have a personal right against the creditor to obtain ownership once the relevant debt has been fully paid. The need for delivery means that the difficulty that is associated with pledge also applies to this type of security. However, the advantage a transfer in security has over pledge is that it provides more extensive automatic powers and can confer all-sums security rights. Unlike pledge, the transfer in security is an improper security.

b) Other non-possessory securities over corporeal moveables

Other voluntary securities over corporeal moveables that do not require delivery of possession have been introduced by statutes. These include ship mortgage, aircraft mortgage and agricultural charge, for which the legislation replaced publicity by possession with publicity by registration.[38]

The commercial inconvenience of the possessory rule was also one of the main reasons why the floating charge was introduced in Scotland by the Companies (Floating Charges) (Scotland) Act 1961.[39] However, it is important to note that the constitution and attachment

---

35 (1894) 22 R (HL) 1.

36 Moveable Transactions (Scotland) Act 2023, s 44. For a background discussion of the issues see Scottish Law Commission, *Report on Moveable Transactions* (Scot Law Com No 249, 2017) paras 25.2ff.

37 See e.g. *Hamilton v Western Bank of Scotland* (1856) 19 D (CSIH) 152. On the need for delivery, see *Clark v West Calder Oil Co* (1882) 9 R (CSIH) 1017.

38 See respectively Merchant Shipping Act 1995, Sch 1 paras 7¬ and 8; Mortgaging of Aircraft Order 1972 (SI 1972/1268), ss 4–7. For international security interests over aircraft objects, see International Interests in Aircraft Equipment (Cape Town Convention) Regulations 2015 (SI 2015/912), reg 16. See also Agricultural Credits (Scotland) Act 1929, s 8 (which introduced the agricultural charge security) – this was later repealed by Financial Services and Markets Act 2000 (Consequential Amendments and Repeals) Order 2001 (SI 2001/3649), art 216. The agricultural charge nevertheless continues to exist, but it is rarely used in practice. The SLC have recommended that such security should no longer be competent. SLC, *Report on Moveable Transactions* (n 36) paras 38.14ff.

39 SLC, *Discussion Paper on Moveable Transactions* (n 8) para 9.1. The current statutory provision that allows the creation of floating charges is now contained in s 462 of the Companies Act 1985 – this is however subject to the implementation of pt 2 of the Bankruptcy and Diligence etc. (Scotland) Act 2007, which is now unlikely to ever be brought into force. For discussion of why the provisions have not been brought into force, see AJM Steven, 'Reform of Security over Moveables: Still a Longstanding Reform Agenda in Scots

of a floating charge are less compliant with the publicity principle than other security rights.[40] Although section 38(3) of the Bankruptcy and Diligence etc. (Scotland) Act 2007 would make floating charges more compliant with the publicity principle by requiring registration for its constitution, it is unlikely that the provision will ever be brought into force.

c) Non-possessory quasi-securities

Businesses have also tried to overcome the difficulty by employing contractual devices that function as securities but without possession. Examples of such devices include retention of title in sale,[41] hire purchase agreements[42] and sale and leaseback with an option to repurchase.[43] These devices enable the creditor to hold ownership over the corporeal moveable property that is being sold, hired or leased to the debtor until the debt is fully satisfied. By owning the property, the creditor's right is protected against the debtor's insolvency. The debtor, for their part, will have possession of the property.[44]

Law' in D Bain and others (eds), *Northern Lights: Essays in Private Law in Memory of Professor David Carey Miller* (Aberdeen University Press 2018) 217, 225.

40 For discussion see ADJ MacPherson, *The Floating Charge* (Edinburgh Legal Education Trust 2020) paras 3.16ff. The current law requires some form of registration relating to the creation and attachment of a floating charge; registration is not, however, a precondition for the creation of the floating charge. See Companies Act 2006, ss 859A and 859H for registration following creation; Insolvency Act 1986, s 53(1) and (2) and 54(3) and (4) for registration upon attachment by receivership; Insolvency Act 1986, s 130(1); Scotland Act 1998, Sch 8 para 23. For registration upon liquidation and in respect of administration, see MacPherson, *The Floating Charge*, paras 3.18–3.19. For criticism of the non-publicity of a floating charge's attachment, see Scottish Law Commission, *Report on Sharp v Thomson* (Scot Law Com No 208, 2008) paras 5.1ff.

41 The retention of title provision involves a sale of the corporeal moveable property by the creditor to the debtor which is subject to a suspensive condition that the title to the property will remain with the creditor until the full price has been paid. Two types of retention of title provisions generally exist: "price only" and "all sums" provisions. The former is specific to the price of the goods sold and typically provides that title will not pass until the price is paid in full. The latter is more extensive and covers the price of the goods and all other sums owed by the buyer to the seller. The validity of these provisions is based on ss 17 and 19(1) of the Sale of Goods Act 1979, which allow parties to postpone the time they intend title to transfer in a contract of sale. It is important that such a provision is characterised as a sale. This is because s 62(4) of that Act disapplies the Act from "sham" sales that operate as securities. It has been held that both the "price only" and "all sums" provisions are valid in Scots law by virtue of ss 17 and 19(1) of the Sale of Goods Act 1979, and that s 62(4) of the Act does not apply since the clause is not a security. See respectively *Archivent Sales & Development Ltd v Strathclyde Regional Council* 1985 SLT (CSOH) 154; *Armour v Thyssen Edelstahlwerke AG* 1990 SLT (HL) 891.

42 The hire purchase arrangement is a hire agreement which gives the debtor/hirer an option to purchase the corporeal moveable property at the end of the hire.

43 In a sale and leaseback arrangement, the corporeal property is already owned and possessed by the debtor. The debtor then "sells" their property to the creditor, and the creditor subsequently leases it back to the debtor. Typically, the transaction will give the debtor an option to repurchase the property at the end of a given period.

44 See GL Gretton, 'The Concept of Security' in DJ Cuisine (ed), *A Scots Conveyancing Miscellany: Essays in Honour of Professor J. M. Halliday* (W Green 1987) 130.

The trust is another device that has the potential to function as a security. It allows the debtor to declare a trust over their asset(s) (i.e. the trust property) for the benefit of the creditor without delivering possession. Although the beneficial right held by the creditor is a personal right against the trustee,[45] the right can be analogous to a real right in some respects. For instance, it will prevail over the claims of the trustee's personal creditors (in respect of the trust property) in the event of the trustee's insolvency.[46] This insolvency effect makes the trust a useful security device since the beneficiary's right in respect of the trust property prevails over the unsecured rights of the trustee's personal creditors. For discussion of the constitution and operation of the trust, see section 5.3.3.

d) Difficulties of the non-possessory securities and reforms

These alternative non-possessory securities and quasi-securities are, however, unsatisfactory. First, the requirement for delivery and possession remains the general rule for constituting a security over corporeal moveables in Scots law.[47] The non-possessory alternatives are just exceptions to the general rule. Second, the application of the non-possessory securities is limited to specific assets,[48] or specific debtors in the case of the floating charge.[49] Another limitation of the floating charge is that the charge ranks behind preferential creditors (including HMRC for certain unpaid taxes),[50] the prescribed part[51] and the expenses of the insolvency process.[52] Upon attachment, a floating charge also ranks behind pre-existing "effectually executed diligence".[53] The default position is that

45 Gretton and Steven, *Property, Trusts and Succession* (n 1) para 23.61.

46 See *Heritable Reversionary Co v Millar* (1892) 19 R (HL) 43, per Lord Watson at 49f. In relation to sequestration, see Bankruptcy (Scotland) Act 2016, s 88(1)(c). This insolvency effect of the beneficiary's right has been explained in terms of the dual patrimony theory. See GL Gretton, 'Trust and Patrimony' in HL MacQueen (ed), *Scots Law into the 21st Century: Essays in Honour of W. A. Wilson* (W Green 1996); GL Gretton, 'Trusts Without Equity' (2000) 49 International and Comparative Law Quarterly 599; KGC Reid, 'Patrimony Not Equity: The Trust in Scotland' in Remus Valsan (ed), *Trusts and Patrimonies* (Edinburgh University Press 2017).

47 This position will change once the Moveable Transactions (Scotland) Act 2023 becomes fully effective.

48 For example, ships and their cargo, aircraft and agricultural products are the only corporeal moveables that are susceptible to a non-possessory security under Scots law.

49 It can only be granted by companies, limited liability partnerships and certain other entities. It cannot be granted by natural persons, ordinary partnerships or limited partnerships under the Limited Partnerships Act 1907.

50 Insolvency Act 1986, s 59. For certain HMRC debts see the Finance Act 2020, ss 98–99.

51 Insolvency Act 1986, s 176A(2)(a) and (b).

52 Insolvency Act 1986, s 60(1)(c) and (d), s 115 and sch B1 para 99(3).

53 Companies Act 1985, s 463(1)(a); Insolvency Act 1986, ss 55(3)(a) and 60(1)(b); Bankruptcy and Diligence etc. (Scotland) Act 2007, s 45(3)(a). On the interpretation of "effectually executed diligence" see *MacMillan v T Leith Developments Ltd (In Receivership and Liquidation)* [2017] CSIH 23, 2017 SC 642. On the general interaction of the law of diligence, floating charges and corporate insolvency processes see ADJ MacPherson, 'The Circle Squared? Floating Charges and Diligence after *MacMillan v T Leith Developments Ltd*' (2018) 4 Juridical Review 230.

floating charges also rank behind fixed securities created after the floating charge.[54] However, that situation rarely arises in practice, as floating charges are almost invariably accompanied by negative pledge clauses, which rank floating charges from their creation date (rather than attachment date) against fixed securities.[55]

The quasi-security devices also have their problems. First, their status as workaround solutions means that parties may incur more transaction costs than would be the case if a proper security were used.[56] Also, quasi-securities like the sale and leaseback arrangement stand the risk of being recharacterised as securities, in which case section 62(4) of the Sale of Goods Act 1979 will apply. As noted above, that section disapplies the Act from "sham" sales that operate as securities.[57] The disapplication of the Act means that the transaction must be valid at common law for it to be legally effective. At common law, delivery of possession is essential for a sale to be effective.[58] Therefore, to ensure the validity of the sale and leaseback arrangement, the debtor has to give up possession to the creditor before the asset is leased back to the debtor. In practice, transaction parties usually try to fulfil the possession requirement by employing artificial delivery techniques, which makes the transaction more costly and complex.[59] In relation to the retention of title provisions, which have been established to be valid under sections 17 and 19(1) of the Sale of Goods Act 1979, the debtor (i.e. the buyer) might be able to transfer good title in the relevant property to a good faith purchaser under section 25(1) of the 1979 Act.[60]

---

54 Companies Act 1985, s 464(4)(a).

55 Companies Act 1985, s 464(1)(a) and (1A). For discussion of the nature of the negative pledge see MacPherson, *The Floating Charge* (n 40) paras 2.29ff.

56 This shortcoming was noted by academics from Aberdeen University in their response to the Scottish Parliament's call for views on the SLC's proposed changes to the law of moveable transactions. Alisdair MacPherson, Donna McKenzie Skene and Euan West, 'Moveable Transactions – Written Submissions' (University of Aberdeen, April 2020) 2 <https://www.parliament.scot/parliamentarybusiness/CurrentCommittees/115002.aspx> accessed 28 May 2024. Other responders, such as UK Finance and Brodies LLP, shared a similar view.

57 For further discussion of the effect of s 62(4) of the Sale of Goods Act 1979 see Gretton, 'The Concept of Security' (n 44) 135ff.

58 Reid, *The Law of Property* (n 1) para 626; Gretton and Steven, *Property, Trusts and Succession* (n 1) paras 5.16f.

59 See e.g. Jenny Hamilton and others, *Business Finance and Security over Moveable Property* (Scottish Executive Central Research Unit 2002) paras 3.130f.

60 See e.g. *Archivent Sales & Development Ltd v Strathclyde Regional Council* 1985 SLT (CSOH) 154. In respect of hire purchase transactions, see Hire Purchase Act 1964, s 27(3). Parties may attempt to draft the retention of title provision such that the buyer agrees to hold proceeds of the sale to third parties in trust for the unpaid seller. While such provisions may be valid in England by virtue of *Aluminium Industrie Vaassen BV v Romalpa Aluminium Ltd* [1976] 1 WLR 676 (CA), they are not valid in Scotland. See *Clark Taylor & Co Ltd v Quality Site Development (Edinburgh) Ltd* 1981 SC (IH) 111, per Lord President Emslie at 116 (where the court held that such provisions lack "the essential ingredients of a trust"). This, however, suggests that such provisions may be valid in Scotland if the essential ingredients of a trust are complied with. For discussion of the essential ingredients of a trust see section 5.3.3.

In respect of the trust, the beneficiary has no property right in the trust property. This means that the trustee can transfer good title (free from any encumbrance under the trust) to a bona fide transferee for value.[61] Since the beneficiary's right is personal, the beneficiary cannot vindicate the property from the third party. This is true even where the transfer is in breach of the trust.[62] The value the trustee received from the bona fide transferee will, however, automatically become trust property.[63]

5.1.2.2 Security over incorporeal moveable property: nature and difficulty

Under Scots law, a proper (or true) security cannot be created over incorporeal moveables.[64] It is impossible to grant a pledge over them as they are incapable of physical possession. Also, there is no Scottish equivalent to the English fixed equitable charge, which would allow the debtor to retain title while granting a subordinate real right to the creditor. While the floating charge may be used over incorporeal moveables, since it can be applied to "all or any part of the property" belonging to an incorporated company,[65] it does not seem to confer any real rights to the charge holder until attachment occurs.[66]

Therefore, the only way a voluntary fixed security can be created over incorporeal moveable property is to transfer title to the creditor.[67] So, if A has a contractual right to receive payments from B and wishes to use the contractual right as security for a loan from C, A must cede their title in the contractual right to C by way of assignation. Since the assignation is in security, A gets a personal right against C to return title when the debt is paid – this is technically known as a right of retrocession. Being an assignation, the general

61 Scottish Law Commission, *Discussion Paper on the Nature and the Constitution of Trusts* (DP 133, 2006) para 2.08.

62 Although the beneficiary has no remedy against the transferee under property law, the beneficiary may have a remedy against the transferee under the law of delict if the transferee takes title in bad faith, or under the law of unjustified enrichment if the transfer was not for value. Nevertheless, a transferee who acquires trust property in bad faith may get a good title in certain circumstances under the Trusts (Scotland) Act 1961, s 2(1).

63 SLC, *Discussion Paper on the Nature and the Constitution of Trusts* (n 61) para 2.10.

64 Gloag and Irvine, *Security* (n 7) 440.

65 Companies Act 1985, s 462.

66 For discussion of the nature of floating charges before attachment see MacPherson, *The Floating Charge* (n 40) ch 2. But even upon attachment, there are doubts as to whether the charge confers a real right (at least in the ordinary sense of the term). This is due to the various limitations that are associated with the charge in terms of enforcement and ranking. See e.g. MacPherson, *The Floating Charge*, ch 6.

67 This is sometimes called *fiducia cum creditore* or fiduciary transfer of title. As Lord Collins once said, "under Scots law the only way in which a fixed security over shares can be taken is by fiduciary transfer of the shares to the creditor". See *Enviroco Ltd v Farstad Supply A/S* [2011] UKSC 16, [2011] 1 WLR 921, at [4]. Though the subject matter of this case was shares, the same principle is true for other incorporeal moveables. See Gloag and Irvine, *Security* (n 7) 469.

rules of assignation apply to an assignation in security.[68] These include the rules on intimation and the *assignatus utitur jure auctoris* rule.[69]

The publicity act required for the security to take effect is intimation to the obligor (i.e. B in the example above).[70] While intimation will be necessary where the assignation involves three parties (i.e. a debtor, an assignor and an assignee), it is possible that the assignation only involves two parties: the assignor and the assignee. This will typically be the case where the incorporeal moveable being assigned is an intellectual property right. Unlike personal rights, they do not generally have debtors or obligors for intimation purposes. Hence, the publicity act required for their transfer is typically registration.[71] One exception to this is copyright, whose assignation only needs to be in writing and signed by the cedent.[72] Thus, creating security over copyrights is another rare exception to the publicity principle in respect of voluntary security, in addition to the floating charge.

Where the incorporeal moveables being assigned are shares, the publicity act required is the registration of the creditor as the holder of the share in the company's register of shareholders.[73] For constitution of security over uncalled capital, it was held in *Ballachulish Slate Quarries Co v Bruce*[74] that the debtor company (i.e. the assignor or cedent) must not only substitute the assignee in its place as at the date of assignment but also intimate to every individual shareholder concerned.

5.1.2.3 Security over corporeal heritable property

The Conveyancing and Feudal Reform (Scotland) Act 1970 (the 1970 Act) provides that a standard security is the only form of heritable security that can be granted over land.[75] A

68 SLC, *Discussion Paper on Moveable Transactions* (n 8) para 7.6.

69 For discussion of the rules on assignation, see section 5.3.2.1.

70 *Gallemos Ltd (In Receivership) v Barratt Falkirk Ltd* 1989 SC (IH) 239 (where Lord Dunpark noted (at [243]) that "[i]ntimation of an assignation to the debtor is the equivalent of delivery of a corporeal moveable and is necessary to complete the title of the assignee"). On the extent to which intimation can be regarded as a publicity act see chapter 8 at footnote 10.

71 See Trade Marks Act 1994, s 25(2) and (3) (with the effect that an unregistered security interest over a registered trademark is ineffective as against a third party who acquires a conflicting interest under the registered trademark without notice of the earlier unregistered security interest); Patents Act 1977, s 33(1) (providing that an earlier unregistered title in a patent will be defeated by a later title that is acquired in good faith, registered or not, in the patent); Registered Designs Act 1949, s 19(5) (providing that an unregistered assignation document of a registered design shall be inadmissible in any court as evidence of title to the said registered design unless the court decides otherwise).

72 Copyright, Designs and Patents Act 1988, s 90(3). See also Laura Macgregor and others, *Commercial Law in Scotland* (6th edn, W Green 2020) 247.

73 Companies Act 2006, ss 770ff. See also *Enviroco Ltd v Farstad Supply A/S* [2011] UKSC 16, [2011] 1 WLR 921.

74 (1908) 16 SLT (CSIH) 48.

75 Conveyancing and Feudal Reform (Scotland) Act 1970, s 9(3) and (4). Although the Act seems to have prohibited other forms of security over land, some securities, aside from the standard security, can still be validly acquired over land. For example, the floating charge can be taken over land. There is also a statutory

standard security is a proper security – the grantor retains their ownership right in the land while granting a subordinate real right to the grantee. The publicity act required for the constitution of standard securities is registration in the Land Register.[76] Where the standard security grantor is a UK company, there is an additional requirement that the standard security must be registered in the Companies Register.[77]

Schedule 2 of the 1970 Act provides two forms of standard security: Form A and Form B. Form A is to be used when the debt obligation is included in the deed containing the standard security. Form B is to be used when the debt obligation is contained in a document separate from the standard security deed. For further discussion of these forms and their accessoriness, see section 5.2.2.1.

5.1.2.4 Security over incorporeal heritable property

The 1970 Act provides that a standard security can be granted over "land or a real right in land". A "real right in land" is defined as:

> any such right, other than ownership or a real burden, which is capable of being held separately and to which a title may be registered in the Land Register of Scotland or recorded in the Register of Sasines.[78]

From the foregoing, three issues may be considered to determine the applicability of a standard security to incorporeal heritable property. These are: (i) whether the incorporeal heritable property is a right other than an ownership right[79] or real burden, (ii) whether it can be held separately, and (iii) whether it is registrable in the Land Register of Scotland (or in the Register of Sasines).

---

power that enables local authorities to take a first-ranking charge over land for debt due to them. See e.g. Housing (Scotland) Act 2006, s 172. These forms of security are known as charging orders – see Roderick RM Paisley, *Land Law* (Green 2000) para 11.32. For recent discussion see William M Gordon and Scott Wortley, *Scottish Land Law*, vol 2 (3rd edn, W Green 2020) paras 22.11ff. It is also possible to obtain a judicial security over land (particularly adjudication, which is due to be replaced with land attachment, but the provisions introducing land attachment are yet to come into force). See Bankruptcy and Diligence etc. Act (Scotland) 2007, ss 79 and 81.

76 Conveyancing and Feudal Reform (Scotland) Act 1970, s 11(1). All registrations are now required to be in the Land Register rather than the Register of Sasines. See Registers of Scotland (Voluntary Registration, Amendment of Fees etc.) Order 2015 (SSI 2015/265), art 3.

77 Companies Act 2006, s 859A. For discussion see section 8.1.2.

78 Conveyancing and Feudal Reform (Scotland) Act 1970, s 9(8)(b).

79 Section 9(2) of the Conveyancing and Feudal Reform (Scotland) Act 1970 makes it clear that a standard security can be taken over land (i.e. corporeal heritable property, which includes any property permanently attached to it).

Take a lease for example. A lease is a subordinate real right (and not an ownership right or a real burden) in land.[80] It can be held separately from other real rights in land – for example, land can have a separate owner and a separate lessee. To answer the third question, it will depend on whether the lease is a long lease (i.e. a duration of over 20 years) or a short lease (a duration of 20 years or less). Long leases are registrable,[81] and so a standard security can be granted over them. Short leases are not registrable,[82] hence they may not be secured by a standard security. Since there is no other statutory authority providing for a special type of security that can be taken over short leases, the Scots common law rule seems to apply. Accordingly, the competent security that may be taken over short leases is an assignation in security which is completed by the assignee taking possession of the premises.[83]

Also, a standard security can be granted over an existing standard security. A standard security is a subordinate real right in land, it can be held separately, and it is also registrable. As for proper liferents,[84] it will appear, from the foregoing principle, that a standard security can be granted over them – proper liferents are real rights in land, they can be held separately, and they are registrable.[85] A standard security may not, however, be granted over the dominant tenement in a praedial servitude.[86] This is because servitude rights are inextricably attached to the dominant land, such that they cannot be held separately from the ownership of the land itself. That is, if the dominant land belongs to X, the servitude right will be enforceable by X, and X alone.[87] A standard security also cannot be granted over floating charges attached to land since they are not registrable in the Land Register. Moreover, uncrystallised floating charges are seemingly not real rights under Scots law.[88]

---

80 This presumes that the required publicity act has been completed in order to make the lease a real right. A lease becomes a real right when the tenant has taken possession, in the case of a short lease (i.e. a duration of 20 years or less), or has registered their interest in the Land Register in the case of a long lease (i.e. a duration of over 20 years). See respectively Leases Act 1449 and Registration of Leases (Scotland) Act 1857, s 20B.

81 Registration of Leases (Scotland) Act 1857, s 1.

82 The registration requirement in s 1 of the Registration of Leases (Scotland) Act 1857 applies only to long leases.

83 See *Clark v West Calder Oil Co* (1882) 9 R (CSIH) 1017.

84 This has been defined as "a real right in land entitling the holder to possess the land for life". See Scottish Law Commission, *Discussion Paper on Heritable Securities: Pre-Default* (DP 168, 2019) para 5.17.

85 Land Registration etc. (Scotland) Act 2012, s 51. See also Paisley (n 75) para 11.3.

86 Praedial servitudes are real rights in land which entitles the owner of a land – the dominant tenement – to do something on a neighbouring land in separate ownership – the burdened tenement.

87 SLC, *Discussion Paper on Heritable Securities* (n 84) para 5.16.

88 See e.g. MacPherson, *The Floating Charge* (n 40) paras 2.01ff (suggesting that an uncrystallised floating charge is not a real right).

5.1.3 *Concluding comments*

This section intended to give the reader a contextual understanding of the nature and constitution of the Scottish law of rights in security. It has done so in a fairly detailed manner, while highlighting the dominant role played by the publicity principle. If the publicity act is not done, no real rights may be constituted. Security rights are real rights; hence their constitution is affected by this principle. As will be seen in the next section, the rules for transferring security rights often reflect how a relevant security right is constituted. This makes the publicity principle a critical factor in determining security rights transfers in Scots law.

5.2 Accessory principle and transfer of security rights under Scots law

5.2.1 *Initial comments*

The *accessorium sequitur principale* principle (hereafter referred to as "the *accessorium* principle") states that when a principal right (e.g. the right to receive payment of a debt) is assigned, any related accessory rights (e.g. a right in security) automatically go with it.[89] In other words, the transfer of the accessory right does not need to be either (i) expressed or referred to in the transfer document, or (ii) publicised.[90] This principle is well recognised under Scots law. Erskine notes that "[a]ssignations, when properly perfected, carry to the assignee all rights which corroborate or strengthen the right conveyed".[91] Security rights are value-adding rights, created to strengthen a creditor's chance of recovering their loans.

In a securitisation transaction, once rights to the debts from the underlying financial assets (e.g. mortgage loans, car loans, commercial loans, trade receivables, etc.) are transferred from the originator to the SPV, the issue arises as to the fate of the security rights originally created for the originator to ensure payment of these debts. Do the security rights follow the transferred receivables automatically, as required by the *accessorium* principle? If the answer is in the affirmative, then it means that the accessory principle does apply, and the focus of research on this subject should be on the transfer of the debts. If the answer is in the negative, it will mean that the security rights are independent of the receivables and should be transferred separately to the SPV.

89 Bell, *Principles* (n 10) para 1298.

90 See *Edinburgh Entertainments Ltd v Stevenson* 1926 SC (IH) 363, per Lord Anderson at 386.

91 Erskine, *Institute* (n 23) III, v, 8. See also Anderson, *Assignation* (n 4) para 2.01.

The following sections discuss the accessoriness of real security rights.[92] Since it is commonplace for businesses in Scotland to use workarounds – like retention of title in sale, sale and leaseback, and hire purchase – as securities over moveable property, the accessoriness of the quasi-security devices will also be examined.

5.2.2 *Accessoriness of real security*

The application of the *accessorium* principle is limited under Scots law. It will be seen below that the applicability of the principle mostly depends on whether the assignation of the debt[93] and the assignation of the related security are governed by the same publicity act. Being a personal right, the publicity act required for the assignation of a debt is intimation.[94] If, for example, registration is the publicity required to assign the related security right, a mere assignation of the debt by intimation may not carry the security right automatically.[95] However, if a single publicity rule governs the assignation of both rights (i.e. the assignation of both rights can be completed by intimation to the obligor), it is likely that the *accessorium* principle will prevail.[96] The applicability of the *accessorium* principle to standard securities, pledges, floating charges, assignation in security and the quasi-security devices is considered in the following sections.

5.2.2.1 Standard security

Section 14 of the 1970 Act sets out the rules governing the assignation of a standard security. It refers to two statutory forms (Forms A and B of Schedule 4) that may be used for assigning the security and provides that registration is necessary to transfer the security.[97] There are two relevant implications of section 14 of the 1970 Act. First, the assignation of the standard security needs to be expressly provided for in a document (rather than arising by operation of law, as would have been the case if the *accessorium* principle applied). Second, the document of assignation has to be registered for the

---

92 As noted, a personal security right rarely features in a securitisation transaction; hence it is excluded from the scope of this section.

93 Strictly speaking, it is the right of claim against the debtor that is being assigned, not the debt. Debts are not assignable since they are obligations and not rights. But the use of assignation of debts is commonplace. See e.g. John Menzies Halliday, *The Conveyancing and Feudal Reform (Scotland) Act 1970* (Green 1970) para 9.0.

94 Gretton and Steven, *Property, Trusts and Succession* (n 1) para 1.29.

95 Using the standard security as an example, MacLeod notes that the publicity rule will prevail over the accessory rule in this circumstance. See John MacLeod, 'Non-Judicial Real Security' in Iain MacNeil (ed), *Scots Commercial Law* (Avizandum Publishing Ltd 2014) 325, para 11.22. This point is discussed in more detail in section 5.2.2.1.

96 See Anderson, *Assignation* (n 4) para 2.17f (expressing a similar point when analysing the accessoriness of the floating charge).

97 Conveyancing and Feudal Reform (Scotland) Act 1970, s 14(1).

standard security to transfer to the assignee. The foregoing requirements effectively exclude the application of the *accessorium* principle to a standard security.

A related issue that is worth considering is whether the assignation of the standard security automatically carries the secured debt (i.e. an inversion of the *accessorium* principle). Section 14 of the 1970 Act is only concerned with the assignation of the standard security. It is silent on what becomes of the secured debt after the assignation of the standard security. Section 14(2) provides that an assignation of a standard security transfers to the assignee the full benefit of all related corroborative or substitutional obligations, the right to recover payments from the debtor all expenses incurred by the creditor in connection with the security, and the entitlement to the benefit of notices served and procedures instituted by the credit in relation to the security. It makes no mention of the secured debt.[98] The question then is whether the assignation of the security by registration automatically carries the debt, or will intimation still be required? A brief illustration of how the two assignation forms in Schedule 4 and the two standard security forms in Schedule 2 interact may be helpful.

The two assignation forms in Schedule 4 are called Form A and Form B. The Form A assignation is a standalone document of assignation. The Form B assignation is used as an endorsement on the standard security document.[99] Unhelpfully, the two standard security forms in Schedule 2 are also called Form A and Form B. In Form A standard security, the security is contained in the same document as the debt. In Form B, the security is contained in a separate document. Section 14 provides that either of the assignation forms may be used to assign the security, leading to four possibilities.[100]

- Possibility 1: Form A standard security is assigned by Form A assignation. Two copies of the assignation document will have to be executed; one copy is required for registration in the Land Register and the other for intimating the debt transfer to the debtor.
- Possibility 2: Form A standard security is assigned by Form B assignation. The endorsed standard security document will have to be re-registered. Since the security document will not be in duplicate, a separate document will have to be drafted for intimation purposes.[101]
- Possibility 3: Form B standard security is assigned by Form A assignation. The security assignation document is registered. The debt will also need to be expressly assigned, either in a separate document or by including in the security assignation document

98 It has been held that s 14(2) of the 1970 Act does not cover the secured personal obligation. *Watson v Bogue (No 1)* 2000 SLT (Sh Ct) 125.

99 For discussion of the extent to which the prescribed wording of both forms is mandatory see section 5.3.2.3.

100 See AJM Steven, 'Accessoriness and Security over Land' (2009) 13 Edinburgh Law Review 387, 407f.

101 SLC, *Discussion Paper on Heritable Securities: Pre-Default* (n 84) para 10.13.

that the debt is also being assigned.[102] Again, intimation to the debtor of the debt transfer will be needed.

– Possibility 4: Form B security is assigned by Form B assignation. The endorsed security document will have to be re-registered. The debt will need to be expressly assigned in a separate document, which is then intimated to the debtor.

The above illustration strictly applies the publicity rule by ensuring that the debtor is intimated to about the debt transfer and that the security transfer is registered. However, having to register the standard security and intimate to the debtor may be commercially inconvenient, especially in cases of bulk transfers. Also, it creates the possibility of a split between the security and the debt, which will occur if intimation and registration are not simultaneous.[103]

The question of whether the registration of the document assigning the standard security should serve to complete the debt transfer has been considered elsewhere. For Form A standard securities, Professor Steven suggests that registration is required to transfer both the security and the debt.[104] He notes that intimation should only be needed to inform the debtor to pay the assignee.[105] The reason being that the debt is closely tied to the standard security, as they are contained in the same document, and the debt cannot be treated separately from the security.[106] Regarding Form B standard security, he suggests that intimation is required to transfer the debt since the debt is constituted in a separate document.[107] He considers a situation where the assignation of the Form B standard security is registered before intimation and suggests that in such situation, registration may be enough to transfer the debt if the wording of the assignation refers to the debt.[108]

Professor Steven's analysis appears to give significant weight to the form in which the standard security is constituted. An alternative way would be to use the form of the assignation as the primary determinant. The standard security is already connected to the

---

102 This was confirmed in *Watson v Bogue (No 1)* 2000 (Sh Ct) SLT 12, where a standard security granted in accordance with Form B of Schedule 2 to the 1970 Act was duly assigned without the debt obligation. It was held that the assignation was only effective to transfer the standard security and not the debt. The court noted that the debt obligation must be expressly described in the document of assignation, or alternatively the debt obligation must itself be assigned by a separate instrument, for it to pass with the standard security.

103 A split between the security and the debt breaches the "unity principle" – this requires the debt and security to be held by the same person, and hence it is exposed to the difficulties arising from such breach. See Anderson, *Assignation* (n 4) para 2.11.

104 Steven, 'Accessoriness and Security over Land' (n 100) 408. Professor Halliday suggested a similar outcome, noting that "[w]here the personal obligation has been created in the standard security, an assignation of the standard security transfers both the debt and the security". See John M Halliday, *Conveyancing Law and Practice in Scotland* (Iain JS Talman ed, 2nd edn, W Green 1997) para 55.15.

105 Steven, 'Accessoriness and Security over Land' (n 100) 408. See also Gordon and Wortley (n 75) para 20.29.

106 Steven, 'Accessoriness and Security over Land' (n 100) 408.

107 ibid.

108 ibid 409.

debt by its very nature as a security, and not necessarily by the form of the standard security.[109] Therefore, where the assignations of the debt and the standard security are contained in the same deed and registration takes place with reference to both, that registration should be enough to transfer both the security and the debt.[110] In this case, registration would serve as constructive intimation.[111] Actual intimation would, however, be needed to inform the debtor to pay to the assignee. Where the assignation of the debt is contained in a separate deed, it is suggested that intimation should be required to transfer the debt. This approach is more likely to reflect parties' intentions since a separate assignation deed will probably be used if parties want the debt and the security to be held separately.

The position of the law in the foregoing remains uncertain. In order to clarify the law, the Scottish Law Commission is consulting on whether registration should be enough to transfer the debt.[112]

5.2.2.2 Pledge

The assignability of a pledge and the rules governing its assignation are uncertain under Scots law. On its assignability, Professor Steven argues that a pledge should not be assignable on the basis that it carries with it an obligation on the part of the pledgee to exercise ordinary care in the handling of the pledged property and to restore the property once the secured debt is discharged.[113] Dr Anderson argues otherwise, contending that a pledge is assignable.[114] One of the four reasons he gives is that the obligations to exercise reasonable care "arise *ex lege* from the fact of the possession", and if the pledged property is delivered to another pledgee, that pledgee will also be bound by operation of law.[115] On the rules governing the assignation of pledge, Anderson suggests that the delivery of possession is not necessary for the assignation to be enforceable and that a mere intimation to the pledgor should suffice.[116] Steven and MacLeod, for their part, suggest that if a pledge

109 The irrelevance of the form of the standard security was confirmed in *UK Acorn Finance Ltd v Smith* 2014 Hous LR (Sh Ct) 50, per Sheriff Mann at [14ff], where the court observed that the question of whether a standard security granted in Form A or B of Schedule 2 is *only* relevant in situations provided under s 10 of the 1970 Act.

110 This reaches the same result as that of Professor Steven in terms of Form A Schedule 2. However, the outcome is different with respect to Form B.

111 This works well for a securitisation transaction, since the transaction sale agreement typically includes the transfer of the debts and the related security rights, and the originator keeps receiving payments from the debtors. See e.g. Finsbury Square 2019-1 Plc (Prospectus, 26 March 2019) 8 and 174.

112 SLC, *Discussion Paper on Heritable Securities* (n 84) paras 10.29ff.

113 Steven, *Pledge and Lien* (n 27) para 4.23. He suggests that the only way a pledge can be assigned is by obtaining the express consent of the pledger – ibid para 4.25.

114 Anderson, *Assignation* (n 4) para 2.06.

115 ibid.

116 ibid.

is assignable at all, the assignee must be put in possession for the assignation to be enforceable.[117]

Dr Anderson's view breaches the publicity principle, which, as shown above, is an important feature of Scots property law. On the other hand, Steven and MacLeod's approach complies with the publicity principle and hence is more acceptable under Scots property law. Therefore, if the publicity principle of Scots property law should be strictly followed, the *accessorium* principle will be excluded, since the transfer of the pledge would depend on the delivery of possession.

In any case, possessory securities, such as pledges, rarely feature in securitisations. This is likely due to the cost and the commercial inconvenience associated with these types of security. The storage cost involved will be particularly inconvenient for the SPV since the SPV is designed to function remotely with very little or no operational base.

5.2.2.3 Floating charge

An important implication of the possibility of creating a floating charge without publicity is that it allows a single rule of assignation to apply to both the floating charge and the debt it secures. In *Libertas-Kommerz*, the court accepted that an assignation of claims under a floating charge which was intimated after attachment and by exchange of letters, transferred both the charge and the debt.[118] The accessoriness of the floating charge was not, however, considered in the case.

While it is clear from the above paragraph that the assignation of the floating charge and the debt it secures is completed by intimation, the position on whether the floating charge automatically follows the assignation of the debt (such that the assignation of the floating charge does not need to be separately provided for and/or intimated) is uncertain.[119]

It is possible for some finance transactions that involve floating charges to be structured in a way that the rights to the debt obligation and the security rights are intended to be

---

117 Steven, *Pledge and Lien* (n 27) para 4.19; MacLeod (n 95) para 327. See also Reid, *The Law of Property* (n 1) para 657. There seems to be judicial support for this argument. See *Guidi v Promontoria (Chestnut) Ltd* 2021 SLT (Sh Ct) 441, at [132], where the Sheriff Court suggests that the method of completing a security transfer depends on how the security was created.

118 *Libertas-Kommerz GmbH v Johnson* 1977 SC (OH) 191. On the previous attempt by the SLC to provide for the registration of assignations of floating charges, see Scottish Law Commission, *Examination of the Companies (Floating Charges) (Scotland) Act 1961* (Memorandum No 10, 1969) para 62; Scottish Law Commission, *Report on the Companies (Floating Charges) (Scotland) Act 1961* (No 14) (Cmnd 4336) (1970) para 19. For a criticism of the current position, see William Lucas, 'The Assignation of Floating Charges' [1996] Scots Law Times (News) 203. The new section 42(1) of the Bankruptcy and Diligence etc. (Scotland) Act 2007 provides for the registration of an assignation of a floating charge, but as noted before, it is unlikely that the provision will ever be brought into force.

119 For discussion, see MacPherson, *The Floating Charge* (n 40) para 2.24.

separately held.[120] This is typically the case in most syndicated loans where a security trustee is appointed to hold the security rights on behalf of the group of lenders. In these circumstances, the transfer of both the debt and security rights must be expressly mentioned and agreed upon before the transferee can acquire rights to the debt and the security.

It is suggested that where the same party holds the debt and the floating charge, the *accessorium* principle should apply as a default rule (since a single rule of assignation applies to both the debt and the floating charge). Parties should, however, be able to depart from the default rule through express provision.

5.2.2.4 The quasi-security devices

The difficulty with applying the *accessorium* principle to the retention of title devices is that they are formally a sale, even though they function as a security.[121] Being a sale and not a security, the retention of title clause preserves the unpaid seller's ownership interest in the goods until the occurrence of a certain event – typically the full payment of the purchase price.[122] The unpaid seller's right is not a *jus in re aliena*[123] since the ownership right in the goods never parted from the seller. It will then be unusual to say that the seller's ownership interest is an accessory to the debts so that the assignation of the debts automatically passes the seller's ownership interest in the goods or vice versa.[124] Therefore, besides transferring the debt by intimation to the debtor, the assignor would also need to, in theory, transfer their ownership right in the corporeal moveable. The same argument can be made for a sale and leaseback arrangement.

5.2.2.5 Assignation in security

As noted above, the assignation in security of certain incorporeal moveables (i.e. registered patents, registered trademarks, registered designs and shares) is subject to publicity acts

120 See Jonathan Hardman, *A Practical Guide to Granting Corporate Security in Scotland* (1st edn, W Green 2018) paras 5.09ff. For the English law position, see HG Beale and others, *The Law of Security and Title-Based Financing* (3rd edn, Oxford University Press 2018) para 2.16.

121 Strictly speaking, a hire purchase is not necessarily a sale agreement since the debtor is not obligated to purchase the relevant property. See Consumer Credit Act 1974, s 189. However, a hire purchase agreement as used here acts as a quasi-security device (and not just an ordinary hire purchase agreement), and it is expected that the buyer in fact intends to buy the goods.

122 See the English case of *Hendy Lennox (Industrial Engines) Ltd v Grahame Puttick Ltd* [1984] 1 WLR 485 (QB). This principle should also apply to Scots law since it is based on a formalist approach – the retention of title arrangement was treated as a sale and not a security device. See *Armour v Thyssen Edelstahlwerke AG* (1990) SLT (HL) 891 (confirming the formalist approach in Scots law). Compare this with the US's functional approach, where such an arrangement is treated as a security and called a "purchase money security interest". See the American Uniform Commercial Code (Secured Transactions) 2010, s 9-103.

123 That is, the seller's right is not derived from the property of the buyer.

124 See also Anderson, *Assignation* (n 4) para 2.20 (citing the difficulties that might arise if the *accessorium* principle were to apply).

other than intimation. For these kinds of property, registration is required for a valid security to be created.[125] The same publicity principle also applies to the assignation of security interests created in these classes of incorporeal moveables, so that no assignation may be effective until it is registered.[126] The implication is that there is a conflict in the rules governing the assignation of security rights in these classes of incorporeal moveables and the assignation of the related debt. This conflict effectively excludes the application of the *accessorium* principle, so that the transfer of the debt cannot carry the security.

The accessoriness of the assignation in security relating to claims should also be considered. There is an absence of attention to this subject in the existing literature. This is surprising, given the issues that could arise from such security rights. An attempt is made here to highlight some of these issues in relation to the *accessorium* principle. Consider the following scenario.

- Stage 1: D owes C £10.
- Stage 2: C owes X £10, and C assigns their claim against D to X in security.
- Stage 3: X wishes to assign their claim against C, as well as the related security, to A.

From the above, the security itself (i.e. the assignation in security at Stage 2) is completed by intimation to D. If the principle of publicity is to be strictly followed at Stage 3, the transfer of the security to A will require intimation to D, and the transfer of the claim will require intimation to C. Alternatively, it may be argued that the *accessorium* principle applies, since the assignation of the claim and the assignation of the security (in Stage 3) are subject to the same publicity principle (i.e. intimation). Therefore, completing the assignation of the claim by intimating to C should carry the security. But the issue is that, though the publicity rules are similar, the debtors to be intimated are different (i.e. D for the security and C for the claim).

Applying the *accessorium* principle will mean that the claim against D will have to transfer to A without intimation. This outcome cannot be achieved for at least two reasons. The first reason is obvious: intimation is a constitutive requirement under Scots law of assignation. Being an assignation, the general rules of assignation apply to an assignation in security, including the rules on intimation.[127] The second reason relates to the policy of debtor protection, which requires that a debtor who is unaware of a transfer should be able to discharge to the creditor last known to them.[128] Applying the *accessorium* principle breaches that policy, since the transfer of the security will immediately become enforceable

125 See above at footnote 71.

126 See Trade Marks Act 1994, s 25(2)(a); Patents Act 1977, s 33(3)(a); Registered Designs Act 1949, s 19(1); Companies Act 2006, s 772.

127 SLC, *Discussion Paper on Moveable Transactions* (n 8) para 7.6. See section 5.3.2.1 for discussion of the rules on assignation.

128 See section 8.2.2 for discussion of the policy of debtor protection.

against D once the debt is transferred. This will be contrary to the principle of Scots property law. It is suggested therefore that the publicity principle will prevail for assignation in security over claims.

The conclusion above seems accurate in theory. But it may present difficulties in practice. Since the assignation of D's debt is in security, A (the ultimate assignee of the claim and the security) would normally wish D to continue to pay to C notwithstanding the assignation. A only needs to collect directly from D if C defaults. For this to work – i.e. for the claim against D to be assigned to X (and in turn A) and yet payable to C until default occurs, it must be permissible under Scots law for the intimation to instruct D to continue paying to C regardless of the assignation. However, it is unclear whether such intimation will be effective under current law.[129] To clarify the law, the Moveable Transactions (Scotland) Act 2023 would abolish any rule of law that renders an assignation ineffective because of an instruction to the debtor to continue paying to the assignor.[130]

Another difficulty is that the assignee (i.e. A in the scenario above) may need to intimate the debtor (i.e. D) twice in the event of a default by the assignor in security (i.e. C). The first intimation will serve to transfer the security while the second intimation will only serve to inform the debtor to pay directly to the assignee. This process will be cumbersome in transactions involving multiple debtors.

5.2.3 *Concluding comments*

The prevalence of the publicity principle in Scots property law means that the *accessorium* principle will most often be excluded. As seen in section 5.2.2, the *accessorium* principle only seems to apply in instances where the constitution of the relevant security right is not subject to publicity. A major example of such security is the floating charge. Yet the application of the *accessorium* principle is not absolute even in these instances, as it will also depend on whether the debt and the security are held by the same party. The *accessorium* principle will apply if they are held by the same party.[131] The doctrine may not however apply if the debt and the charge are held separately. This is normally the case in syndicated loan arrangements where a trustee is typically appointed to hold the security for the benefit of the lenders.

129 The SLC suggests that the validity of such intimation is doubtful. See SLC, *Discussion Paper on Moveable Transactions* (n 8) para 11.14, at footnote 28. Cf RG Anderson and JWA Biemans, 'Reform of Assignation in Security: Lessons from the Netherlands' (2012) 16 Edinburgh Law Review 24, 29f; Hardman, *A Practical Guide to Granting Corporate Security in Scotland* (n 120) para 7.30.

130 Moveable Transactions (Scotland) Act 2023, s 17(1)(b).

131 See e.g. *Libertas-Kommerz GmbH v Johnson* 1977 SC (OH) 191.

5.3 Solutions available for transferring security rights in securitisations under Scots law

5.3.1 *Initial comments*

Having shown why it is necessary to expressly include security rights as part of rights being transferred under the securitisation sale agreement, this section discusses the transfer mechanisms available in Scots law for transferring security rights. It focuses on two transfer mechanisms: (i) assignation and (ii) the Scottish trust. The section examines the formalities associated with these transfer mechanisms, with a view to explaining why the Scottish trust is the preferred transfer solution for securitisations in Scotland under the current law.

The analysis on assignation begins in section 5.3.2.1 with the definition of assignation and a discussion of the current rules for assigning claims and the difficulties posed by the rules in the context of securitisation. This initial focus on the assignation of claims (rather than security rights, which are the focus of this book) is necessary for three reasons. First, it gives the reader a background knowledge of the general rules of assignation under Scots law. Second, since claims are principal rights, a discussion of their assignation is relevant to determine the transfer of security rights that are subject to the *accessorium* principle (i.e. the floating charge). Thirdly, the discussion of the general assignation rules presents a context for the subsequent discussion (in section 5.3.2.2) of the newly introduced assignation by registration under the Moveable Transactions (Scotland) Act 2023. Section 5.3.2.3 considers the assignation of security rights in the context of securitisation. The discussion of the Scottish trust begins in section 5.3.3.

5.3.2 *Assignation*

5.3.2.1 Meaning, current rules and difficulties

Assignation is a means by which incorporeal property can be transferred from one person to another.[132] Suppose A has a right against B to receive x amount and decides to transfer the said right to C. Assignation is the process by which the transfer can be effected under Scots law.[133] The transferor (A) is known as the cedent (or assignor). The transferee (C) is

132 GL Gretton and KGC Reid, *Conveyancing* (5th edn, W Green 2018) para 24.01. Note that earlier sources have used the term "assignation" for the transfer of corporeal moveable property. See e.g. J Graham Stewart, *A Treatise on the Law of Diligence* (Green 1898) 151, 154 and 157 (referring to the "assignation" of corporeal moveables). See William W McBryde, *The Law of Contract in Scotland* (3rd edn, Thomson/W Green 2007) para 12.20 (noting the "perplexing tendency" in the past to use the term "assignation" for corporeal moveables).

133 Gretton and Steven, *Property, Trusts and Succession* (n 1) para 1.29.

called the assignee. B is known as the debtor (or the obligor), while the right to receive x amount is the incorporeal property. In a securitisation transaction, the originator is typically the cedent while the SPV is the assignee. The incorporeal property, in the context of the present work, are the debts owed by the obligors to the originator and the related security rights.

Modern Scots law on assignation is a three-step process.[134] The first step is the entry into an agreement to assign the incorporeal property. The second step is the act of assignation, which is normally represented by the delivery of a deed of assignation. The last step is intimation (that is, the giving of formal notice of the assignation to the obligor). In practice, the first two steps take place at the same time, and they are not required to be in writing.[135] If parties choose to have the contract and the deed in writing, which is typically the case, there is no formality regarding words to use, provided that the cedent makes clear in the documents their intention to assign.[136]

Unlike the first two steps, the last step (intimation) is formalised. Unhelpfully, especially for transactions (such as securitisations) involving bulk transfers, the right is only transferred at the last step.[137] Bankton was clear about this:

> [t]he assignation is not completed by executing and delivering it to the assignee, but it must likewise be intimated to the debtor, till which is done, the cedent is not understood in our law to be denuded.[138]

The three formal methods of intimation are prescribed under common law and the Transmission of Moveable Property (Scotland) Act 1862 (the 1862 Act). The common law method requires a schedule of intimation (including a copy of the assignation) to be notarised and signed by a procurator before delivery to the obligor.[139] The assignee is then required to retain an instrument of intimation, signed by the notary as evidence of the intimation.[140]

In a bid to make intimation much simpler than the common law method, the 1862 Act introduced another form of notarial intimation as well as a non-notarial intimation.[141] The

134 Anderson, *Assignation* (n 4) para 1.11.

135 See *Guidi v Promontoria (Chestnut) Ltd* 2021 SLT (Sh Ct) 441, at [130]. See also Requirements of Writing (Scotland) Act 1995, s 1(1).

136 *Carter v McIntosh* (1862) 24 D (CSIH) 925; *Brownlee v Robb* 1907 SC (IH) 1302.

137 *Gallemos Ltd (In Receivership) v Barratt Falkirk Ltd* 1989 SC (IH) 239. The most an assignee gets from an unintimated assignation is a personal right against the cedent. See Erskine, *Institute* (n 23) III, v, 3; Bell, *Principles* (n 10) para 1462.

138 Bankton, *Institute* (n 17) III, i, 6. See also Stair (n 23) III, i, 6.

139 Bell, *Principles* (n 10) para 1463.

140 ibid para 1464.

141 Transmission of Moveable Property (Scotland) Act 1862, s 2. The Act preserves the common law method of intimation. See s 3 of the Act.

notarial intimation involves the delivery of a certified copy of the assignation by a notary to the obligor in the presence of two witnesses.[142] The notary then issues a certificate of intimation, in the form provided in Schedule C of the 1862 Act, to the assignee as evidence of the intimation. The non-notarial method involves the delivery of a certified copy of the assignation to the obligor by post and requires a written acknowledgement of receipt to be obtained from the obligor.[143]

These formal methods of intimation can be prohibitively costly and will present great difficulty for securitisations involving thousands or tens of thousands of obligors, as is typically the case with securitisations backed by mortgage and auto loan receivables respectively.

Two equivalents to intimation have also been recognised at common law. The first arises where the obligor acts in a way that shows that they are aware of the assignation (e.g. by making payment to the assignee after hearing about the assignation informally). In this case, the obligor may be personally barred from claiming to be unaware of the assignation.[144] Also, an intimation may arise where the obligor is a party to a judicial proceeding that is based on the assignation.[145]

But these equivalents offer little or no solution to the difficulty presented by formal intimation in respect of securitisations. The SPV and, in turn, the investors would want to be certain that the asset pool is transferred from the originator to the SPV at the commencement of the transaction. A formal intimation to the obligor is the only way to achieve this certainty. On the contrary, the equivalents do not provide such certainty since they depend on the happening of a future event (e.g. an obligor exhibiting the relevant conduct or the institution of a judicial proceeding against an obligor) for the transfer to occur. Accordingly, they tend to rectify a defective "assignation".

Other less formal methods of intimation have also emerged from modern practice. These include intimation by correspondence (without enclosing a copy of the assignation)[146] and by sending stamped invoices to debtors showing that the debts have been transferred and the details of the assignee.[147] In *Christie Owen and Davies Plc v Campbell*[148] the court

142 Bell, *Principles* (n 10) para 1464.

143 ibid.

144 Stair (n 23) III, i, 9 (noting that "[a]ny writ under the debtor's hand, acknowledging the production of the assignation, will be sufficient intimation").

145 In *Carter v McIntosh* (1862) 24 D (CSIH) 925, at 934, Lord Justice-Clerk Inglis described judicial intimation as the "best of all intimations". See also *Promontoria (Ram) Ltd v Moore* [2017] CSOH 88, 2018 SCLR 299, per Lord Bannatyne at [43] and [94].

146 In *Libertas-Kommerz GmbH v Johnson* 1977 SC (OH) 191, the assignor merely informed the obligor by letter about the assignation and the obligor acknowledged. The court held the communication to be an effective intimation.

147 Scottish Law Commission, *Business and Regulatory Impact Assessment: Draft Moveable Transactions (Scotland) Bill 2017* (Scot Law Com No 249, 2017) 7.

148 [2009] CSIH 26, 2009 SC 436 (where an unacknowledged intimation by post was held to be valid).

suggested that the methods provided under the 1862 Act are not mandatory.[149] However, since the effectiveness of the informal intimation was not tested against a competing assignation, the binding effect of the case in circumstances where there are two competing claimants has been questioned.[150]

The foregoing indicates that there are still doubts regarding the validity of the informal methods.[151] Indeed, it has been advised that the only legally safe way around the difficulty posed by intimation for transactions such as securitisation is to adopt the formal methods, even if they are commercially inconvenient.[152] This brings formal intimation and its associated difficulty in respect of securitisation back to the fore.

The necessity of intimation in the Scots law of assignation also makes securitisations of future flow receivables impracticable. Indeed, intimation (and hence transfer) will be impossible where the obligors are yet to be identified at the time of transfer. However, the position is not entirely clear in circumstances where the future obligor is identifiable and in fact intimated. Suppose the originator has an identifiable class of customers it usually sells goods to on credit. The originator assigns its future rights against these identifiable customers to an SPV for securitisation purposes and intimates each of them of the assignation of their respective future debts. Would such intimation be enough to transfer the debts to the SPV immediately after the debts arise?

It was suggested that the doctrine of accretion[153] would apply to make such assignations effective immediately after the debts are created.[154] The SLC is, however, of the view that accretion should not apply, even where the obligor is identifiable and in fact intimated before the right arises.[155] The SLC reasons that the intimation "does not seem to be valid in itself, because the person to whom intimation is made is not the account party [debtor]" at the time the intimation is made.[156] In *Bedwells and Yates v Tod*,[157] the Court of Session

149 See also *Promontoria (Ram) Ltd v Moore* [2017] CSOH 88, per Lord Bannatyne at [96] – the court simply states that the terms of the 1862 Act are "permissive not prescriptive".

150 RG Anderson, 'A Strange Notice' (2009) 13 Edinburgh Law Review 484, 485. The same limitation also applies to *Libertas-Kommerz GmbH v Johnson* 1977 SC (OH) 191.

151 See Anderson, *Assignation* (n 4) para 7.15; Gretton and Steven, *Property, Trusts and Succession* (n 1) para 5.44.

152 McBryde (n 132) para 12.95.

153 The doctrine of accretion is a general principle of property law, which arises where a party purportedly transfers to another party a right it has no title to, but it later acquires title to the right. The doctrine operates to grant the transferee the title immediately upon the transferor acquiring it. For general discussion of the doctrine, see Reid, *The Law of Property* (n 1) para 677.

154 Gloag and Irvine, *Security* (n 7) 441. See also *Buchanan v Alba Diagnostics Ltd* 2004 SC (HL) 9, at [19] (where Lord Hoffmann asserted the application of the doctrine to the assignation of future incorporeal property in Scots law); for the criticism of Lord Hoffmann's assertion, see RG Anderson, '*Buchanan v Alba Diagnostics*: Accretion of Title and Assignation of Future Patents' (2005) 9 Edinburgh Law Review 457, 463.

155 SLC, *Discussion Paper on Moveable Transactions* (n 8) para 4.63.

156 ibid 4.65. This view was adopted in the Report. See SLC, *Report on Moveable Transactions* (n 36) para 5.92.

157 2 December 1819 FC (CS) 50.

held the assignation of a legacy to be invalid because the intimation occurred when the testator was still alive, and the executor had not assumed office. The foregoing reasoning was adopted in the more recent case of *Bank of Scotland Cashflow Finance v Heritage International Transport Ltd*.[158] But it does not seem that the courts fully considered the effect of the doctrine in these cases.[159]

The foregoing demonstrates the uncertainties that exist as to the extent to which future rights are assignable under the current Scottish law.[160] But even if by any chance they were found to be assignable, the formality of intimation would still pose difficulties for securitisation.

5.3.2.2 The registration solution

The Scottish Parliament passed the Moveable Transactions (Scotland) Bill on 4 May 2023, following which the Bill received Royal Assent on 13 June 2023. The resulting Act, the Moveable Transactions (Scotland) Act 2023 (hereafter "the Moveable Transactions Act"), introduces significant reforms to the law of assignation and the law of security over moveable property in Scotland.[161] This section considers aspects of the Act that involve assignations.[162]

An area of current Scottish assignation law that is viewed as "most unsatisfactory" is intimation.[163] This is especially so for securitisation transactions, as it creates difficulties for future flows securitisations and securitisations involving bulk sales. The registration solution, which will be introduced when the Moveable Transactions Act becomes fully effective, is principally aimed at resolving these difficulties.[164] The scope of the reform is limited to the assignation of a "claim" rather than the assignation of "incorporeal property" as a whole. A "claim" in this context is defined in the Act as "a right to the performance of

158 2003 SLT (Sh Ct) 107.

159 See SLC, *Discussion Paper on Moveable Transactions* (n 8) para 4.63.

160 The Moveable Transactions (Scotland) Act 2023 would disapply the rule of accretion in assignation of claims when it becomes fully effective. See s 3(3)(b) of the Act.

161 The reform introduced by the Act has been described as "revolutionary rather than evolutionary in nature". Jonathan Hardman, 'Clarificatory Evolutionary Reform – The Importance of the Scottish Law Commission's Discussion Paper on Heritable Securities: Pre-Default' (2020) 2 Juridical Review 96, 100. It is expected that the Act will fully come into force in the second half of 2024.

162 For a brief analysis of the nature of the two reforms see Hamish Patrick and AJM Steven, 'Moveable transactions law reform coming in Scotland?' (2018) Butterworths Journal of International Banking and Financial Law 71.

163 SLC, *Report on Moveable Transactions* (n 36) paras 3.16 and 5.1ff.

164 Various provisions are also included in the Act to clarify areas of the current law that are unclear.

an obligation".[165] Essentially, these are rights whose transfer requires intimation.[166] Other rights that are subject to special transfer rules (such as rights under intellectual property rights, negotiable instruments, company shares, bonds) are excluded.[167] It also follows that security rights like standard securities and, possibly, pledges, whose transfer is subject to special transfer rules, would be excluded. Moreover, a real security right is neither a personal right nor "a right to the performance of an obligation".[168] It is a real right and, therefore, outwith the definition of claim.

A major reform presented by the Moveable Transactions Act in respect of assignation of claims is the introduction of a registration system that would serve as an alternative way of completing title.[169] A public register would be established for the registration, which would be called the Register of Assignations.[170] Entries into the Register would mainly include the particulars of the assignor and assignee, the assignation document, and the date and time of registration.[171] The SLC also proposes an electronic-only registration to make filing simple and inexpensive.[172] Unlike the current law, the assignation document would be required to be in writing and signed by the assignor.[173] No particular form of writing would be required.

In keeping with the specificity rule of property law,[174] the registration solution requires that the assignation document identifies the claim(s) it relates to.[175] A class identification rather than specific identification would be allowed where multiple claims are involved.[176] For example, a company that wishes to assign its present and future customer invoices would not need to describe the invoices individually. This would have been difficult and even impossible where future claims are involved. Rather, the registration solution allows

165 Moveable Transactions (Scotland) Act 2023, s 41(1). Though this would mainly involve monetary claims, it also extends to non-monetary claims. In respect of incorporeal heritable property, only monetary claims relating to land are included in the definition. Monetary claims relating to land are included because of the value and popular use of rents as security property and the need to facilitate the use of such assets as security. The SLC also considered the fact that assignation of rents does not require registration in the Land Register – only leases of land exceeding 20 years are registrable. See SLC, *Report on Moveable Transactions* (n 36) paras 4.13ff.

166 Being a right against a debtor or an obligor, the debtor or obligor would need to be intimated to before the right can be assigned under current law.

167 SLC, *Report on Moveable Transactions* (n 36) paras 1.18 and 3.4.

168 Cautionary obligation, being a personal right, should be included in the definition.

169 Moveable Transactions (Scotland) Act 2023 (hereafter "Moveable Transactions Act"), s 3(2)(b)(i) and (ii); SLC, *Report on Moveable Transactions* (n 36) paras 5.9ff.

170 Moveable Transactions Act, s 19(1); SLC, *Report on Moveable Transactions* (n 36) para 6.7.

171 Moveable Transactions Act, s 21(1); SLC, *Report on Moveable Transactions* (n 36) paras 7.3ff.

172 SLC, *Report on Moveable Transactions* (n 36) paras 6.33ff.

173 Moveable Transactions Act, s 1(1); SLC, *Report on Moveable Transactions* (n 36) paras 4.19ff.

174 This is an established principle of property law which requires that the subject of a transfer must be properly identified. See Gretton and Steven, *Property, Trusts and Succession* (n 1) paras 4.14ff.

175 Moveable Transactions Act, s 1(2).

176 ibid s 1(3).

a reference to be made to an identifiable class of claims. Therefore, a transfer will occur if a claim can be "identifiable as a claim to which the assignation document relates".[177] The examples provided by the SLC of what would amount to an identifiable class are references to a class that is limited by date, services or goods. For example, the SLC notes that the following description would pass as an identifiable class: "all plumbing invoices" and "all plumbing invoices issued in July 2018".[178]

But it is not clear if a wide and comprehensive description such as "all present and future claims held by the Assignor" would pass as an identifiable class. It has been suggested that such comprehensive description may provide a higher degree of identification, since an interested party only needs to ascertain whether a claim is held by the assignor to determine if the claim has been assigned.[179] Indeed, such description makes identification easier when compared with some vaguer references to a limited class. It is submitted that such comprehensive description should be enough to transfer to the assignee claims that have arisen and are held by the assignor. In this case, it would be vital for parties to properly define what "claims" entail in the assignation document. They may well adopt the definition provided under the Moveable Transactions Act.

The new registration option would certainly facilitate securitisations involving bulk sales, as parties only need to register a single assignation document that identifies the class of claims being transferred. Although the current law does not prohibit the transfer of multiple claims in a single assignation document, it however requires the originator to intimate to every debtor separately. Such a requirement makes securitisation prohibitively costly.

Registration would also enable future flows securitisation. Unlike the current law where the existence of the debtor is necessary for intimation (and, in turn, transfer) to be completed, the registration option would not require the existence of the debtor – the particulars of the debtor are not needed for filing. The main transfer requirement for future claims under the registration regime seems to be specificity – a future claim will only transfer to the assignee when it becomes "identifiable as a claim to which the assignation document relates". Hence, where the claim is described as "all present and future claims held by the Assignor", a non-existent claim is not held by the assignor and so cannot be transferred. However, the transfer would occur immediately once the claim arises and is held by the assignor.[180] Where the future right arises after the assignor

177 ibid ss 1(3) and 3(2)(c).

178 SLC, *Report on Moveable Transactions* (n 36) para 4.26.

179 See ADJ MacPherson, 'The Future of Moveable Security in Scots Law? Comments on the Scottish Law Commission's Report on Moveable Transactions' (2018) 2 Juridical Review 98, 102.

180 Moveable Transactions Act, ss 1(4) and 3(2)(a); SLC, *Report on Moveable Transactions* (n 36) para 5.96. The Moveable Transactions Act lists four conditions that must be met for a claim to transfer: (i) the assignor has to be the holder of the claim; (ii) the assignation must have been intimated or registered; (iii) the claim must

becomes insolvent, the assignation with respect to those future rights would be ineffective.[181]

Since the definition of a claim in the Moveable Transactions Act does not extend to security rights, or at least those subject to special transfer rules (e.g. standard securities and perhaps pledges), it is essential to examine the Act's provisions related to the *accessorium* principle. The Act provides that the principle would apply as a default rule,[182] even where the claim and the related security right are subject to conflicting transfer rules. Sections 16(2) and (3) of the Moveable Transactions Act provide:

> (2) Subject to anything which requires to be done under subsection (3), the assignee acquires, by virtue of the transfer of the claim, any security (in so far as the security is transferable) which relates to, and only to, the claim transferred.
> (3) Where the performance of some act by the assignor is necessary for the security to transfer to the assignee, the assignor must –
> a. perform that act, and
> b. do so as soon as reasonably practicable after the claim is transferred.

The explanatory note to section 16(2) clarifies that the provision "has the effect that the assignation will transfer any security (or, where formalities are required, the right to any security) which relates to the claim assigned". The transfer will occur even if the security right is subject to a special transfer rule.[183]

But it is not entirely clear how section 16(2) fits into the provision of section 16(3). Section 16(3) deals with the situation where the security right is subject to a special transfer rule. In the explanatory note to section 16(3), it is stated that "if the assignee acquires a security under this section then the assignor is required as soon as reasonably practicable to perform any steps necessary to transfer the security". The last part of that statement seems to suggest that the security right would only transfer when the additional formality is complied with. A similar suggestion appears in the Report on Moveable Transactions, where the SLC notes that "[w]ith some security rights it would be necessary for more to be done to vest the security in the assignee".[184] This uncertainty may be best explained by an example.

---

be identifiable; and (iv) where the claim is subject to a condition, the condition must have been fulfilled. See s 3(2) of the Act.

181 Moveable Transactions Act, s 4(2) and (3). For discussion see sections 8.2.4.2(d) and 8.3.3.

182 The two exceptions to the default rule are where the security is not restricted to the assigned claim and where the claim is partially assigned. In both exceptions, the security right would remain with the assignor unless parties expressly agree otherwise. Moveable Transactions Act, s 16(1) and (2).

183 See e.g. Example 1 of the note.

184 SLC, *Report on Moveable Transactions* (n 36) para 13.32.

Assuming Max borrows £100,000 from Ben and grants Ben a standard security to secure the loan. Ben assigns his right to the £100,000 to Paul on 15 May. On 25 May, the standard security is assigned in accordance with section 14 of the Conveyancing and Feudal Reform (Scotland) Act 1970. Would Paul acquire complete title to the security on 15 May or 25 May? It may be argued that the effect of section 16(3) is that Paul acquires the right to obtain the standard security on 15 May, and then he acquires the standard security itself on 25 May. But that is unlikely to be correct, given the unititular nature of Scots property law. According to Professor Reid, "[t]here is no such thing as a personal right of ownership: ownership is necessarily a real right."[185]

A related issue may arise where Max fraudulently assigns the same standard security to a third party and the third party completes title on 20 May. Will section 16(2) and (3) afford Paul the priority to reclaim title after the registration on 25 May? It seems unlikely, as it appears that Paul's right is personal, and not real, and so unenforceable against third parties.

There is also an apparent confusion which arises from the examples provided in the explanatory notes to section 16(2) and (3).[186] Example 1 of section 16(2) is to the effect that a standard security will automatically pass with the assigned debt. But the note to section 16(3) states otherwise: that an automatic transfer of the standard security will not occur since an extra act of registration in the Land Register is needed by virtue of section 14 of the Conveyancing and Feudal Reform (Scotland) Act 1970. It may be said that since section 16(2) is subject to section 16(3), the provisions of section 16(3) and the accompanying note will prevail. But it would have been clearer if the examples specify the security rights for which section 16(3) will and will not be relevant. It is expected that the security rights for which section 16(3) will be relevant will include standard securities and possessory pledges.[187] But it is not clear if it will also include assignations in security, so that the intimation of the underlying debtor will be considered as an extra act that will have to be completed before the transfer of the assignation in security can be valid.[188]

Another uncertainty in section 16(3) relates to the consequence of the assignor's failure to carry out the requisite act or where the requisite act is carried out but not within a reasonable time. If it was accepted that the assignee acquired completed title to the security at the time the claim was assigned, would the title return to the assignor? Furthermore, what precisely would be a reasonable time in this context? Could, for example, the 21-day

185 KGC Reid, 'Unintimated Assignations' [1989] Scots Law Times (News) 267, 269.

186 See the notes to s 16(2) and (3) of the Moveable Transactions Act.

187 The SLC indicates that the section will apply to possessory pledges – see SLC, *Report on Moveable Transactions* (n 36) para 13.32. It will not, however, apply to the newly introduced statutory pledge since its assignation does not require additional formality – see Moveable Transactions Act, s 57(2).

188 See section 5.2.2.5 for discussion of the accessoriness of an assignation in security.

rule used under section 859A(4) of Companies Act 2006 for registration of charges be adopted as a guide, or would a "reasonable time" be determined on a case-by-case basis?

The supporting notes provided for section 16(3) do not clarify these issues and how section 16(3) would operate precisely. Accordingly, it would most likely require clarification from case law. In the meantime, it is expected that parties would generally complete the additional formality required to transfer the related security without delay. This makes the reform seem to be of little significance when compared to current law, especially for transfers involving standard securities, possessory pledges and potentially assignations in security. This is because the originator would still need to complete any additional formality required to transfer the security right. The ideal situation for securitisation would have been for the assignation of the claim to automatically give the assignee title to the related security, regardless of whether the security is subject to a special transfer rule or not. This way, the registration regime would indirectly apply to security rights.[189]

Several other changes are introduced under the Moveable Transactions Act. For example, a debtor who performs in good faith to the assignor would be protected,[190] the *assignatus utitur jure auctoris* rule would be placed on a statutory footing,[191] and an instruction to the debtor to keep performing to the assignor even after transfer would be valid.[192] On intimation, the changes would recognise only three methods of intimation, namely: intimation by a written notice delivered to the debtor by or on behalf of the assignor or assignee (the written notice could be delivered personally, electronically or by post);[193] intimation by debtor's acknowledgement; and judicial intimation.[194] The changes would also confirm that a copy of the assignation would not be required to be delivered to the debtor.[195]

5.3.2.3 Assignations of security rights

Sections 5.2.2 and 5.3.2.2 have shown that despite the *accessorium* principle, parties will still be required to perform any additional formalities necessary to transfer the relevant security right. Hence, for security rights whose transfer is subject to special transfer rules, parties will need to, in addition to completing the transfer of the debt, take necessary steps to complete the transfer of the relevant security right. These additional steps are discussed below, with particular attention paid to standard securities.

189 See sections 8.2.7.2 and 8.3.2 for discussion of the publicity issues that may arise from such automatic transfer and how such issues may be addressed.
190 Moveable Transactions Act, s 10.
191 ibid s 14.
192 ibid s 17(1)(b).
193 ibid s 8(5).
194 ibid s 8(1)(a) and (b).
195 See ibid s 8(3) – setting out what the notice should consist of. See also SLC, *Report on Moveable Transactions* (n 36) para 5.46.

a) Standard security

In the case of standard securities, the necessary steps required to complete their transfer are prescribed under section 14 of the Conveyancing and Feudal Reform (Scotland) Act 1970 (the 1970 Act). That section provides that:

> [a]ny standard security duly [registered or] recorded may be transferred, in whole or in part, by the creditor by an assignation in conformity with Form A or B of Schedule 4 to this Act, and upon such an assignation being duly [registered or] recorded, the security, or, as the case may be, part thereof, shall be vested in the assignee as effectually as if the security or the part had been granted in his favour.

In other words, the assignation of a standard security has to (i) conform with one of the forms prescribed in Schedule 4[196] and (ii) be registered in the Land Register.

Schedule 4 sets out two forms of assignation:

> Form A
> Assignation of Standard Security
> I, AB (designation), in consideration of £..... hereby assign to CD (designation) a standard security for £..... (or a maximum sum of £....., to the extent of £..... being the amount now due thereunder.....
>
> Form B
> [To be endorsed on the standard security]
> As above save that instead of the words "a standard security for £...." (or otherwise, as the case may be) insert "the foregoing standard security". Where the security is for a fluctuating amount whether subject to a maximum or not, add "to the extent of £..... being the amount now due thereunder".

Seven notes are attached to Schedule 4. Note 2(1) requires that where the standard security is for an uncertain debt amount, the assignation document should specify the amount of indebtedness due at the time of the assignation.

The permissive wording used in section 14 for the conformity requirement (i.e. "may") suggests that other forms of assignation may be used. Section 53 of the Act makes it clear that exact adherence to the relevant forms is not essential: the assignation only needs to conform "as closely as may be", and the creditor is allowed to include "any additional

196 For discussion of Forms A and B of Schedule 4, and how they interact with Forms A and B of Schedule 2, see section 5.2.2.1.

matter" which they consider relevant. This confirms that a degree of latitude is permitted. This is necessary given that the prescribed wording in the forms is limited and does not envisage bulk assignations of standard securities. But to what extent are parties allowed to deviate from the prescribed forms? The law in this area was not entirely clear until recently.

The controversy in this area had mainly bordered on whether the requirement of Note 2(1) can be omitted. In *OneSavings Bank Plc v Burns*,[197] a decision of Sheriff P Mann confirmed that the forms could be adapted to include bulk assignations. The sheriff, however, held that an assignation that failed to specify the amount of debt due, as required by Note 2(1), is ineffectual to transfer the real right in the standard security.[198] This suggests that the Note 2(1) requirement is mandatory.

Two months later, the Outer House of the Court of Session reached a contrary decision that the failure to specify the amount due was not serious. The court took a subjective approach in that the decision was founded mainly on the basis that the debtor had not been "affected in any way, far less materially by [the] omission."[199] Two later decisions (of the sheriff court) adopted a similar subjective approach.[200]

More recently, the Inner House of the Court of Session formally overruled the decision in *OneSavings* and held that an assignation does not need to specify a precise amount of debt owed at the time of transfer for it to be valid.[201] The court also rejected the conclusion reached at the court of first instance that section 14 of the 1970 Act requires the assignation document to be a unilateral deed drawn up solely to transfer standard securities (and not any other interests).[202] This decision of the Court of Session provides welcome clarification in this area of law and confirms that the statutory wording can be adapted to meet new commercial realities. In any case, the SLC has recommended that no mandatory form of deed for assigning a standard security should be required.[203]

b) Others

For pledges, in addition to intimating to all the debtors, parties may need to deliver possession of the corporeal moveable to the assignee for the security transfer.[204] Additional registration requirements also apply to security rights created over certain other assets,

197 2017 SLT (Sh Ct) 129.
198 ibid [22]–[28].
199 *Shear v Clipper Holding II SARL* (26 May 2017) (CSOH) [unreported], per Lord Bannatyne at [3].
200 *Promontoria (Henrico) Ltd v The Firm of Portico Holdings (Scotland)* [2018] SC GRE 5, 2018 GWD 6; *Clipper Holding II SARL v SF and SFX* (Sheriff Holligan, 18 January 2018) [unreported].
201 *Guidi v Promontoria (Chestnut) Ltd* [2023] CSIH 4, 2023 SCLR 417, at [15].
202 ibid [16]–[20].
203 SLC, *Discussion Paper on Heritable Securities: Pre-Default* (n 84) para 10.38.
204 See discussion at section 5.2.2.2.

such as registered patents, designs, trademarks, ships and aircraft.[205] For the assignation in security, parties may have to intimate the debtors connected to the security in addition to intimating the debtors connected to the claims (see discussion above in section 5.2.2.5). These added formalities make the use of assignation as a transfer mechanism for security rights in securitisation difficult.

5.3.3 *Trust*

5.3.3.1 Nature of Scottish trust law

Scottish trust law and English trust law are functionally similar. First, both institutions compel a person (or group of persons) who has been vested with a property to hold and use the said property for the exclusive benefit of another person (or group of persons).[206] The person holding and using the property is called the trustee, and the person for whose exclusive benefit the property is held and used is the beneficiary. The person who creates the trust and transfers property into it is the settlor in English law or the truster in Scots law. The property transferred into the trust is regarded as the trust property.

Also, both institutions separate the trust property from the trustee's general property, so that the beneficiary's right in the trust property takes precedence over the trustee's personal creditors' rights during the trustee's insolvency. This function is hereafter called the "insolvency effect".

Yet the paths through which the English trust and the Scottish trust achieve these functions differ. In particular, the English trust law is a product of equity.[207] It is based on a division between ownership in law and ownership in equity, with the trustee being the owner of the trust property in law and the beneficiary the owner in equity.[208] The prevalent view in English law is that the beneficiary's right is a real right,[209] which takes precedence over the rights of the trustee's creditors. In contrast, equity is not known to Scots law. Thus, Scottish trust law is based on a unitary ownership system, of which sole ownership is vested in the trustee.[210] The beneficiary's right is only a personal right against the trustee.[211]

205 See footnote 71 above. See also Merchant Shipping (Registration of Ships) Regulations 1993 (SI 1993/3138), regs 60 and 61; Air Navigation Order 2016 (SI 2016/765), s 28(2).

206 William A Wilson, AGM Duncan and WA Elliott, *Trusts, Trustees and Executors* (2nd edn, W Green 1995) para 1.63.

207 William Swadling, 'Property: General Principles' in Andrew Burrows (ed), *English Private Law* (3rd edn, Oxford University Press 2013) para 4.141.

208 For discussion of the separation of ownership in English trusts, see Sarah Worthington, *Equity* (2nd edn, Oxford University Press 2006) 63.

209 See Gretton, 'Trusts without Equity' (n 46) 604.

210 Stair (n 23) I, xiii, 7.

211 Gretton and Steven, *Property, Trusts and Succession* (n 1) para 23.61.

This personal nature of the beneficiary's right has raised difficulty in explaining the doctrinal basis of the trust's insolvency effect in Scots law. Personal rights only affect the obligor (i.e. the trustee) – they do not extend to third parties, such as the trustee's personal creditors. The dual patrimony theory has, however, been used to explain the trust's insolvency effect.[212] The trustee is considered as having two patrimonies: a personal patrimony and a trust patrimony. The personal patrimony encompasses the trustee's personal assets and liabilities. The trust patrimony encompasses the trust assets and liabilities. These two patrimonies are independent of each other and the (in)solvency of one does not affect the (in)solvency of the other.

5.3.3.2 Scottish trust as a mechanism for transferring security rights in securitisation

Businesses have used the Scottish trust to avoid the difficulties posed by assignation in securitisations. The originator can sign a deed of trust, declaring that it will hold the Scottish receivables and their related security rights as sole trustee for the benefit of the SPV. This type of trust (i.e. where the truster is also the trustee) is called a "truster-as-trustee trust".[213] Since the originator only transfers the assets into its trust patrimony, there is no need to intimate to the obligors. All that is required by law is to: (i) declare the trust in writing;[214] (ii) name at least one existing asset that is to constitute the trust property;[215] and (iii) intimate the trust to the beneficiary (or at least one beneficiary where there is more than one).[216]

Therefore, the originator only needs to intimate to the SPV (or at least one investor where investors are named as the direct beneficiaries of the trust) to transfer the security

212 This approach for Scots law was developed by Professors Gretton and Reid. See the citations at footnote 46 above. The SLC also preferred the double patrimony theory to the option of conferring legal or juristic personality on trusts. SLC, *Discussion Paper on the Nature and the Constitution of Trusts* (n 61) paras 1.4 and 2.39ff.

213 The practice of a truster declaring themselves as trustee is judicially validated in *Allan's Trustees v Inland Revenue Commissioners* 1971 (HL) SLT 62.

214 Requirements of Writing (Scotland) Act 1995, s 1(2)(a)(iii). However, see the exceptions in s 1(3) and (4) of the Act. In contrast, where the truster and the trustee are different parties, the trust does not need to be in writing. See s 1(1) of the Act.

215 In *Joint Administrators of Rangers Football Club Plc, Noters* [2012] CSOH 55, 2012 SLT 599, per Lord Hodge at [33], a trust was held to be ineffective on the ground that none of the trust assets existed.

216 *Allan's Trustees v Inland Revenue Commissioners* 1971 SLT (HL) 62. In *Clark Taylor & Co Ltd v Quality Site Development (Edinburgh) Ltd* 1981 SC (IH) 111, Lord President Emslie suggested (at [117ff]) that other acts of delivery, aside intimation to the beneficiary, may be enough to bring a truster-as-trustee trust into operation. The SLC also suggests that registering the trust in the Books of Council and Session or sheriff court book, or intimating to the beneficiary's agent, should also be sufficient. For discussion of the constitution of trust more generally, see SLC, *Discussion Paper on the Nature and the Constitution of Trusts* (n 61) pt 3.

rights from its personal patrimony to the trust patrimony.[217] At this stage the SPV only acquires personal rights against the originator in respect of the trust property.[218]

Scots trust law also recognises future flows securitisation. In *Tay Valley*, the court held that a regular intimation to the beneficiary of the list of assets that have arisen since the last intimation is sufficient to transfer those assets to the trust patrimony. It is, however, unclear if a transfer of future trust assets would be achieved through other means than a regular intimation to the beneficiary.

Suppose the originator intimates to the SPV about the existence of a trust that comprises both existing and future assets, and the originator makes the future assets ascertainable by reference to an identifiable class of assets or debtors. The author is of the opinion that such an act should be enough to transfer the future assets immediately as they arise. The main basis for intimating to the beneficiary in a truster-as-trustee trust is to ensure that the trust is made irrevocable.[219] An irrevocability outcome can be reached if the future assets are made ascertainable, since the truster can no longer revoke or deny the existence of the trust in respect of the future assets whenever they arise. A further intimation should only be required for future assets that are generally described but not ascertainable. However, in practice, to avoid the uncertainty in this area, parties declare supplemental trusts on an ongoing basis to cover future assets that have arisen.[220]

The utility of the trust is further strengthened by virtue of the non-application of the Business Contract Terms (Assignment of Receivables) Regulations 2018 to contracts

---

217 In *Heritable Reversionary Co v Millar* (1892) 19 R (HL) 43, a bankrupt held a heritable property in trust for Heritable Reversionary Company Ltd. The trust was not recorded in the Register of Sasines, and the question before the court was whether the heritable property formed part of the bankrupt's sequestrated estate. The House of Lords held that the heritable property did not form part of the bankrupt's estate, and thus did not vest in the trustee of the estate. This supports the argument that the registration of trust involving a standard security may not be required for the validity of the trust.

218 Gretton and Steven, *Property, Trusts and Succession* (n 1) para 23.61. But the right can be analogous to a real right in some respects. For instance, the right will prevail over the claims of the trustee's personal creditors in the event of the trustee's insolvency. See *Heritable Reversionary Co v Millar* (1892) 19 R (HL) 43, per Lord Watson at 49f. It is important, and indeed common, to support the trust by including express provisions (in the transaction document) that oblige the originator to transfer ownership rights in the trust assets to the SPV on the occurrence of certain perfection events, like the occurrence of a credit rating downgrade or imminent insolvency in respect of the originator. See e.g. Cardiff Auto Receivables Securitisation 2011-1 PLC (Prospectus, 7 February 2011) 76 <https://www.ise.ie/debt_documents/Prospectus%20-%20Standalone_2ce37b2a-18b8-4add-a220-f1a66fa89056.PDF> accessed 28 May 2024; Finsbury Square 2019-1 Plc (n 111) 115.

219 *Tay Valley Joinery Ltd v CF Financial Services Ltd* 1987 SLT (CSIH) 207, per Lord Dunpark at 216 (noting that "[w]hat is required is something equivalent to the delivery of the trust property to the beneficiary so as to make the trust irrevocable). In *Cameron's Trustees v Cameron* (1907) 14 SLT (CSIH) 720, Lord Kyllachy (at 724) describes the requisite act as "some overt extraneous and ostensible act, which involves acceptance of the trust, and marks definitely the character of the trustee's possession".

220 See Marion MacInnes, Bruce Stephen and Peter Brading, 'Scotland: Securitisation Laws and Regulations 2020' (ICLG 2020) para 4.11 <https://iclg.com/practice-areas/securitisation-laws-and-regulations/scotland> accessed 28 May 2024.

governed by Scots law. The Regulations only apply to contracts governed by the laws of England and Wales or the law of Northern Ireland.[221] This means that anti-assignation clauses remain effective in Scots law. On the consequences of a breach of anti-assignation clauses, Scottish law follows the English law rule in *Linden Gardens Trust Ltd v Lenesta Sludge Disposals Ltd*[222] to render the purported assignation ineffective not just as between the debtor and the assignor but also as against the assignee.[223]

A related issue worth considering is whether an anti-assignation clause extends to trusts. In *Don King*, the English Court of Appeal held that: (i) an assignment of contractual rights is "different in character" from a declaration of trust over such rights; (ii) a clause prohibiting assignments does not extend to declarations of trust; and (iii) where a restriction on trust declaration is intended, the contract should expressly provide so.[224] Though English cases are not binding in Scotland, it is likely that a Scottish court will find the decision in *Don King* persuasive. This is because the Scottish trust is equally different in character from assignation. For example, it does not involve the transfer of contractual rights to the beneficiary. Only a beneficial interest is created, a personal right against the trustee albeit with insolvency effect. Also, the trust does not prejudice the right of the obligor – the rights of the beneficiary flow from the trust itself and not from the underlying agreement between the originator and the obligor.[225]

Another related issue is the enforceability of an anti-trust clause (i.e. where the contract expressly provides that rights arising from it are not to be held by any of the parties in trust for any other party). It is probably very rare to see such clauses, since, unlike an assignation, declaring a trust may not prejudice the rights of the obligor since the obligor will remain liable to the same party they are contracted to. In this sense, i.e. where the trust does not prejudice the debtor, there is force in the argument that such anti-trust clause would constitute an unjustified restraint on the creditor's right to freely use or hold their property and therefore should be unenforceable on the ground of public policy.

Yet it is not inconceivable that a trust will prejudice the debtor. This is because even though the trustee is the legal owner of the trust property, they are under a fiduciary obligation to always put the interest of the beneficiary ahead of theirs while administering the property. This opens up the possibility that the trustee may be forced to take actions (against the debtor) they would not have taken if not for the fiduciary obligation. Another possibility is where the debtor also serves as a creditor to the other party. The debtor will

221 Business Contract Terms (Assignment of Receivables) Regulations 2018 (SI 2018/1254) (Explanatory notes to the Regulations, para 1).

222 [1994] 1 AC 85 (HL).

223 See Reid, *The Law of Property* (n 1) para 652. The SLC recommends in its report that the status quo should be maintained, and this is adopted under the Moveable Transactions Act, s 6. See SLC, *Report on Moveable Transactions* (n 36) paras 13.2ff.

224 *Don King (Productions) Inc v Warren* [2000] Ch 291 (CA), per Aldous LJ at 320ff.

225 *Allan's Trustees v Inland Revenue Commissioners* 1971 SLT (HL) 62, per Lord Reid at 64.

have a genuine commercial reason to include an anti-trust clause in order to avoid the trust's insolvency effect, which may be detrimental to the debtor's chances of realising their credit. Moreover, even if the debtor's position will not be prejudiced, rendering the clause unenforceable would undermine the established rule in the Latin maxim *pacta sunt servanda* (i.e. "agreements must be kept"). It is suggested in the present work that unless excluded by statute or case law, anti-trust clauses should be enforceable under Scots law regardless of whether they are justified or not.[226] In any case, anti-trust clauses rarely occur in practice and do not diminish the utility of trust as a transfer solution for Scottish securitisations.

5.4 Conclusion

The Scottish trust's ability to separate "ownership" from "benefit" without invoking the publicity principle makes it the preferred transfer solution that is currently available in Scots law. It requires the originator to declare itself the owner of the security rights when transferring the beneficial rights to the SPV. Since ownership remains with the originator, no intimation to the debtors is required. All that is required for the trust to come into effect is for the originator to intimate to the SPV.

The usefulness of the trust institution is also strengthened because anti-assignation clauses are valid in Scots law, so that parties can validly prohibit or restrict assignations in Scotland, making the trust the only viable transfer mechanism available for parties. This reinforces the position of the trust as the preferred solution under current Scots law.

The analysis undertaken in this chapter (for the preferred solution) is limited to solutions that are currently available under Scots law. It does not consider the registration solution adopted under the Moveable Transactions (Scotland) Act 2023, which is expected to come into full force in the second half of 2024. For discussion of how the registration solution compares with the trust and the preferred solutions in England and France, see section 8.2.

226 English case law suggests that anti-trust clauses are enforceable. See e.g. *Don King (Productions) Inc v Warren* [2000] Ch 291 (CA), per Aldous LJ at 321. It is unclear whether reg 2 of the Business Contract Terms (Assignment of Receivables) Regulations 2018 (SI 2018/1254) extends to anti-trust clauses, so that anti-trust clauses are also rendered ineffective under English law. Given the suggestions in *Don King*, it may be argued that an assignment is not the same with a declaration of trust, thereby making reg 2 inapplicable to anti-trust clauses. Cf Paul MacMahon, 'Rethinking Assignability' (2020) 79 The Cambridge Law Journal 288, 306f.

6 TRANSFER OF RIGHTS UNDER ENGLISH LAW

This chapter examines the legal solutions available for transferring security rights in securitisations under English law. The aim is to identify the preferred transfer solution and demonstrate why it is so preferred.

The chapter proceeds as follows. Section 6.1 discusses the accessoriness of security rights to their related debts and its effect on the transfer of security rights under English law. It demonstrates that the transfer of rights to debt does not always mean that the related security rights will automatically pass under English law. Section 6.2 discusses four main solutions available under English law for transferring security rights in securitisations. These solutions include novation, legal assignment, equitable assignment and trust. This chapter concludes in section 6.3 that the flexible and low-cost nature of the equitable assignment makes it the preferred method of transferring security rights in securitisations under English law.

It will be seen that, in comparison to Scots law, the publicity principle plays a less significant role under English law.[1] This is mainly due to the influence of equity, which allows property rights to be created without publicity. Also, unlike Scots law, which has a unititular property law system, English law has a divided property law system that recognises two property rights: equitable rights and legal rights.[2]

6.1 Accessory principle and transfer of security rights under English law

6.1.1 *Overview of the English law of security rights*

English law recognises four categories of voluntary real security: a mortgage, a charge, a pledge, and a contractual lien.[3] A mortgage is a non-possessory security which involves

1 See also section 8.1.3.

2 For a comparison, see HL MacQueen, 'Scots Law' in JM Smits (ed), *Elgar Encyclopedia of Comparative Law* (2nd edn, Edward Elgar 2012) 790.

3 *Re Cosslett (Contractors) Ltd* [1998] Ch 495 (CA), per Millet LJ at 508. See also HG Beale and others, *The Law of Security and Title-Based Financing* (3rd edn, Oxford University Press 2018) para 1.17.

the transfer of title in security.[4] The title transferred can be legal (i.e. legal mortgage) or equitable (i.e. equitable mortgage). Publicity is not required for constituting an equitable mortgage but is generally required for constituting a legal mortgage.[5] A charge is a creation of equity.[6] It is a non-possessory security which merely creates an encumbrance over the security property. It can arise without publicity.[7] The charge may be fixed or floating.[8] Given their flexibility and the fact that their validity does not depend on possession, the mortgage and the charge can be created over all property classes.[9]

A pledge is a common law security which can only be constituted by the actual or constructive delivery of possession of the security property.[10] The contractual lien also depends on possession. It grants the creditor the right to detain the goods of the debtor for security.[11] It differs from a pledge because the goods being detained are initially delivered to the creditor for some purposes other than security.[12] Also, a pledge grants an implied power of sale where the debtor defaults, but this is not the case with a contractual lien, unless parties expressly agree to it.[13] Since they depend on possession, the pledge and the

4 Louise Gullifer (ed), *Goode and Gullifer on Legal Problems of Credit and Security* (7th edn, Sweet & Maxwell 2022) para 1.52; Ewan McKendrick (ed), *Goode and McKendrick on Commercial Law* (6th edn, Penguin Books 2020) para 22.21. It should be noted that a legal mortgage over land has ceased to operate as a title transfer since the introduction of the Law of Property Act 1925. Instead, it now operates as "a demise [or subdemise] of the land to the mortgagee for a term of years absolute" – see ss 85–87 of the Law of Property Act 1925.

5 See Goode and Gullifer, *Legal Problems* (n 4) paras 1.12f.

6 One exception is the legal charge over land, which is a creation of statute – Law of Property Act 1925, s 85(1); Land Registration Act 2002, s 51.

7 Goode and Gullifer, *Legal Problems* (n 4) para 1.53. But note the effect of the registration scheme under ss 859A and 859H of the Companies Act 2006, which applies where the chargor is a company. See section 8.1.3.2 for discussion.

8 Goode and McKendrick, *Commercial Law* (n 4) para 22.25.

9 ibid paras 22.23 and 25.09. Property under English law may be classified the same way as under Scots law, except for differences in terminology. It can be tangible or intangible (compare corporeal and incorporeal under Scots law). Property can also be real or personal (compare heritable and moveable under Scot law). It can further be classified as tangible personal property (i.e. choses in possession), intangible personal property (choses in action), tangible real property (land and the right of ownership in land) and intangible real property (other interests in land). See generally FH Lawson and Bernard Rudden, *The Law of Property* (3rd edn, Oxford University Press 2002) ch 2.

10 Goode and Gullifer, *Legal Problems* (n 4) para 1.44; Goode and McKendrick, *Commercial Law* (n 4) para 22.17.

11 Goode and Gullifer, *Legal Problems* (n 4) para 1.51; Goode and McKendrick, *Commercial Law* (n 4) para 22.20.

12 Goode and Gullifer, *Legal Problems* (n 4) para 1.51; Goode and McKendrick, *Commercial Law* (n 4) para 22.20.

13 Goode and Gullifer, *Legal Problems* (n 4) para 1.51; Goode and McKendrick, *Commercial Law* (n 4) para 22.20.

contractual lien can only be taken over tangible assets, such as choses in possession and land.[14]

The pledge and contractual lien may also be taken over documentary intangibles. A pure intangible property is different from a documentary intangible property. Documentary intangibles are evidenced in a document, and the document represents title to the rights under the document. Hence, the possession of the document means entitlement to the rights under it.[15] Common examples include bills of lading and promissory notes. On the other hand, pure intangibles may be evidenced in a document, but the document does not represent title. This makes possession impossible. Examples include rights to debts, intellectual property and registered shares.[16] Therefore, the term "share pledges" is misleading since shares are non-pledgeable in the strict sense.

The possessory requirement that applies to the pledge and the contractual lien means that their utility for commercial transactions is limited. However, the flexible nature of the mortgage and the charge, and their general applicability, means that businesses in England do not face the difficulty their Scottish counterparts face.[17] The availability of mortgage and charge also means that the need for complex functional security arrangements, such as a sale and leaseback arrangement and the trust, is reduced under English law.

6.1.2 *The accessory principle*

The extent to which the *accessorium sequitur principale* rule (the *accessorium* principle) applies to real securities under English law is uncertain. First, it is difficult to trace the application of the general accessory rule in leading literature. Professor Steven observes that the mention of the word "accessory" in relation to real security is "less visible" in English law sources when compared to personal security.[18] He identifies two reasons this may be so in relation to a mortgage over land. The first reason relates to the nature of the mortgage as an instrument of transfer. The security extinguishes not merely upon the discharge of the debt but upon the reconveyance of title. Hence, the aspect of the accessory

---

14 Although in practice the securities are rarely taken over land. See e.g. Goode and Gullifer, *Legal Problems* (n 4) para 1.45.

15 Goode and McKendrick note that "the document is treated as a chattel" – Goode and McKendrick, *Commercial Law* (n 4) para 2.56.

16 See generally Goode and Gullifer, *Legal Problems* (n 4) paras 1.45ff.

17 For the position in Scotland see section 5.1.2.1.

18 AJM Steven, 'Accessoriness and Security over Land' (2009) 13 Edinburgh Law Review 387, 390 (and the authorities cited). For example, the word "accessory" is used to describe a guarantor's obligation in Lionel Smith, 'Security' in Andrew Burrows (ed), *English Private Law* (Oxford University Press 2013) para 5.161; Goode and McKendrick, *Commercial Law* (n 4) para 30.14. But both texts do not use the word in their analysis of real security.

principle which requires that the security automatically extinguishes upon the discharge of the debt does not apply.

The second reason relates to a suggestion made by Professor Sparkes regarding the effect of the common law remedy of forfeiture.[19] That remedy gives the mortgagee the right to take mortgaged land where the debtor fails to pay the related debt, regardless of any difference in the value of the land and the amount of the debt. Hence, the accessory principle, which requires the value of the security to reflect the amount owed, does not apply.[20] Sparkes goes on to suggest that "equity imposes accessoriness" through the equity of redemption rule, which gives a mortgagor the right to redeem the mortgaged property on the discharge of the debt.[21]

Other reasons for the difficulty can be identified. Primarily, the influence of equity in English law makes the principle irrelevant.[22] Equity considers as done that which ought to be done.[23] Therefore, if an assignment of a claim is for value but the assignation document is silent on the transfer of the related security, equity may intervene to confer property rights over the security to the assignee. This may explain why Professors Goode and McKendrick's *Commercial Law* refers to the trust, rather than the *accessorium* principle, as the mechanism to apply where the debt is transferred without expressly including the security.[24] The point also supports Sparkes's suggestion (in relation to land mortgage) that "equity imposes accessoriness".[25]

Furthermore, publicity plays a less important role in English law when compared with Scots law.[26] This is because equitable security rights do not require publicity for their validity and transfer.[27] This, therefore, reduces the importance of the *accessorium* principle since the second limb of the rule (i.e. publicity of the transfer is not required) is achievable through equity.

Besides the difficulty in tracing the application of the accessory principle, the position on the application of the *accessorium* principle to real security is not conclusive. As noted above, Professors Goode and McKendrick, citing *Morley v Morley*,[28] suggest that the

19 Peter Sparkes, *European Land Law* (Hart 2007) 399.
20 See ibid 398f.
21 ibid 300 (citing *Seton v Slade* (1802) 7 Ves 265, per Lord Eldon LC at 273).
22 Unlike Scots law, which has a unititular system of property law, English law has a divided system of property law which recognises two property rights: legal rights and equitable rights.
23 See e.g. *Tebb v Hodge* (1869) LR 5 CP 73 (Ex Ch); *Tailby v Official Receiver* (1888) 13 App Cas 523 (HL).
24 Goode and McKendrick, *Commercial Law* (n 4) para 23.56 (suggesting that the assignor will hold the security right in trust for the assignee and citing *Morley v Morley* (1858) 53 ER 633). See discussion below on *Morley*.
25 Sparkes (n 19) 399.
26 David L Carey Miller and Malcolm M Combe, 'The Boundaries of Property Rights in Scots Law: Report to the XVIIth Congress of Comparative Law' (2006) 10 Electronic Journal of Comparative Law 1, 3.
27 See sections 8.1.3.1 and 8.1.3.2.
28 (1858) 53 ER 633 (Ch).

assignor will hold the security right in trust for the assignee.[29] In other words, the security right does not pass automatically with the transferred debt: the legal title to the security right remains with the assignor, who will hold the title for the benefit of the assignee.

But the circumstances were different in *Morley*. The issue in that case was whether an assignor who transferred a debt but *expressly excluded* the transfer of the related mortgage was entitled to foreclose on the mortgage. The Court of Chancery rejected the argument that the security automatically passed with the debt and held that the assignor was entitled to foreclose. The assignor would then hold the money recovered in trust for the assignee.[30] The decision was based mainly on the fact that the security was expressly excluded from the transfer. It is, therefore, not a good authority for the present issue in focus (i.e. where the debt is transferred, and no mention is made of the related security right).

The court in *Morley*, however, observed that "[i]f the deed had remained *simpliciter* [i.e. without the express exclusion of the mortgage], … it would have carried this mortgage with it."[31] In other words, the "*accessorium* rule" would have applied if the debt was transferred without any reference to the mortgage. But the comment is *obiter* and hence not legally binding as a precedent. Also, the reasoning behind the *obiter* statement was not given – i.e. whether it is based on the *accessorium* principle or the principle of equity, since both principles would have produced different legal effects. If the *obiter* was based on the principle of equity, then the transferee's right in the security would be in equity and therefore subject to the general limitations of equitable rights.[32] If it was based on the *accessorium* principle, the transferee's right would probably be at law, putting the transferee in a better standing compared to an equitable right. The position on the applicability of the *accessorium* principle in relation to the charge, the pledge and the contractual lien is equally unclear.

The law, however, seems to be more clear-cut in the converse case – i.e. where the security is transferred without the debt. Goode and McKendrick note that a transfer of a mortgage with no reference to the debt operates to transfer the debt by implication of law.[33] Section 114(1) of the Law of Property Act 1925 affirms that position by providing that the transfer of a mortgage carries with it "the right to demand, sue for, recover, and

29 Goode and McKendrick, *Commercial Law* (n 4) para 23.56.
30 *Morley v Morley* (1858) 53 ER 633 (Ch), at 636.
31 ibid at 635.
32 See section 8.2.6.2.
33 Goode and McKendrick, *Commercial Law* (n 4) para 23.56.

give receipts for, the mortgage money".[34] Goode and McKendrick presume that the foregoing position also applies to the transfer of a charge.[35]

The foregoing is interesting, given that it suggests that the principal (i.e. the debt) follows the accessory (the security). That outcome inverts the *accessorium* principle. A related issue is whether the operation of the inverted *accessorium* principle can be excluded by parties so that only the security is transferred. Section 114(1) is made subject to parties' intention in relation to a mortgage, making it possible for parties to exclude its application. It is suggested that a similar approach will apply to a charge.

6.1.3 *Concluding comments*

The foregoing shows that the application of the *accessorium* principle in relation to real security (i.e. the security follows the debt) is unclear under English law. The law in fact suggests that the position is truer in the converse case (i.e. the debt follows the security). Therefore, care should be taken to expressly refer to security rights in a securitisation transaction. Also, where the transfer of the security requires the performance of some additional acts, care should be taken to perform those acts for the transfer to be completed.

6.2 Solutions available for transferring security rights in securitisations under English law

6.2.1 *Initial comments*

This section discusses the mechanisms available for transferring security rights in securitisations under English law. The perfection and documentation issues associated with the identified transfer mechanism and why equitable assignment is the most commonly used transfer mechanism for securitisations under English law will also be discussed in this section.

34 In *Jones v Gibbons* (1804) 9 Ves Jr 407 (Ch), Sir W Grant noted at [411f] that "he, who has the estate, has in effect the debt; as the estate can never be taken from him except by payment of the debt." It should be noted that s 114(1) does not apply to "a transfer of a bill of sale of chattels by way of security" – see s 114(5) of the Law of Property Act 1925.

35 Goode and McKendrick, *Commercial Law* (n 4) para 23.56.

6.2.2 Novation

Commercial contracts generally comprise obligations and rights. As a general rule, contractual rights are freely and unilaterally transferrable.[36] In contrast, contractual obligations cannot be transferred unilaterally without first obtaining the consent of the other party to the contract.[37] Novation arises when such consent is obtained for the transfer of the contractual obligations and contractual rights. In other words, where lender "B" with undrawn commitments under a loan agreement with obligor "A" wishes to transfer its obligations (i.e. the undrawn amounts) and its rights arising from the said agreement to C, who also agrees, novation (i.e. an agreement between all the parties – A, B and C) is the only way B can ensure that it will be fully discharged from its payment obligations. Thus, a novation is defined as "a tripartite agreement by which an existing contract between A and B is discharged and a new contract is made between A and C, usually on the same terms as the first contract."[38] Strictly speaking, a novation does not transfer B's rights and obligations to C. Rather, it cancels all of B's rights and obligations, while C assumes new (albeit similar) rights and obligations in B's place.[39]

An important advantage of a novation in a financial transaction is that it is the only way a lender can fully transfer its contractual obligations to a third party under English law.[40] If the lender wishes to achieve this result with other methods of transfer (like assignment), the lender will have to procure an undertaking or a similar commitment (in the transfer agreement) from the transferee that it will perform the lender's contractual obligations. This type of arrangement does not discharge the lender from its obligations under the original contract with the obligor. The obligor can pursue the lender for the performance of outstanding obligations. Also, since novation puts the "transferee" in a direct contractual relationship with the obligor, the "transferee" can enforce its rights under the novation agreement against the obligor without having to join the original lender in an action. Despite these advantages, there are reasons why a novation is rarely

36 Simon Whittaker, 'Contract Law and Other Legal Categories' in HG Beale (ed), *Chitty on Contracts* (35th edn, Sweet & Maxwell 2023) para 3.090. The exceptions to this rule include cases where there is a contractual prohibition or restriction on assignments and cases where the rights are of a personal nature. See B McFarlane, 'Assignment and Novation' in HG Beale (ed), *Chitty on Contracts* (35th edn, Sweet & Maxwell 2023) para 23.043ff. See also section 6.2.4 below.

37 *Tolhurst v Associated Portland Cement Manufacturers Ltd* [1902] 2 KB 660 (CA), at 668 (where Collins MR said "[i]t is, I think, quite clear that neither at law nor in equity could the burden of a contract be shifted off the shoulders of a contractor on to those of another without the consent of the contractee"). See also *Nokes v Doncaster Amalgamated Collieries Ltd* [1940] AC 1014 (HL).

38 Stephen Furst and others, *Keating on Construction Contracts* (11th edn, Sweet & Maxwell 2016) 429, para 13.003.

39 McFarlane (n 36) para 23.089.

40 *Tolhurst v Associated Portland Cement Manufacturers Ltd* [1902] 2 KB 660 (CA), per Collins MR at 668.

used for transferring debts and security rights in securitisation transactions. These reasons mainly flow from the nature of novation as a new contract and the consent requirement.

6.2.2.1 The consent requirement: implications in a securitisation transaction

The key issue with securitisations is that they normally involve multiple debtors. For example, mortgage-backed securities could involve tens of thousands of underlying mortgagors.[41] In a novation, the consent of the mortgagors must be obtained for the debt and security rights to be effectively novated. This requirement can be prohibitive, given the number of mortgagors involved. Suppose the security was provided by a party other than the debtor. In that case, it means that the consent of the security provider must equally be obtained for the novation to be binding with respect to the security. This is because a novation is effectively a new contract, and the consent of all the parties involved in the original transaction must be obtained for it to be binding.[42] Otherwise, the security will no longer be enforceable since the secured debt has been extinguished and replaced with a new debt. The accessory right (i.e. the security) is worthless without the principal right (i.e. the secured debt).[43]

It is important to note the difference between the necessity of "notification" in a legal assignment and "consent" in a novation. The validity of a legal assignment does not depend on the obligor agreeing or consenting to the assignment; the assignor/assignee is only required to notify the obligor of the assignment (provided there are no transfer restrictions in the original contract). Conversely, the requirement for consent in a novation means that the obligor must agree to the novation for it to be binding. This implies that the requirement can make securitisation impossible as it gives obligors the opportunity to "block" the proposed transfer by withholding their consents. Moreover, the originator may not want the obligors to know about the transfer for commercial reasons. Such reasons might be the need to maintain a long-term commercial relationship with the obligors or avoid sending a negative or incorrect signal to the obligors, who might think that the originator is selling its assets because it has financial problems.

Lastly, the necessity of the obligor's consent makes securitisations of future flow receivables impossible. Future flows securitisations involve the transfer of receivables

41 See e.g. Elland RMBS 2018 Plc (Prospectus, 13 December 2018) 114f <https://www.rns-pdf.londonstockexchange.com/rns/5340K_1-2018-12-14.pdf> accessed 28 May 2024 (involving 39,000 mortgages).

42 McFarlane (n 36) para 23.089.

43 See the Scottish case of *Watson v Bogue (No 1)* 2000 SLT (Sh Ct) 125, per Sheriff Principal Nicholson at 129 (quoting Sheriff Andrew Bell's description of a security without an underlying debt as "a mere husk, empty of any content").

arising from future contracts which are non-existent, and the obligors are unknown at the time of transfer.[44]

6.2.2.2 Novation as a new contract: implications for security

The effect of a novation as a new contract is that a novated security in a securitisation transaction effectively becomes a new security. This means that the usual perfection requirements necessary for creating a new security will have to be observed. The requirements would include registration of the security at Companies House (if the obligor is a UK company), registration at the relevant asset registry, delivery of possession or control of the security asset to the special purpose vehicle (SPV) in the case of a pledge or contractual lien, payment of new charges and taxes for mortgages, etc.

Another effect of a novated security is that it resets hardening periods. This makes the novated security vulnerable to the risk of being set aside under sections 238, 239, 240 and 245 of the Insolvency Act 1986. The provisions of the first three sections empower an insolvency practitioner to seek to set aside a security transaction where (i) the transaction is entered into at an undervalue or is preferential, and (ii) the transaction occurs within six months of the borrower going into liquidation or two years in circumstances where the transaction involves a connected person (e.g. a director or spouse of a director).

Section 245 automatically renders a floating charge void if the charge is created within twelve months of the chargor going into insolvency (in circumstances where the chargor is unable to pay its debts at the time of creating the charge) or within two years in circumstances where the charge is created in favour of a connected person. However, the application of section 245 is exempted to the extent that the charge holder advanced value to the chargor at the same time as, or after, the creation of the charge.[45]

The original security transaction may have fallen outside the hardening periods (i.e. it has existed for more than six months, twelve months or two years respectively, so it is no longer vulnerable to being set aside under sections 238, 239, 240 or 245 of the Insolvency Act 1986). Novating the security transaction means creating a new security. This, in turn, restarts the period within which the security will be vulnerable under the relevant provisions. This is a real concern, particularly in collateralised loan obligations (CLOs) where the obligors usually are companies. Also, concerning section 245, the value for the floating charge would have been advanced *before* the creation of the new charge, making it more likely that the charge will not be exempt from the avoidance effect of the section.

Furthermore, since the novated security effectively becomes a new security, priority issues may arise. The investors might find that they rank behind a creditor whose security was created after the original agreement but before the novation.

---

44 For more on future flows securitisation see John Deacon, *Global Securitisation and CDOs* (Wiley 2004) 125.

45 See s 245(2) of the Act.

6.2.2.3 Summary on novation

Novation can achieve the function of a transfer of security rights. But it is rarely used in practice for securitisation transactions because of the difficulties arising from its requirement for consent and the implications of it being a new contract. Moreover, a security usually confers benefits (and not obligations) relating to the security rights on the secured party, and securitisations do not generally require the transfer of obligations because they typically involve fully drawn loans. This diminishes the usefulness of novation in a securitisation transaction.

6.2.3 *Assignment*

6.2.3.1 Overview and history

Assignment is another mechanism through which security interests can be transferred under English law. It is defined as "the transfer from one person (the assignor) to another (the assignee) of the whole or part of an existing right or interest in intangible property presently owned by the assignor".[46] In the context of this passage, the assignor is the originator; the assignee is the SPV, and the rights are the receivables and the related security rights. Unlike novation, an assignment does not require the obligor's consent.[47] It also does not involve the creation of a new contract between the debtor and the assignor since assignments only transfer existing rights in the original contract to the assignee.[48] Therefore, an assignment of a debt or its related security will not affect the priority of the security already taken; neither will it reset the hardening period. Also, an assigned security right does not need to be reconstituted.[49] The assignment of registered legal mortgages over land, intellectual property rights, aircraft or ships will, however, need to be registered at the relevant asset registry in order to reflect the details of the assignee as the new proprietor of the security.[50]

Prior to the Judicature Act 1873,[51] the common law saw contractual rights merely as procedural rights to sue and considered them unassignable so as to pass the right of action

---

46 Ying Khai Liew (ed), *Guest on the Law of Assignment* (4th edn, Sweet & Maxwell 2021) para 1.01.

47 Note, however, that consent will be needed if there is a valid non-assignment clause. For discussion of the validity of non-assignment clauses see section 6.2.4.2.

48 Liew (n 46) para 1.01.

49 See section 6.2.2.2 for discussion of the implications of novation as a new contract.

50 See respectively Land Registration Act 2002, s 27; Patents Act 1977, s 33 (similar provision also applies to trademarks and designs); Air Navigation Order 2016 (SI 2016/765), s 28(2); Merchant Shipping (Registration of Ships) Regulations 1993 (SI 1993/3138), regs 60 and 61.

51 Before the 1873 Act, common law courts and courts of equity operated separately and in a parallel manner. Traditionally, English law distinguishes between legal rights and equitable rights. The courts of common law only entertained claims arising from legal rights while the Court of Chancery entertained claims arising from equitable rights. As a result of this division, it was important to categorise choses in action into legal choses in action and equitable choses in action. The Judicature Acts of 1873 and 1875, among other things,

at law.[52] One way of achieving such a result (i.e. the ability of the transferee to bring a direct action at law against the debtor) was by novation.[53] The result could also be achieved through a power of attorney, but this solution would not fully protect the transferee since powers of attorneys were revocable.[54]

Contractual rights were unassignable at common law because they were seen as too personal in nature and incapable of being assigned.[55] It was suggested that this "personal nature" justification was based on the dire consequences a debtor could face if they defaulted on their debt (which included imprisonment).[56] Therefore, it was necessary to let the debtor have a say on who became their creditor. Another reason was the concern that allowing assignments would lead to "intermeddling in litigation in which the intermeddler has no concern".[57]

Contractual rights – both legal and equitable – were, however, assignable in equity.[58] Equity viewed contractual rights as procedural rights to sue and as a piece of property that could be assigned. Therefore, the court of equity permitted the assignee to sue in their own name if the rights were equitable rights (e.g. rights under a trust or a legacy).[59] If the rights were legal rights (e.g. debts due under a contract), the assignee could obtain an order from the court of equity, compelling the assignor to allow the assignee to use their name in a common law suit.[60] Cozens-Hardy LJ explained these points in his judgment in *Fitzroy v Cave* as follows:

> At common law a … debt was looked upon as a strictly personal obligation, and an assignment of it was regarded as a mere assignment of a right to bring an action at law against the debtor. … But the Courts of Equity took a different view. They admitted the title of an assignee of a debt, regarding it as a piece of

---

fused the two courts into a new single Supreme Court of Judicature (consisting of the High Court of Justice and the Court of Appeal) where all rights – both legal and equitable – became enforceable. This fusion made the categorisation of choses in action less important. WT Major, 'The Assignment of Things in Action' in *Basic English Law* (Macmillan Education UK 1990) 239.

52 *Durham Brothers v Robertson* [1898] 1 QB 765 (CA), per Chitty LJ at 770. Exceptions applied in relation to rights assigned to, or held by, the Crown and rights arising from negotiable instruments. See McFarlane (n 36) para 23.001.

53 Stanley Bailey, 'Assignment of Debts in England from the Twelfth to the Twentieth Century' (1932) 48 Law Quarterly Review 547, 550.

54 McFarlane (n 36) para 23.001.

55 ibid.

56 Bailey (n 53) 549.

57 Edwin Peel and GH Treitel, *The Law of Contract* (14th edn, Sweet & Maxwell 2015) 672.

58 McFarlane (n 36) para 23.002.

59 ibid.

60 ibid.

> property, an asset capable of being dealt with like any other asset, and treating the necessity of an action at law to get it in as a mere incident.[61]

Section 25(6) of the Judicature Act 1873[62] introduced statutory provisions that allowed the assignment of choses in action. A chose (or a thing) in action is a form of personal property which can only be claimed or enforced by action. It contrasts with a chose in possession, another form of personal property, which can be claimed or enforced by taking actual physical possession of the thing.[63] Examples of a chose in action include rights arising from a contract, rights under a trust, intellectual property rights and insurance policies. Section 25(6) of the Judicature Act 1873 was later replaced by section 136(1) of the Law of Property Act 1925 (the 1925 Act).

Although the Judicature Acts of 1873 and 1875 ended the institutional separation of common law and equity, the separation remains important in relation to English substantive laws.[64] Therefore, assignments effected in accordance with section 136(1) of the 1925 Act are referred to as statutory or legal assignments. Assignments that fall short of the requirements of the 1925 Act are effective as equitable assignments.[65] The nature and requirements of the two forms of assignment are discussed below.

6.2.3.2 Statutory assignment

Section 136(1) of the 1925 Act governs assignments of choses in action. A right to a debt is an example of a chose in action. Certain conditions must be met for an assignment under section 136(1) to be effective. These conditions are that the assignment must be absolute, written, and notified to the debtor. As noted above, the main issues normally encountered when using such assignment as the mode of transfer in securitisations is the notification requirement. A brief description of the notification requirement is given in the paragraph below.

---

61 *Fitzroy v Cave* [1905] 2 KB 364 (CA), per Cozens-Hardy LJ at 372.

62 Supreme Court of Judicature Act 1873, s 25(6).

63 Explaining the difference, Blackstone noted that a property in possession subsists where "a man hath both the right and also the occupation of the thing", while a property in action subsists where "a man hath not the occupation, but merely a bare right to occupy the thing in question; the possession whereof may however be recovered by a suit or action at law". W Blackstone, *Commentaries on the Laws of England* (Clarendon Press 1766) ii, 396.

64 It has been argued that this separation in English law is needless and should be eradicated. Andrew Burrows, 'We Do This At Common Law But That In Equity' (2002) 22 Oxford Journal of Legal Studies 1.

65 *William Brandt's Sons & Co v Dunlop Rubber Company, Limited* [1905] AC 454 (HL), per Lord Macnaghten at 462 (stating that "[t]he statute does not forbid or destroy equitable assignments or impair their efficacy in the slightest degree").

The notice must be expressed in writing.[66] Hence, oral notification is not sufficient.[67] The fact that the debtor had paid to the assignee on the account of the debt is not sufficient to exclude the debtor from relying on the statute.[68] The written notice does not have to comply with any formal requirements for it to be valid.[69] But it must be clear that an assignment has occurred so that the debtor knows what has been assigned and to whom they have to pay the debt in the future.[70] The Act does not give a specific time within which the notice must be given. It provides that the legal right to the chose in action being assigned, which gives the assignee the power to enforce or discharge the same without the concurrence of the assignor, only passes from the date the written notice has been given to the debtor.[71] Clearly, having to send a written notification to every debtor will be costly for securitisations involving multiple debtors. Furthermore, for reasons shown in section 5.3.2.1, notification makes the securitisation of future receivables impracticable.

In respect of the related security rights, section 6.1.2 demonstrates that the position of the law regarding the application of the *accessorium* principle is uncertain. The secured lender who wishes to transfer the legal title in a security (along with the secured debt) should therefore refer to the transfer of the security in the assignment document and perform any act which is requisite for the transfer of the security. Hence, where the assignment involves registered legal mortgages over land, intellectual property rights, aircrafts or ships, the assignment (in addition to giving notice to the debtor) will need to be registered at the relevant asset registry.[72] If the assignment involves a pledge, delivery to the assignee will be necessary. Also, where the assignment involves a legal mortgage over claims, a written notice of the security transfer may need to be given to the underlying debtors for the assignment to be effective. These formalities (that is notification, registration and possession) pose difficulties for transactions involving multiple obligors and/or future rights.

---

66 Law of Property Act 1925, ss 136(1) and 196(1).

67 *Hockley and Papworth v Goldstein* (1920) 90 LJKB 111 (where the assignor knew that the debtor could not read and gave an oral notice. It was held that a written notice is essential).

68 ibid. See also Liew (n 46) para 2.29.

69 *Denney v Conklin* [1913] 3 KB 177 (KB), per Atkin J at 180.

70 *Van Lynn Developments Ltd v Pelias Construction Co Ltd* [1969] 1 QB 607 (CA), per Lord Denning MR at 61ff (holding that a written demand to the debtor for payment was a sufficient notice).

71 Law of Property Act 1925, s 136(1).

72 See Land Registration Act 2002, s 27; Patents Act 1977, s 33 (similar provision also applies to trademarks and designs); Air Navigation Order 2016 (SI 2016/765), s 28(2); Merchant Shipping (Registration of Ships) Regulations 1993 (SI 1993/3138), regs 60 and 61.

6.2.3.3 Equitable assignment of security rights

An assignment that fails to fulfil any of the statutory requirements may still be valid in equity.[73] Therefore, notice is not required to bring an equitable assignment into effect.[74] However, it should be noted that section 53(1)(c) of the 1925 Act requires a disposition of an equitable interest or trust to be in writing. In other words, the assignment of an equitable chose in action will be void if done orally.

Where the equitable assignment involves the transfer of registered legal mortgages over land, intellectual property rights, aircraft or ships, registration at the relevant asset registry is not necessary for the assignment to be effective. This flexible nature of the equitable assignment makes it an important method of assigning choses in action in English law. Most especially, the fact that notice and other relevant registration requirements are unnecessary in equitable assignment makes it attractive for securitisation.

In practice, where the equitable assignment is used in a securitisation transaction, the perfection requirements (i.e. notice and registration) are avoided until the occurrence of certain notification events.[75] This solution enables the originator to save considerable costs and, at the same time, minimises the risk of the SPV's (and ultimately the investors') title being defeated by a subsequent legal title in the same receivable(s) and related security which is acquired for value and without notice of the SPV's equitable title.[76]

Equitable assignment also enables future flows securitisations. The *locus classicus* on this is *Tailby v Official Receiver* (1888) 13 App Cas 523, where the House of Lords held that an agreement to assign future rights (i.e. rights which the assignor hopes to acquire under a contract that is not yet in existence) will be effective in equity to transfer the future rights as soon as they come into existence, provided that the assignee provides a valuable consideration for the transfer and the future rights are sufficiently identifiable under the agreement.

Equitable assignment, however, has its own downsides which present considerable risks for the SPV (and ultimately the investors). Where an assignment of security rights is effected without the notice of the security providers, the legal title to the security will remain with the originator, while only the equitable title passes to the SPV. This means that the assignee may not be able to bring an independent action against the security provider

---

73 *William Brandt's Sons & Co v Dunlop Rubber Company, Limited* [1905] AC 454 (HL); *Gorringe v Irwell India Rubber and Gutta Percha Works* (1886) 34 Ch D 128 (CA).

74 See Liew (n 46) para 3.13.

75 See e.g. Elland RMBS 2018 Plc (Prospectus, 13 December 2018) 114–115 <https://www.rns-pdf.londonstockexchange.com/rns/5340K_1-2018-12-14.pdf> accessed on 28 May 2024 (including notification events such as court order for a notification, insolvency event in respect of the originator, and a servicer termination event). See also JJ de Vries Robbé, *Securitization Law and Practice: In the Face of the Credit Crunch* (Kluwer Law International 2008) para 2.20 (including events such as the downgrade of the originator's credit rating and non-compliance by the originator of any material obligation).

76 *Dearle v Hall* (1828) 3 Russ 1 (Ch).

without joining the assignor.[77] Also, an equitable assignment without notice takes effect subject to new equities[78] having priority over the title of the assignee.[79] Furthermore, an equitable assignment is subject to a later legal assignment that is taken for value and without notice of the earlier equitable assignment.[80] See section 8.2.6.2 for discussion of the disadvantages of the equitable assignment.

6.2.4 *Trust*

6.2.4.1 **Overview**

Where novation or assignment is used as the instrument of transfer in a securitisation transaction, the originator's title to the underlying security rights and the related receivables is sold to the SPV.[81] The SPV, in turn, funds the acquisition by issuing bonds to investors. The title in the receivables and related security rights will vest in the SPV and be used as collateral against the bonds issued.[82] Where a trust is adopted instead, the transaction structure will depend on how the originator chooses to constitute the trust. There are two possibilities.[83] First, the originator may declare itself as a trustee of the

77 The assignee will need to join the assignor in the suit as either claimant or defendant. This requirement has, however, been held to be only a matter of procedural practice and can be waived. See *Central Insurance Co Ltd v Seacalf Shipping Corp (The Aiolos)* [1983] 2 Lloyd's Rep 25 (CA), per Oliver LJ at 32; *Charnesh Kapoor v National Westminster Bank Plc* [2011] EWCA Civ 1083, [2012] 1 All ER 1201; *Bexhill UK Ltd v Abdul Razzaq* [2012] EWCA Civ 1376, [2012] 10 WLUK 745.

78 These include the obligor's rights of set-offs or counterclaims agreed between the originator and the security providers after the equitable assignment has been effected.

79 While all assignments (both statutory and equitable) are subject to existing equities (see Law of Property Act 1925, s 136), new equities only bind an equitable assignee since the security providers are entitled to continue dealing with the assignor until a notice is given. See *Business Computers Ltd v Anglo-African Leasing Ltd* [1977] 1 WLR 578 (Ch); *Bibby Factors Northwest Ltd v HFD Ltd* [2015] EWCA Civ 1908, [2016] 1 Lloyd's Rep 517. See section 8.2.2.3.

80 The priority of competing assignments of a chose in action is governed by the rule in *Dearle v Hall* (1828) 3 Russ 1 (Ch), which is that an assignee who notifies the debtor first and takes title for value and without notice of an earlier assignment gets priority over the earlier assignment. *Dearle v Hall* was about competing equitable assignments of equitable choses in action (i.e. beneficial interest in a trust fund). But subsequent case law has extended the rule to competing equitable assignments of legal choses in action such as debts. See e.g. *Gorringe v Irwell India Rubber and Gutta Percha Works* (1886) 34 Ch D 128 (CA), per Cotton and Bowen LJJ at 132 and 135 respectively; *Marchant v Morton, Down & Co* [1901] 2 KB 829, per Channell J at 831; *Lyle (BS) v Rosher* [1959] 1 WLR 8 (HL), per Lord Morton at 16; *Compaq Computer Ltd v Abercorn Group Ltd* [1991] BCC 484 (Ch), per Mummery J at 497.

81 The SPV in this case is organised typically as a specially formed orphan company whose shares are owned by charitable trustees so that the shares are not traceable to the originator. The objective is to ensure that the assets of the SPV are not treated as those of the originator in the event of the originator's insolvency.

82 Typically, the SPV's assets (which includes the transferred security rights) are mortgaged or charged to a security trustee who will hold the security for the benefit of the investors.

83 *Milroy v Lord* (1862) 45 ER 1185 (QB), per Knight Bruce LJ at 1189; Graham Virgo, *The Principles of Equity & Trusts* (5th edn, Oxford University Press 2023) 145f.

receivables and the related security (i.e. the originator-as-trustee method).[84] For this method, the legal title will remain with the originator in its capacity as trustee while the SPV gets the beneficial interests and the personal rights against the originator. The SPV's assets (i.e. the beneficial interest and the personal rights against the originator) may then be used as security for the bonds.[85]

Alternatively, the originator may vest title in the SPV and declare that the title is to be held for the investors' benefits (i.e. the SPV-as-trustee method).[86] In this case, the SPV holds legal title as trustee while the investors acquire (i) the beneficial interests in the trust property and (ii) personal rights against the trustee.[87] Since the trust is created voluntarily, the relevant type of trust for securitisation is an express trust. The next two paragraphs briefly discuss the requirements of creating and constituting an enforceable express trust under English law.

First, the trust must be certain about (i) the settlor's intention to create a trust, (ii) the subject matter of the trust (or the trust property) and (iii) the identity of the beneficiaries of the trust (or the objects of the trust).[88] These are typically called the "three certainties".[89] The second requirement relates to the formalities required for declaring a trust. Generally, there are none.[90] Hence, a trust can be declared orally.[91] However, where statutory formalities are applicable to a relevant property, it has to be complied with. For instance, section 53(1)(b) of the Law of Property Act 1925 requires that a trust over land or any interest therein should be in writing and signed by the settlor.[92]

The third requirement relates to formalities required for constituting the trust. A mere declaration of trust is not enough to make the trust effective. It is necessary that the settlor does everything necessary to vest title in the trust property in the trustee.[93] The trust

---

84 This method is equivalent to the Scottish truster-as-trustee method. See section 5.3.3.

85 See e.g. Marke Raines, 'Cutting Edge Close-up: Sumitomo's Aurora CLO' (1998) 17 International Financial Law Review 6. The article discusses the Aurora CLO transaction of 1998, which was the first securitisation transaction in Europe that used the declaration of trust as transfer mechanism. In the Aurora CLO transaction, the originator declared a trust in favour of the SPV (holding 99% of the beneficial interest) and itself (holding 1%). The SPV in turn charged its beneficial interest in the trust to a note trustee on trust for the noteholders. The SPV also granted an irrevocable power of attorney to the note trustee to secure the performance of the SPV's obligations under the trust and delegate to the note trustee the SPV's personal rights under the originator's trust.

86 Philip Wood, *Title Finance, Derivatives, Securitisations, Set-off and Netting* (Sweet & Maxwell 1995) para 4.8; Alastair Hudson, *The Law of Finance* (2nd edn, Sweet & Maxwell 2013) para 44.11.

87 Hudson (n 86) para 44.11.

88 See *Wright v Atkyns* (1823) Turn & R 143 (Ch); *Knight v Knight* (1840) 3 Beav 148 (Ch).

89 For discussion see Virgo (n 83) ch 4. See also Hudson (n 86) para 21.07.

90 Hudson (n 86) para 21.08; Virgo (n 83) 123f.

91 This is especially the case for personal property, such as money and chattels. See *Paul v Constance* [1977] 1 WLR 527 (CA).

92 Where a trust over land is not evidenced in writing, the trust will be unenforceable (rather than void). See Virgo (n 83) 123f.

93 The leading case on this is *Milroy v Lord* (1862) 45 ER 1185 (QB), per Knight Bruce LJ at 1189f.

becomes fully "constituted" and effective from the point title is vested in the trustee.[94] The logic behind "title transfer as constitutive requirement" is that the trust becomes irrevocable once title is transferred.[95]

Therefore, the trust will be automatically constituted where the originator-as-trustee method is used, since the originator already has title.[96] On the other hand, the SPV-as-trustee method requires title to be vested in the SPV for it to be constituted.[97] Normally, the settlor will be required to fully divest themselves of the legal title they have in the property.[98] This means that where the settlor has legal title in the property, the legal title has to be vested in the trustee. Therefore, a statutory assignment will have to be completed if the trust property is a legal interest in contractual rights, such as a debt.[99] And if the related security is a legal charge over registered land, the transfer must take the form of a deed[100] and must also be registered in the Land Register.[101]

The above requirements for the SPV-as-trustee method result in the notification/registration difficulty, which is discussed above. This would make the SPV-as-trustee method unhelpful in the circumstance. However, equity may intervene to validate the trust if a transfer of an equitable title (rather than legal title) is completed. This is especially so given that the beneficiaries in this case are not "volunteers" – investors in a securitisation transaction would normally give consideration and have a direct right of action against the settlor to transfer legal title.[102] Such right of action makes the trust irrevocable and capable of being constituted.

The subsequent analysis of the trust vis-à-vis the equitable assignment will be based on the originator-as-trustee method. This is because of the method's relative simplicity and suitability for securitisation compared to the SPV-as-trustee method. The additional title transfer formality that is required for the SPV-as-trustee method explains why it may be less favourable for securitisation. Moreover, as will be seen below, an important utility of the trust mechanism used to be its ability to circumvent anti-assignment clauses in receivables finance.[103] The SPV-as-trustee method could not have achieved this purpose since the assignment of the receivables would be essential for the trust to be constituted.

94 ibid. See also Philip Henry Pettit, *Equity and the Law of Trusts* (12th edn, Oxford University Press 2012) 102; Virgo (n 83) 144f.

95 See e.g. *Re Bowden* [1936] Ch 71.

96 Virgo (n 83) 145.

97 ibid 138.

98 *Milroy v Lord* (1862) 45 ER 1185 (QB), per Knight Bruce LJ at 1189. See also Pettit (n 94) 102; Virgo (n 83) 144f.

99 Law of Property Act 1925, s 136(1).

100 Law of Property Act 1925, s 52(1).

101 Land Registration Act 2002, s 27(1) and (3)(a).

102 See Pettit (n 94) 101; Virgo (n 83) 154.

103 That is before the Business Contract Terms (Assignment of Receivables) Regulations 2018 (SI 2018/1254) came into force.

In contrast, the originator-as-trustee method could achieve the purpose since it requires no actual assignment for its constitution.

6.2.4.2 Trust vs equitable assignment

The originator-as-trustee structure produces a similar outcome to the equitable assignment in certain respects. First, it can be used to circumvent the publicity difficulties (i.e. notification, registration and delivery of possession) that arise in relation to the transfer of the receivables and the related securities. Also, both the equitable assignment and the originator-as-trustee structure result in the SPV holding a beneficial interest in the securitised assets. This means that the trust is subject to similar limitations associated with equitable interests.[104] Yet the equitable assignment is considered the most popular solution for the transfer of receivables and the security rights in securitisation under English law.[105] The literature provides scant reasons for why the equitable assignment is preferred to the trust.[106] An attempt is made in the following paragraphs to fill this gap.

First, the two mechanisms are different in their approaches. An assignment generally involves the transfer of existing rights, while a trust involves the creation of new rights. Under a trust, the benefits due to the beneficiary flow from the trust itself and not from the underlying agreement between the originator and the debtors. In contrast, the equitable assignee's rights flow from the underlying agreement. An important implication of this is that there is a direct relationship between the equitable assignee and the debtor, and the equitable assignee can sue the debtor in their own name as a matter of course.[107] On the other hand, there is no such direct relationship in a trust, and the trust beneficiary can only sue in exceptional circumstances.[108]

---

104 For example, the beneficial interest could be defeated if the trustee transferred the legal title (in breach of trust) to a purchaser for value and without notice of the breach. See *Independent Trustee Services Ltd v GP Noble Trustees Ltd* [2012] EWCA Civ 195, [2012] 3 WLR 597, per Lloyd LJ at [106].

105 See e.g. Philip Wood, *Law and Practice of International Finance* (Sweet & Maxwell 2008) paras 28.19 and 28.34 (suggesting that the sale structure (through the equitable assignment mechanism) is "by far the most common"); Robbé, *Securitization Law and Practice* (n 75) para 2.19. See also Wood, *Title Finance* (n 86) para 5.2.

106 At least, none of the sources cited in footnote 105 provide any reason. Though the sources make general comments about the benefits of using the equitable assignment, they make no comparison of the equitable assignment with the trust.

107 See *First Abu Dhabi Bank PJSC v BP Oil International Limited* [2018] EWCA Civ 14, [2018] 1 WLUK 203, per Gloster LJ at [37]. Although the equitable assignee is required to join the assignor (either as claimant or defendant), the requirement is only a matter of procedural practice and can be waived. See *Central Insurance Co Ltd v Seacalf Shipping Corp (The Aiolos)* [1983] 2 Lloyd's Rep 25 (CA), per Oliver LJ at 32; *Charnesh Kapoor v National Westminster Bank Plc* [2011] EWCA Civ 1083, [2012] 1 All ER 1201; *Bexhill UK Ltd v Abdul Razzaq* [2012] EWCA Civ 1376, [2012] 10 WLUK 745.

108 See *Hayim v Citibank NA* [1987] AC 730 (PC), per Lord Templeman at 748. See also PG Turner, 'Prohibitions on Assignment: Intellectualism v. Law' (2018) 134 Law Quarterly Review 532, 535. The general rule is that only the trustee can sue under a trust. Where, however, the trustee refuses to sue, the beneficiary may sue in their own name, joining the trustee as a defendant. See *Vandepitte v Preferred Accident Insurance Corp of*

Secondly, a written equitable assignment can be converted into a legal assignment (e.g. by the assignee giving notice); however, a trust cannot.[109] To acquire legal title in a trust, the beneficiary will have to ask the trustee to transfer the interest. Thirdly, trusts generally impose fiduciary and administrative duties on trustees.[110] These include, for example, a duty to be active in "getting in the debts" and to promptly sue for recovery of the debts where necessary,[111] a duty not to profit from their position as trustee and a duty to act in utmost good faith. The originator may be unwilling to take on such a wide range of duties. In contrast, assignors' duties generally do not include fiduciary duties.[112]

Furthermore, the equitable assignment is a direct mechanism for transferring choses in action.[113] This makes it fit for the securitisation purpose. On the other hand, the trust structure typically serves as a workaround which is used to circumvent restrictions on the use of assignments for securitisation purposes.[114] (One such obstacle is the effect of anti-assignment clauses on securitisation, which is discussed below.) As a workaround, it will typically be the case that the trust structure will require other workarounds to be fit for the securitisation purpose. For example, under the trust structure, title to the securitised assets remains with the originator (as trustee) and the SPV's rights (as beneficiary) in the assets can only be enforced through the trustee as a matter of course.

In order to de-link the securitised assets from the originator's default risks, parties normally resort to an irrevocable power of attorney instrument. The power of attorney will be issued by the originator and will entitle the SPV to enforce the originator's rights under the receivables/securities agreements in the event of the originator's breach of duty or insolvency. Also, to secure the performance of the SPV's powers under the originator's power of attorney, a further power of attorney which delegates the SPV's powers to a bond trustee[115] may be required.[116] These structures can make the transaction complex and more costly.

New York [1933] AC 70 (PC), per Lord Wright at 79. It has been held that the effect of such an action instituted by the beneficiary is to enforce the right under the trust in favour of the trustee and not in favour of the beneficiary. See *Harmer v Armstrong* [1934] Ch 65 (CA), per Lawrence LJ at 88.

109 *Barbados Trust Co Ltd v Bank of Zambia & Anor* [2007] EWCA Civ 148, [2007] 2 WLUK 645, per Waller LJ at [43].

110 *Don King (Productions) Inc v Warren* [2000] Ch 291 (CA), per Aldous LJ at 317. See also Lynton Tucker, Nick Le Poidevin and James Brightwell, *Lewin on Trusts* (20th edn, Sweet & Maxwell 2020) ch 34.

111 *Lewin on Trusts* (n 110) paras 34.020ff.

112 *Don King (Productions) Inc v Warren* [2000] Ch 291 (CA), per Aldous LJ at 317f. See also Turner (n 108) 532, 535f.

113 See the Law of Property Act 1925, s 136(1). See also Greg Tolhurst, *The Assignment of Contractual Rights* (2nd edn, Hart 2016) para 1.01 (defining assignment as involving "a transfer of a contractual right from the owner (assignor) to the transferee (assignee)").

114 See e.g. Deacon (n 44) 39.

115 The bond trustee will hold the power on behalf of the bond holders.

116 For discussion of the structure of Sumitomo's Aurora CLO see Raines (n 85) 6.

Moreover, the utility of the English trust as a transfer mechanism for securitisation has diminished since the introduction of the Business Contract Terms (Assignment of Receivables) Regulations 2018. The Regulations invalidate clauses that purport to prohibit or restrict the assignment of receivables in business-to-business contracts.[117] Prior to the Regulations, anti-assignment clauses were enforceable.[118] The House of Lords in *Linden Gardens* held that an assignment in contravention of such clauses is ineffective to transfer the contractual rights.[119] This suggests that even an equitable assignment effected in contravention of the prohibition may be void.[120]

Following the decision in *Don King* that a clause prohibiting assignments does not extend to declarations of trust,[121] the trust became a popular solution for circumventing the anti-assignment restrictions.[122] This utility has now been diminished by the 2018 Regulations. The Regulations, however, do not cover: (i) receivables that are owed to large enterprises or SPVs;[123] and (ii) various types of contracts, including contracts concerning interests in land, certain derivatives contracts and contracts in connection with prescribed financial services.[124] The effect is that the prohibitions falling under the exemptions will generally be enforceable and the trust mechanism may continue to be useful in those limited cases.

6.3 Conclusion

The objective of this chapter has been to identify the preferred transfer solution under English law and demonstrate why it is so preferred. The chapter first examined the extent

117 See reg 2 of the Regulations.

118 *Linden Gardens Trust Ltd v Lenesta Sludge Disposals Ltd* [1994] 1 AC 85 (HL).

119 ibid 108.

120 For discussion of whether the decision in *Linden Gardens* extends to equitable assignments see Roy M Goode, 'Contractual Prohibitions against Assignment' (2009) 3 Lloyd's Maritime and Commercial Law Quarterly 300 (suggesting (at 305) that the correct position would be that a prohibition purporting to render an assignment void, even as between the assignor and assignee, is of no effect on the ground of repugnancy and public policy, since such prohibition will interfere with the assignor's property right of alienation). Cf GJ Tolhurst and JW Carter, 'Prohibitions on Assignment: A Choice to be Made' (2014) 73 The Cambridge Law Journal 405. In *First Abu Dhabi Bank PJSC v BP Oil International Ltd* [2018] EWCA Civ 14, [2018] 1 WLUK 203, per Gloster LJ at [30], the Court of Appeal questioned the House of Lord's decision in *Linden Gardens* on the enforceability of the prohibition against equitable assignments. The Court, however, accepted that it was bound by the decision in *Linden Gardens* and held that the prohibition was enforceable to render an equitable assignment invalid.

121 *Don King (Productions) Inc v Warren* [2000] Ch 291 (CA). For discussion of the case see section 5.3.3.2.

122 See Deacon (n 44) 39.

123 Reg 3 of the 2018 Regulations defines a large enterprise as an enterprise which is not a sole trader, partnership or unincorporated association or a company or LLP qualifying as small or medium-sized under the relevant legislation.

124 See reg 4 of the Regulations.

to which the *accessorium* principle applies in English law. It demonstrated that the position under English law is uncertain, and care should be taken to expressly refer to both subjects of transfer – i.e. the debts and security rights – if the transferee (i.e. the SPV) intends to acquire both rights.

The chapter then considered the preferred transfer solution and the reasons why such solution is so preferred. It finds that the equitable assignment is the preferred solution, ahead of the trust, statutory assignment and novation solutions. The equitable assignment affords securitisation parties a flexible and low-cost means of solving the consent, notification and registration problems inherent in novations and legal assignments. Although the trust solution also affords similar solutions (i.e. it can be used to circumvent the consent, notification and registration difficulties), the beneficiary's right under the underlying contractual agreement is limited compared to that of the equitable assignee.

Also, since the trust functions more as a workaround for the transfer purpose in securitisation, it will typically require other steps for it to fit the securitisation purpose. This makes the trust mechanism more complex and costly. Moreover, the usefulness in relation to anti-assignment clauses has been whittled down since the introduction of the Business Contract Terms (Assignment of Receivables) Regulations 2018, which invalidates clauses that purport to prohibit or restrict the assignment of receivables under business-to-business contracts.[125]

125 This is subject to the exceptions under regs 3 and 4 of the 2018 Regulations.

7 TRANSFER OF RIGHTS UNDER FRENCH LAW

This chapter discusses the different transfer mechanisms available for transfer of security rights under French law. The objective is to identify the preferred solution and demonstrate why it is so preferred.

The French legal framework for securitisations differs from the English and Scottish frameworks in two ways. First, France has a special piece of legislation for securitisation. Second, *accessorium sequitur principale* has a wider application under French law, and the extent to which it applies to the transfer solutions discussed here varies.

The chapter is structured as follows. Section 7.1 gives a general overview of the French securitisation law. It examines the nature of the French securitisation entity and how it was modernised over time. Sections 7.2, 7.3, 7.4 and 7.5 respectively examine the four solutions available under French law for transferring security rights in a securitisation. These solutions include assignment under the French Civil Code, the subrogation of rights, the Dailly assignment and assignment under the French securitisation law. Given that the *accessorium sequitur principale* rule (hereafter "the *accessorium* principle") applies differently to these solutions, the doctrine will be discussed within each of the relevant sections. This chapter concludes, in section 7.6, that the assignment under the French securitisation law is the preferred solution.

7.1 Introduction to the French securitisation legal framework

7.1.1 An overview of the French legal framework prior to the French Securitisation Act of 1988

An important feature of the French legal framework on securitisation is the existence of securitisation-specific legislation. This legislation was introduced in 1988[1] to facilitate

1 Law No 88-2001 of 23 December 1988, implemented by Decree No 89-158 of 9 March 1989 <http://vinodkothari.com/seclawfr/> accessed 28 May 2024 (hereafter "the 1988 Act"). Following the amendment to the 1988 Act by Law No 2003-706 of 1 August 2003 and Decree No 2004-155 of 24 November 2004, the French securitisation law has since been codified in the French Monetary and Financial Code (as amended by Law No 2019-486 of 22 May 2019) (hereafter "the MFC"), and the law is currently set out under arts L214-166-1 to L214-190 of the MFC.

different aspects of securitisation.[2] Prior to its introduction, there was an obvious need for a special securitisation law in France, as some important aspects of securitisation were not facilitated under the general commercial laws of France. The concept of trust was not recognised at that time and so trust structures could not be used.[3] Another option would be to use a private company specially incorporated for the purpose of the securitisation, but this also had its limitations. Companies were required to have a minimum share capital under the French Commercial Code.[4] Also, since companies incorporated in France were subject to the French insolvency rules, there was a risk that private companies used as securitisation vehicles would not be insolvency proof.[5] This was particularly relevant where the securitisation vehicle engages in activities that increase its insolvency risks (such as borrowing and providing liquidity support for the transaction). The foregoing points contrast with the position in England and Scotland where trust structures existed and there were no requirements for minimum share capital for private companies incorporated under United Kingdom (UK) company laws.

Even if trust structures existed in France or the transaction cost of the minimum share capital requirement was inconsequential, securitisation would have been restricted only to banks. This is because French laws considered the acquisition of receivables to be a credit activity,[6] in which only French-licensed credit institutions[7] or EU-passported credit

---

2 It has been suggested that the legislation was the first securitisation-specific legislation to be enacted in Europe. See Arthur F Salomons, 'Deformalisation of Assignment Law and the Position of the Debtor in European Property Law' (2007) Centre for the Study of European Contract Law Working Paper Series No. 2007/01, 6 <http://www.ssrn.com/abstract=968654> accessed 28 May 2024.

3 The French trust, *fiducie*, was introduced in 2007 by Law No 2007-211 of 19 February 2007 and is now codified in arts 2011 to 2030 of the French Civil Code (FCC). The *fiducie* is similar to the Scottish trust in some respects – it recognises the concept of segregating the special (trust) patrimony from the general (personal) patrimony. But some differences exist. For example, a *fiducie* contract must be express, it must contain certain minimum provisions, and it must be registered within one month of creation (see respectively arts 2012, 2018, 2019 and 2020 of the FCC). Also, art 2013 of the FCC nullifies *fiducies* that are established gratuitously or for inheritance purposes, and art 2015 of the FCC limits the type of persons who can act as trustees for a *fiducie* to financial institutions and legal advocates.

4 The French Commercial Code, art L224-2.

5 Making a securitisation vehicle insolvency proof is important for two reasons: it ensures (i) that the securitisation entity is not affected by the insolvency of the originator (either as a result of an improper separation of the two entities or an improper segregation of the securitised assets from the estate of the originator), and (ii) that the entity is one that has little or no chance of becoming subject to any insolvency proceedings. See Michael Cohn, 'Asset Securitization: How Remote Is Bankruptcy Remote?' (1998) 26 Hofstra Law Review 929, 931f.

6 The MFC, art L313-1 provides that "[a] credit transaction constitutes any act by which a person acting for consideration makes or promises to make funds available to another person or makes, in the latter's interest, a commitment by signature such as an endorsement, bond, or guarantee." This English translation is based on Légifrance <https://www.legifrance.gouv.fr/codes/article_lc/LEGIARTI000006652080> accessed 01 May 2024.

7 A credit institution is defined as "an undertaking the business of which is to take deposits or other repayable funds from the public and to grant credits for its own account." See the combination of art L511-1 of the

institutions[8] could engage. This rule is known as the French banking monopoly rule.[9] Consequently, non-bank institutions, including a company specially incorporated for the purpose of securitisation, could not buy unmatured debts and the related security rights.[10]

An additional difficulty encountered in using the French general commercial laws for securitisations was the significant role notification played and the formalised nature of its execution under the former article 1690 of the French Civil Code (FCC).[11] Under the old law, notification was a prerequisite not just for enforceability of the assignment against third parties, but also for enforceability between the assignor and the assignee.[12] And for the obligor to be validly notified, the notification required to be delivered to them through a bailiff (*huissier*) – this method of notification was called *signification*. As an alternative to *signification*, the old law required the obligor to acknowledge the assignment by a notarised deed. These two instances were the only certain ways to make assignments valid against third parties (including the obligor) under the FCC. Just like Scots law, French law has a unititular system of property law and considers the right of property to be absolute.[13] Hence, the equitable assignment solution was not available to circumvent the formality of *signification*.

The other two alternative transfer methods available under French law were subrogation and the simplified Dailly assignment (discussed below at sections 7.3 and 7.4). But these alternatives also had their limitations. A subrogation required the full value of the receivables to be paid by the purchaser for them to be fully entitled to the proceeds from the debtor.[14] This raises issues with securitisations since asset sales in the transaction are done on a discount. A Dailly assignment, on its part, was subject to the French banking monopoly rule and its related problems. In addition, the assignment could only be used in relation to receivables arising from the debtor's (or obligor's) business or professional activities.[15] This rule raised difficulties because it excluded important consumer receivables

---

MFC and art 4(1) of Council Regulation (EC) 575/2013 on prudential requirements for credit institutions and investment firms and amending Regulation (EU) No 648/2012 [2013] OJ L176/1.

8 EU-passported credit institutions are foreign credit institutions licensed to carry out banking activities in France under the Council Directive 2000/12/EC of 20 March 2000 relating to the taking up and pursuit of the business of credit institutions [2000] OJ L126/1.

9 See art L511-5 MFC. A failure to comply with this rule is punishable by three years of imprisonment and a €375,000 fine – art L571-3 MFC.

10 In the context of securitisation, the trade of purchasing receivables was considered as a credit activity that could only be performed by banks under the French Banking Act 1984.

11 A modified provision is now contained in arts 1321ff of the FCC, which was implemented pursuant to Ordinance No 2016-131 of 10 February 2016 (hereafter "Order 2016").

12 James Leavy, 'France' in Harry C Sigman and Eva-Maria Kieninger (eds), *Cross-Border Security over Receivables* (Sellier European Law Publishers 2009) 123.

13 The FCC, art 544.

14 See the former art 1250 of the FCC (now art 1346 of the Civil Code as amended by Order 2016).

15 The MFC, art L313-23.

(like residential mortgages, auto loans, credit card loans, trade receivables, etc.) that did not relate to any business or professional activities of the debtors.

Given the internationalisation of financial markets and the need for the French markets to remain competitive, legislative intervention to enable securitisations in France was considered necessary.

7.1.2 *The 1988 Act and its reforms*

The 1988 Act was introduced to address these difficulties and make securitisations more efficient under French law. A central innovation of the 1988 Act was the creation of a dedicated securitisation vehicle called *Fonds Commun de Creances* (i.e. a mutual debt fund, hereafter referred to as "the Fund"). The Fund had no legal personality, and its sole purpose was to acquire receivables and issue units representing the receivables.[16] It did not require a share capital, board of directors or employees for it to be set up or managed. The originator only needed to appoint a management company[17] and a custodian,[18] who would set up the Fund by creating its regulations in accordance with the 1988 Act.[19] Thereafter, they would draft and negotiate (with relevant parties, mainly the originator) the receivables purchase agreement, the servicing agreement, various other ancillary agreements, and the prospectus. While the management company administered the Fund on behalf of the investors and represented the Fund in relation to third parties and in all court proceedings, the custodian acted as the depository of the Fund's assets and the supervisor of the management company.[20]

Since the Fund had a statutory mandate to acquire receivables and issue units representing the receivables, the Fund was effectively exempted from the French banking monopoly rule. In addition, its unique nature as a "fund" without legal personality meant that the Fund was not subject to the French laws on minimum share capital requirement and insolvency proceedings. The 1988 Act also adopted a simplified transfer mechanism (hereafter called "French *bordereau*"), which made assignments of receivables enforceable against third parties without the *signification* requirement.[21]

---

16 The 1988 Act, art 34(i) and (iii).

17 The management company must be a commercial company, approved by the Stock Exchange Operations Commission, whose sole object was to manage Funds. See the 1988 Act, arts 37(ii) and 40(ii).

18 The custodian must be either a French credit institution, an EU-passported credit institution, or any other institutions authorised by the French Minister of the Economy. The 1988 Act, art 40(iii).

19 The 1988 Act, art 37.

20 See the 1988 Act, art 40(ii) and (iii). The originator would typically act as the custodian. See John Deacon, *Global Securitisation and CDOs* (Wiley 2004) 278.

21 The 1988 Act, art 34(ix). See section 7.5 for discussion of this method of assignment.

The 1988 Act underwent several reforms to make the Fund more robust and efficient.[22] These reforms allowed the Fund to purchase additional receivables after the first purchase,[23] issue units of less than two years' tenor,[24] issue additional units after an initial issue,[25] purchase assets and issue securities denominated in currencies other than French francs,[26] manage more than one compartment of funds,[27] purchase future receivables,[28] purchase receivables from non-bank corporate originators,[29] issue debt securities,[30] and enter credit derivatives.[31]

7.1.3 New securitisation entities under French law

In 2008, the concept of *organismes de titrisation* (i.e. securitisation organisations or OTs) was introduced to replace the Fund.[32] OTs expanded the scope of the Fund by introducing an alternative option of setting up a securitisation vehicle as a company. Hence, OTs can take the form of securitisation mutual funds (i.e. *fonds commun de titrisation* or FCTs – a co-ownership without legal personality, which functions like the Fund) or securitisation companies (i.e. *sociétés de titrisation* or SDTs – a legal entity created as a limited liability company).[33]

Being a limited liability company, an SDT has a minimum share capital requirement, it issues shares, it may hold general meetings and it has directors.[34] However, SDTs are managed by a management company and their assets are held by a custodian,[35] and most provisions and requirements that apply to companies under the French Commercial Code (hereafter "the Commercial Code") do not apply to the SDT.[36] In practice, sponsors use the SDT when they are looking to benefit from favourable international tax treaties.

The French securitisation vehicle structure was further modified in 2018 with the introduction of a new category of entities, called *organismes de financement* (i.e. financing

22 For a detailed account of these reforms, see Deacon (n 20) 274.
23 Law 93-6 of 4 January 1993, implemented by Decree No 93-589 of 27 March 1993.
24 ibid.
25 ibid.
26 Law No 96-597 of 2 July 1996, implemented by Decree No 97-919 of 6 October 1997.
27 ibid.
28 Law No 98-546 of 2 July 1998, implemented by Decree No 98-1015 of 6 November 1998.
29 ibid.
30 Law No 2003-706 of 1 August 2003, implemented by Decree No 2004-155 of 24 November 2004.
31 ibid.
32 This was in pursuance to Ordinance No 2008-556 of 13 June 2008 and Decree No 2008-711 of 17 July 2008 (hereafter "Order 2008").
33 The MFC (as amended by Order 2008), art L214-42-1(ii).
34 The MFC (as amended by Order 2008), art L214-49-3-I(1)–(6).
35 The MFC (as amended by Order 2008), arts L214-49-1 and L214-49-2. This also applies to FCTs. See art L214-49-7(i) and (ii) of the MFC (as amended by Order 2008).
36 See for example, art L214-49-3.-I of the MFC (as amended by Order 2008).

organisations or OFs).[37] OFs comprise the existing OTs and a newly introduced *organismes de financement spécialisé* (i.e. specialised financing organisations or OFSs).[38] Just as with OTs, OFSs can be formed either as a co-ownership without legal personality (i.e. *fonds de financement spécialisé* or FFS) or as a limited liability company (i.e. *societe de financement spécialisé* or SFS).[39] While OFSs share most of the features of the OTs, OFSs are authorised under the EU Regulation on European long-term investment funds (the ELTIFs Regulation)[40] and managed by management companies authorised under the EU Directive on alternative investment funds (AIFMD).[41]

The new OFSs were introduced to boost non-banking financing in France and to benefit from the European Long-Term Investment Funds (ELTIFs) framework which makes ELTIFs marketable to both professional and retail investors across the EU.[42] FCTs or SDTs may also be eligible to become ELTIFs if they are managed by a management company authorised under the AIFMD and they comply with the requirements of the ELTIFs Regulation.[43] Otherwise, they may not be marketable to retail investors across the EU.[44] These securitisation entities will be collectively referred to as the "FCT" in this chapter.

7.2 ASSIGNMENT OF RIGHTS UNDER THE FCC

7.2.1 *Introduction and general overview*

Article 1321 of the FCC defines assignment of rights as "a contract by which the assigning creditor transmits, for consideration or free of charge, all or part of his debt against the assigned debtor to a third party called the assignee."[45] This method of assignment can transfer present and future rights, as well as a single right or a pool of rights.[46] To be valid,

37 This was in pursuance to Ordinance No 2017-1432 of 4 October 2017, which entered into force on 3 January 2018 (hereafter "Order 2017").

38 The MFC (as amended by Order 2017), art L214-166-1.

39 The MFC (as amended by Order 2017), art L214-168(I).

40 Council Regulation (EU) 2015/760 of 29 April 2015 on European long-term investment funds [2015] OJ L123/98.

41 Council Directive 2011/61/EU of 8 June 2011 on Alternative Investment Fund Managers and amending Directives 2003/41/EC and 2009/65/EC and Regulations (EC) No 1060/2009 and (EU) No 1095/2010 [2011] OJ L174/1.

42 ELTIFs Regulation, art 31.

43 ELTIFs Regulation, art 6.

44 AIFMD, art 43 (which suggests that only management companies authorised under the AIFMD may market alternative investment funds to retailers).

45 This English translation is based on Légifrance <https://www.legifrance.gouv.fr/codes/article_lc/LEGIARTI000032042026> accessed 01 May 2024.

46 The FCC, art 1321(ii).

the assignment must be evidenced in writing.[47] The *assignatus utitur jure auctoris* rule applies to this method of assignment, so that the assignee does not get a better right than the assignor would have had against the obligor.[48] Hence, a notified obligor may still be entitled to the defences available under the receivables agreement (such as nullity, the defence of non-performance, and set-off rights). Also, the obligor may be entitled to the defences arising from their relationship with the assignor before the assignment became valid against them.[49]

The important difference between the FCC assignment and its English statutory assignment and Scottish assignation counterparts lies in the act that must be done for the assignment to be constituted against third parties. Under the English statutory assignment and the Scots assignation, notification is essential.[50] But notification is not required under the FCC assignment.[51] The assignment becomes effective from the date it is signed, not just between the assignor and the assignee, but also against third parties (excluding the obligor).[52] Third parties would include the assignor's creditors and liquidators, so that an executed FCC assignment is enough to remove the assigned rights from the estate or patrimony of the assignor.

Notification is only required under an FCC assignment where the assignee wishes to obtain payment from the obligor or enforce the assignment against the obligor.[53] In such case, the FCC simply requires that the obligor should be notified of the assignment.[54] The notification is not required to take any special form or be undertaken through a special mode of delivery for it to be valid. Thus, it may be done by post or electronically, provided that it informs the obligor of what has been assigned and who they should perform to in the future. The FCC also provides for two other ways (aside from notification) of making the assignment enforceable against the obligor: the obligor may simply acknowledge the assignment or give their consent prior to (or at the time of) the assignment.[55] It is important to note that the transfer of future rights takes effect, as between the assignor and the assignee and against third parties, from the date of the transfer (and not when the rights come into existence).[56] This effect was introduced in 2021, under article 26 of Order No

47 The FCC, art 1322.
48 The FCC, art 1324(ii). For discussion of the doctrine see section 8.2.2.3.
49 ibid.
50 Law of Property Act 1925, s 136(1) (England); *Gallemos Ltd (In Receivership) v Barratt Falkirk Ltd* 1989 SC (IH) 239 (Scotland). The equitable assignment is a major exception under English law, which can arise without notification. See section 6.2.3.3 for discussion.
51 The FCC, arts 1322f.
52 The FCC, art 1323.
53 The FCC, art 1324(i).
54 ibid.
55 ibid.
56 The FCC, art 1323.

2021-1192, to protect the validity of such assignments if the future receivables arise after the assignor's insolvency.[57]

The foregoing points on notification signify a radical shift from the previous position under the former article 1690 of the FCC (see discussion in section 7.1.1). The reform is important for a securitisation transaction since it makes it possible to achieve a true sale outcome without the need to notify the large number of debtors typically involved in the transaction. But the unnotified FCC assignment has its limitations. These limitations are discussed in section 7.2.3.

7.2.2 *The accessoriness question under articles 1321ff of the FCC*

The advantage of completing title with no formality is true with assignment of debts.[58] But the case may be different in relation to assignment of security rights. Chapters 5 and 6 have shown that the assignment of security rights may be governed by special rules that require publicity acts other than notification. This is especially so in the case of real security rights – real rights are enforceable against the whole world, thus the external act required for their constitution and assignment tends to be a public act (i.e. either through registration or delivery of possession). In contrast, personal rights (such as debt rights and sureties) are enforceable against a person or group of persons, thus the external act required for constituting their assignments tends to be a private or silent "publicity" (i.e. through the notification of the debtor against whom the right is held).

The difference in publicity, as highlighted above, would not be an issue if the *accessorium* principle always prevails.[59] Where the doctrine prevails, then the assignment of the principal rights suffices to transfer the security rights regardless of any other additional formalities that may apply to the security rights.

Generally, the FCC recognises the *accessorium* principle. Article 1321(iii) of the FCC states that the assignment of a debt "extends to accessories to the debt". The provision in the old law was clearer on this. The former article 1692 of the FCC provided that "the sale or assignment of a money claim includes its accessories such as security, privileges, and hypothecs". Similar provisions have also been made in relation to some security rights. For example, article 2473 of the FCC provides that "[t]he mortgage is transferred automatically with the secured debt."[60]

57 See section 8.2.4 for discussion of the issues arising from the transfer of future receivables during the assignor's insolvency.

58 The FCC, arts 1321ff are general provisions that regulate the assignment of incorporeal property under the FCC.

59 See section 5.2.1 for discussion of the meaning of the principle.

60 This English translation is based on Légifrance <https://www.legifrance.gouv.fr/codes/article_lc/LEGIARTI000006449687/2019-04-19> accessed 01 May 2024.

However, the application of the *accessorium* principle may be limited in respect of security rights for which proprietary (or third-party) effects[61] and priority rankings are dependent on a public act.[62] Before discussing this limitation, it is important to first give a brief overview of the real securities (i.e. securities over assets) available under French law and how they attain their proprietary effects.[63]

7.2.2.1 Overview of French law on real securities after the 2006 reform

The FCC was substantially reformed in 2006 to modernise and simplify the law on security.[64] It was further reformed in 2021 to address the shortcomings of the 2006 reform, particularly its failure to adequately address the fragmentation in the law regarding moveable securities.[65] The combined reform resulted in the introduction of a new Book IV in the FCC, which is dedicated to security issues (i.e. real and personal securities). While Title I of the new Book IV focuses on personal securities, Title II focuses on real securities. The FCC classifies real securities according to the moveable or immoveable nature of the encumbered property. A property is recognised as moveable either by its nature or by prescription of law.[66] Hence things or animals that can move or be moved from one place to another are moveable properties by nature[67] – these are essentially considered corporeal (or tangible) moveables. Incorporeal (or intangible) moveables like money claims, contractual rights, shares and annuities are moveable properties by prescription of law.[68]

For immoveables, land, buildings and objects that form part of the land or building – such as trees and their unharvested fruits, and water mills – are recognised as immoveable property by their nature.[69] Corporeal moveables that are placed on, or attached to, the land or building permanently or for the service of the property are recognised as immoveable by destination.[70] These include animals committed to farming, beehives, water pipes, factory equipment and other fixtures. Incorporeal moveables connected to land or buildings, such as servitudes, usufructs of immoveable things and claims to recover

61 Generally, a right with a proprietary effect is one that is enforceable against the whole world.

62 This is demonstrated in section 5.2.2.

63 The focal point here is real security, because, as demonstrated in section 5.1, the underlying security rights used in backing securitisations are rights held over assets.

64 The reform was enabled by Law No 2005-842 of 26 July 2005, and implemented by Decree No 2006-346 of 23 March 2006 (hereafter "2006 Decree").

65 This reform was enabled by Ordinance No 2021-1192 of 15 September 2021 (hereafter "2021 Ordinance"). The Ordinance came into force on these provisions on 1 January 2022. For a detailed account of the shortcomings of the 2006 reforms, see Jean-Francois Riffard, 'The Still Uncompleted Evolution of the French Law on Secured Transactions Towards Modernity' in Louise Gullifer and N Orkun Akseli (eds), *Secured Transactions Law Reform: Principles, Policies and Practice* (Hart 2016) 382.

66 The FCC, art 527.

67 The FCC, art 528.

68 The FCC, art 529.

69 The FCC, arts 518 and 519.

70 The FCC, arts 524 and 525.

immoveable things, are considered immoveable property by the object to which they apply.[71]

French law recognises three categories of voluntary security over immoveable property, namely mortgages (*hypothèques*), real estate pledge (formerly called *antichresis*) and the retention of title as security.[72] For moveable property, there are three general voluntary securities specified under the FCC, plus various other asset-specific securities specified across the FCC, the Commercial Code, the Monetary and Financial Code (hereafter "the MFC") and the Intellectual Property Code.

The three general moveable securities are pledge over corporeal (*gage*) and incorporeal (*nantissement*) moveables,[73] retention of title as security[74] and fiduciary transfer for security purpose (*fiducie à titre de garantie*).[75] These securities are general in the sense that they are applicable to a wide range of moveable asset classes. The asset-specific moveable securities include transfer of cash in security,[76] pledges over intellectual property rights,[77] registered motor vehicles,[78] securities accounts,[79] and businesses as a going concern.[80]

---

71 The FCC, art 526.

72 See the FCC, art 2375.

73 This is an all-purpose security that can be created over corporeal and incorporeal moveable assets, or a pool of such assets. It can also be created over fixtures (i.e. corporeal moveables that are immoveable by destination) – art 2334 FCC. The security may be possessory or non-possessory – the latter was introduced by the 2006 Decree to allow for registration as an alternative to the traditional possessory pledge. While both the possessory and non-possessory forms can be created over corporeal moveables, the non-possessory form can only be taken over incorporeal moveables since they are incapable of possession. See generally arts 2333ff and 2355 of the FCC.

74 Retention of title as security became recognised as a security interest under arts 2367ff of the FCC. It is a form of a conditional sale agreement, where the ownership of a property sold is retained by the vendor as security until such time as the buyer fully discharges the purchase obligation.

75 This involves the transfer of a moveable asset (corporeal or incorporeal), or a pool of such assets, under a trust agreement for security purposes. It is a non-possessory security involving three parties: a beneficiary as the secured creditor, a settlor as the security grantor and a trustee who manages the trust assets. See generally arts 2372-1ff and 2011ff FCC. The rules governing its creation and perfection are the same as those applicable to the general trusts under arts 2011ff FCC.

76 This security enables the secured creditor (or transferee) to set off the sum of money transferred against the debt owed in the event of the debtor's default. See generally arts 2374 to 2374-6 FCC.

77 The French Intellectual Property Code makes provisions for pledges over various intellectual property rights, including patents, trademarks and designs.

78 See art 2338 FCC, as implemented by Decree No 2023-97 of 14 February 2023.

79 This relates to financial securities and their "fruits and products". It involves registering the stated assets under a special account held by an intermediary or financial institution and pledging the account as security. The security becomes effective against the parties, the security issuer and third parties simply by a written declaration signed by the security grantor (i.e. the account holder). See art L211-20 of the MFC.

80 The special pledge over business is a non-possessory security. Once constituted, it automatically covers the business's trademark, goodwill and leasing rights. It may extend to other specified assets like intellectual property rights, commercial furniture, equipment and tools, if the security contract so expresses. The following assets are, however, excluded from the scope of the security: receivables, inventories, real estate property, contractual rights (other than leasehold) and bank accounts. See arts L142-1ff of the French Commercial Code.

Regarding receivables, there are two types of security available under the FCC, namely pledge over receivables (*nantissement de créances*) and assignment of receivables in security (*cessions de créances à titre de garantie*).[81] The latter is a notable change introduced under the 2021 reform. Previously, a security assignment of receivables (as opposed to an absolute assignment) could only be granted under the Dailly law, which was subject to the bank monopoly rule and its related difficulties (see the discussion in sections 7.1.1 and 7.4). The French *Cour de Cassation* held in a prominent case that any attempt to grant such an assignment outside of the conditions permitted under the Dailly law would automatically be recharacterised as a pledge of receivables (rather than as an assignment) and would therefore be subject to the formalities and limitations applicable to such a pledge.[82] The FCC has now removed these constraints under articles 2373 to 2373-3, by expressly permitting security assignments of all receivables (including non-professional debts) to non-financial institutions.

A key goal of the 2006 and 2021 reforms was to integrate the pre-existing security regimes, which were formerly located across different parts of French laws, with the new securities introduced in the new Book IV of the FCC.[83] This goal has been achieved in respect of personal securities (now entirely contained in Title I, Book IV of the FCC) and securities over immoveable property (now entirely contained in articles 2375 to 2488-5 of the FCC). However, the goal is only partially achieved in relation to moveable securities. While some pre-existing asset-specific security rules previously located in different parts of French law have been repealed and integrated into the rules applicable to the general pledge over moveable assets under articles 2333 to 2350 of the FCC,[84] other asset-specific securities (as mentioned above) still remain. Additionally, new asset-specific securities located within the FCC have been introduced following the 2021 reform, namely the transfer of cash in security and the assignment of receivables in security.

7.2.2.2 The application of the *accessorium* principle to real securities under French law

A notable feature in all the moveable and immoveable securities is that their proprietary effect is mostly dependent on a public act. For example, the priority ranking of a mortgage counts from the date it is registered.[85] For the real estate pledge, the security grantor is

81 See respectively arts 2355ff FCC and arts 2373 to 2373-3 FCC.
82 Cour de Cassation, 19 December 2006, *N° de pourvoi* 05-16.395.
83 For discussion of the relevant French security rules before the reform see M Gdanski, 'Taking Security in France' in MG Bridge and Robert H Stevens (eds), *Cross-Border Security and Insolvency* (Oxford University Press 2001) 59.
84 For example, pledges over equipment and machine tools and pledges over inventory, which were previously located in the French Commercial Code, have been abolished.
85 See art 2418 of the FCC.

required to give up possession of the immoveable property for the security to be effective.[86] Similar publicity acts of registration and possession apply to moveable securities. The general non-possessory pledge over moveables and the possessory pledge respectively require registration and possession to be valid against third parties.[87] With respect to the fiduciary transfer for security, while the security becomes effective against the transaction parties and third parties from the date of the agreement, the trust contract and any amendments made to it must be registered in a national trusts register within one month of its creation or modification for it to remain valid.[88] If the trust assets include debt claims, the assignment of the debts only becomes enforceable against the obligor upon notification.[89] The special pledges over business, registered vehicles and intellectual property rights all require registration to be enforceable against third parties,[90] and the transfer of cash by security requires dispossession of the cash by way of remittance to the secured creditor.[91] Regarding the pledge over receivables and assignment of receivables in security, although they are valid against the security parties and third parties, they require notification for their validity against the obligor.[92]

The question, therefore, is whether there is a special provision of law that requires a public act for the assignment of these real securities. For if the answer is negative, then the application of the doctrine poses no difficulty – a simple assignment of the debt would be enough to pass the security rights without further formalities. This appears to be the case with mortgages, as article 2473 of the FCC confirms that "a mortgage is transferred automatically with the secured debt."

86 The FCC, art 2379. Although the secured creditor can lease the property back to the debtor while still retaining the security. See art 2382 of the FCC.

87 Arts 2337 and 2338 FCC. Regarding incorporeal moveables, see art 2355 FCC, which indicates in its last paragraph that the pledge over incorporeal moveables (with the exception of receivables) is subject to the same publicity rules applicable to the pledge over corporeal moveables. The non-possessory pledge requires registration in a unified register called the "Register of Security Interests over Moveable Property and Other Related Transactions". This register was introduced under Decree No. 2021-1887 of 29 December 2021 and became operative on 1 January 2023. It aims to harmonise the rules and procedures governing the publication of security interests over moveable property, which were until now largely fragmented. While this harmonisation has been achieved with respect to most moveable securities, some asset specific registers – such as those applicable to vehicles, trusts and intellectual property rights – still exist (see below).

88 Arts 2372-1 and 2019 FCC.

89 Art 2018-2 FCC.

90 The pledge over business requires registration in the unified register of security interests over moveable property – arts L142-3 and R521-2(4) of the French Commercial Code, while the pledge over registered vehicles needs to be registered in a special register that is integrated into the general vehicle registration system in France and kept by the Minister of Interior. See art 2338 FCC, as implemented by Decree No 2023-97 of 14 February 2023. For the pledge over intellectual property rights see the Intellectual Property Code, arts L513-3 (registered design), L613-9 (registered patent) and L714-7 (registered trademark).

91 See art 2374-2 FCC.

92 See respectively arts 2361 and 2362 FCC and art 2373 FCC.

The difficulty arises where the answer is in the affirmative, since assignment of the debt without more will not confer on the assignee a proprietary title in respect of the security rights. This appears to be the case under article 2425 of the FCC, which expects parties to record, in the form of notes in the margin of existing registrations, any changes in the person or domicile of the creditor who benefits from a registered mortgage. While the wording of article 2425 is mandatory – it uses the word "shall" – it is not clear what the consequence will be in the event of non-compliance. Considering the mandatory word used in the provision, compliance with the requirement of article 2425 of the FCC is recommended.

There is, nevertheless, an apparent conflict between articles 2425 and 2473 of the FCC in respect of mortgages. Article 2473 states that mortgages transfer with the secured debt by operation of law, while article 2425 provides a formality to be complied with in order to complete the transfer of a registered mortgage. As already noted, it is not clear what the consequence will be if article 2425 is not complied with. The provision does not appear to be a prerequisite for constituting the transfer either as between the assignor and the assignee or as against third parties. If it was, the FCC would have made it clear, as it does with the creation and recharge of mortgages.[93] It may therefore be concluded that while article 2425 of the FCC remains a requirement for the transfer, it is not a constitutive requirement and does not affect the operation of article 2473. Therefore, a completed transfer of title in the mortgaged claim should automatically pass the title in the mortgage security without any further formality.

The application of the *accessorium* principle to assignments of pledges over registered trademarks, registered designs, registered patents, registered vehicles and the fiduciary transfer in security is, however, limited. In these cases, there are express provisions that require such assignments to be registered for them to be enforceable against third parties.[94] Since no other similar provisions apply to other securities, the general rule of article 1321(iii) of the FCC should apply to make the securities pass automatically with the transferred debts.[95]

---

93 See e.g. art 2418 FCC. A mortgage recharge involves the granting of a mortgage over a property that is already subject to an earlier mortgage.

94 See respectively arts L714-7, L513-3 and L613-9 of the Intellectual Property Code; art 7 of Decree No 2023-97; arts 2372-1 and 2019 of the FCC.

95 Under the old rules, retention of title was not recognised as a security interest and therefore was not considered subject to the accessory principle. In 1988 the Cour de Cassation held that a secured lender would need to be contractually substituted for the seller's right of retention to pass – see Cour de Cassation, 15 March 1988, JCP G 1989, II 21348. Given that the FCC now expressly recognises title retention as a form of security interest, it is submitted that the old position does not apply under current law, and such security would be subject to the general accessory rule under art 1321(iii) FCC. See art 2367 FCC.

7.2.3 *Limitations of assignment of rights under the FCC*

Section 7.2.2.2 demonstrates that the *accessorium* principle generally applies to real securities in France, with the fiduciary transfer in security and pledges over registered designs, registered trademarks, registered patents and registered vehicles being the few exceptions. This makes the FCC assignment appear attractive for securitisations, since its creation and perfection do not require any formalities – the transfer of the receivables and related security rights is effective between the parties and enforceable against third parties (excluding the obligor), as at the date the assignment is signed. However, the FCC assignment also has its downsides in the context of securitisation. An unnotified FCC assignment limits the rights of the FCT (i.e. the securitisation entity) on the assigned debts and related security rights, since such assignment cannot be enforced against the debtor and the security holder (if different from the debtor).

The limitation in respect of the debt is that the debtors will be entitled to continue making payments to the originator, who, in turn, can validly discharge the debtors of the debts without the concurrence of the FCT. This makes the FCT take on a double credit risk (the double credit risk). It is exposed not only to the debtors' credit default risks but also to the originator's credit default risk. Also, since the originator will remain in charge of the debt collection, there is a risk that the receivables collected will be commingled with the originator's assets during its insolvency (the commingling risk).

Commingling risks can be mitigated through the provisions of articles L214-173 and L214-228 of the MFC. These provisions enable the FCT's management company and the originator to enter into a dedicated account agreement that makes all relevant receivables payable to an account opened for the sole benefit of the FCT. Such payments can either be made directly by the debtors into the dedicated account (e.g. in respect of monies payable by direct debits) or indirectly (e.g. regarding monies paid to the originator's account by cheque or payment methods other than direct debits). The MFC provides that the creditors of the originator (or any other entity responsible for the collection) will have no right to the monies paid into the dedicated account, even if the originator is subject to any insolvency proceedings under Book VI of the French Commercial Code.[96]

The limitation in respect of the assigned security rights is that the originator may validly discharge the security provider from their security obligations without the concurrence of the FCT. Also, only the originator can enforce the relevant security interests in the event of any payment defaults. Though the management company can ensure that the FCT is protected in these areas by including specific covenants in the receivables purchase agreement, this will only grant the FCT a personal right against the assignor. It does not disturb the defences the debtor or security provider may have as a

96 The MFC, art L214-173.

result of their relations with the originator in pursuance to the receivables agreement (such defences may include, for example, the debtors' right of set-off, discharge from debt, release from security obligations, etc.) – see article 1324(i) FCC. Again, where the originator becomes insolvent after enforcing the assigned security rights, there is a risk that the monies obtained from such enforcement will be commingled with other assets of the insolvent originator. It is suggested that the FCT should also be able to benefit from the dedicated account solution under article 214-173 of the MFC by making the dedicated account agreement cover proceeds obtained as a result of the enforcement of the assigned security rights.

7.3 Transfer by way of subrogation

7.3.1 *An overview of French law on subrogation*

Subrogation is another mechanism through which security rights can be transferred in French law. Under this method, a third party pays the creditor to satisfy the debtor's debt. As result, the third party assumes the rights (principal and ancillary) the creditor would have otherwise had against the debtor, but only to the extent to which their payment discharges the debtor.[97]

Subrogation may be initiated by the creditor or the debtor. In either case, it must be express and, subject to limited exceptions, must coincide with the time the creditor receives the payment.[98] In practice, these requirements would be achieved through a formal subrogation receipt (*quittance subrogative*) given by the creditor to the third party, acknowledging receipt of the payment satisfaction and stating that the creditor substitutes the third party for themselves in respect of their rights under the relevant debt receivables and the associated security interest(s).[99]

Where the subrogation is initiated by the debtor, i.e. where the debtor takes a loan from a lender to satisfy the debt and then subrogates the lender to the initial creditor's rights, the consent of the creditor must be sought and the subrogation receipt must indicate the source of the funds.[100] The creditor's consent will not, however, be required where the debt has fallen due or where payment was set for the benefit of the debtor. In

97 The FCC, art 1346-1.

98 The FCC, arts 1346-1 and 1346-2.

99 See e.g. Cars Alliance Auto Loans France V 2018-1 (Prospectus, 29 March 2018) <https://www.rcibs.com/_content/TITRISATION/Prospectus_(29032018).pdf> accessed 28 May 2024.

100 The FCC, art 1346-2(i).

such a case the loan instrument with the new lender and the subrogation receipt must be notarised.[101]

The transfer of the receivables by way of subrogation becomes enforceable against third parties (without any further formality) from the date of the subrogation.[102] In respect of the debtor, the transfer only becomes enforceable when they are notified of it or when they acknowledge it.[103] The related security rights (being ancillary rights) are transferred automatically with the receivables,[104] except for fiduciary transfers in security and pledges over registered patents, registered trademarks, registered designs and registered vehicles, which would all need to be registered.

The *assignatus utitur jure auctoris* rule applies to subrogation, so that a notified debtor will continue to be entitled to defences available under the receivables agreement (such as nullity, the defence of non-performance, and set-off rights).[105]

7.3.2 *Subrogation: advantages and disadvantages for securitisations*

In the context of a securitisation transaction, the FCT is the third party, the originator is the initial creditor, and the obligors represent the debtors. Since securitisation transactions are typically initiated by originators, the subrogation should take place on the initiative of the creditor – this makes sense since the number of debtors involved in a securitisation would make a debtor-initiated subrogation a near impossibility.

The fact that no formality (like notification, registration or notarisation) is involved in effecting the transfer of receivables and the associated security rights against third parties, subject to the above exceptions, works well for securitisations. But since notification (or acknowledgement by the obligors) is required for the transfer to be enforceable against the obligors, the limitations of assignment as highlighted in section 7.2.3 apply to subrogation.

An additional limitation of subrogation is that it applies only up to the extent of the payment satisfaction.[106] Suppose C (a dealer) sells a motor vehicle to D on credit at a total cost of €1,000, using retention of title as security. If A pays C €8,000 in satisfaction of D's debt, the consequent subrogation will only apply to the €8,000 and C would have a priority claim over A in respect of the remaining €2,000 and its equivalent security. This may raise issues with securitisations since asset sales in a securitisation are transacted on a discount.[107]

101 The FCC, art 1346-2(ii).
102 The FCC, art 1346-5(ii).
103 The FCC, art 1346-5(i).
104 The FCC, art 1346-4.
105 The FCC, art 1346-5(c).
106 The FCC, art 1346-3.
107 Buying the securitised assets on a discount enables over-collateralisation, which is one of the ways of enhancing the credit rating of the securitisation bonds. See Andrew Davidson and others, *Securitization:*

Another limitation applies in respect of future receivables. A transfer in the context of subrogation only occurs when there has been a payment satisfaction. This presupposes the existence of a debt and indicates that the subrogation of a debt and the related security right will only be effective from the date the debt and security rights come into existence. The risk here is that the subrogation of future debts and security rights that arise after the insolvency of the originator may be rendered ineffective.

7.4 Assignment under the Dailly law

7.4.1 *General overview of Dailly assignment of receivables*

The Dailly assignment of receivables is another mechanism available under French law for transferring security interests in securitisations.[108] It was introduced in 1981 to simplify assignments of receivables in professional funding arrangements by expunging the notification regime that existed under the former article 1690 of the Civil Code. Both existing and future receivables are assignable under this method.[109]

To constitute the assignment, the assignor is only required to sign and deliver to the assignee a dated written list of the assigned receivables (the Dailly assignment document), which must contain: (i) the designation "deed of assignment of receivables"; (ii) a declaration that the assignment is subject to the provisions of articles L313-23 to L313-34 of the MFC; (iii) the name of the assignee; and (iv) the description of each of the receivables assigned or, for future receivables, a description of the elements that can be used to determine each of them whenever they arise (e.g. by indicating the type of debtors, the place of payment or the estimated value of the debt).[110] The assignment becomes enforceable between the assignee and the assignor, and against third parties (including the obligor), as of the date specified in the Dailly assignment document without further formalities, regardless of the origination or the maturity date of the receivables and regardless of the law applicable to the assigned receivables or the national law of the debtors.[111] One of the important effects of the preceding sentence is that the Dailly assignment of future receivables becomes effective not from the dates the contracts

Structuring and Investment Analysis (Wiley 2003) 25.

108 Loi Dailly (Law No 81-1 of 2 January 1981), as amended by Law 84-46 of 24 January 1984. Now codified in arts L313-23ff of the MFC. The Dailly assignment is named after Senator Étienne Dailly, the sponsor of the enabling law.

109 The MFC, art L313-23(ii).

110 The MFC, art L313-23(iii).

111 The MFC, art L313-27(i). See also Cour de Cassation, 5 July 1994, RTD com 1995, 172; Cour de Cassation, 3 January 1996, JCP G 1996, II 22682; Cour de Cassation, 13 February 1996, Banque 1996, No 569, 91.

creating the receivables come into existence (as it is with the subrogation), but from the date specified in the Dailly assignment document.

Regarding the security interests attached to the receivables assigned, article L313-27(iii) of the MFC provides that the delivery of the Dailly assignment document to the assignee automatically passes to the assignee all the security rights attached to each of the receivables assigned and their enforceability against third parties with no further formalities. Being a special provision covering commercial financial transactions, article L313-27(iii) will prevail over the provisions discussed in section 7.2.2.2 above on the limitations of the *accessorium* principle.

Although the transfer of the receivables and the attached securities is enforceable against all third parties (including the obligor) as of the date indicated in the Dailly assignment document, the obligor may validly continue to pay the debts to the assignor until such time as the assignee notifies the obligor of the assignment and demands that payments be made to them. In other words, the only purpose notification serves under the Dailly assignment is to instruct the obligor to make payments to the assignee or their nominee.[112] In respect of the related securities, notification serves no purpose – the automatic transfer of the securities becomes enforceable against the security provider (and other third parties) without any further formality. This is unlike the FCC assignment and subrogation where notification serves the purpose of enforceability against the debtor, so that only the assignor can bring an action against an unnotified debtor in respect of the assigned debt and the related security rights.

7.4.2 *Dailly assignments: advantages and disadvantages for securitisations*

This foregoing simplification of assignment works well in the context of securitisation. Importantly, it guarantees the unlimited application of the *accessorium* principle, so that the security rights automatically pass with the related receivables with no further formalities. This means that the limitations highlighted in section 7.2.2.2 above in respect of the *accessorium* principle do not apply to Dailly assignments.

Also, the fact that the FCT can enforce the assignment against the obligor with no formality means that the limitations in section 7.2.3 regarding the assignee's lack of an independent enforcement right do not apply. Furthermore, since the Dailly assignment of future receivables becomes effective as at the date specified in the assignment document, and not the date the future receivable arises, the assignment of future receivables under the Dailly assignment is insolvency proof.[113]

112 The MFC, art L313-28.

113 For more discussion see Leavy (n 12) 140ff. See also section 8.2.4.

The double credit risk, however, still applies to this method. Since an unnotified Dailly assignment enables the obligor to keep paying to the originator, and the originator may, in turn, validly release the obligors of the debt without the concurrence of the securitisation vehicle, there is the risk that the obligor or the originator may default in their obligation to pay to the assignee. In relation to the security rights, it may be contended that the originator cannot validly release the security provider from the securities, since the securities are legally transferred to the securitisation vehicle regardless of notification – notification only serves the purpose of changing the recipient of payments arising from the receivables contract and does not affect the already assigned security rights. However, this argument may be criticised on at least two grounds.

First, the accessorial transfer of the security rights is a derivative of the principal transfer of the debts, hence it can only go as far as the principal transfer. Accordingly, if the originator retains the right to discharge the obligors for the debts in an unnotified Dailly assignment, the originator should also have the same rights in respect of the ancillary rights attached to debts. Second, even if the FCT had the sole right to enforce or release the securities attached to the discharged debts, the security rights may be of no value because of the effect of two other aspects of the accessory principle which stipulate that: (i) the extinction of the debt automatically ends the accessory right;[114] and (ii) the enforcement of security is predicated on the existence of a debt.[115] The consequence is that if the originator discharges the obligors of the debts, either or both of the following may apply: (i) the security rights are automatically extinguished regardless of who has the right; (ii) the holder of the security rights would have no reason to enforce the rights since the debt is now non-existent.

Furthermore, since the unnotified obligors may keep making payments to the originator in a Dailly assignment, there is the risk that the monies collected may be commingled with other assets of the originator should the originator become subject to insolvency. The dedicated account arrangement can, however, be used to mitigate this commingling risk.

Another constraint, which is possibly the most significant, is the limitations that apply to the kind of receivables that can be sold under the assignment and the status of the purchaser.[116] A Dailly assignment is only applicable where: (i) the assignee is a credit institution duly licensed in France, an EU-passported credit institution, or a French

114 This rule is recognised by French law. See e.g. art 1350-2 of the FCC (in respect of a guarantee); art 2474(1) of the FCC (in respect of a mortgage); and art 2384(1) of the FCC (in respect of a real estate pledge). It should be noted that there may be a need to record the discharge in the asset registry where the security was initially registered; in this case, the debtor may need to take further steps to record the extinguished security in the register.

115 For general discussion of these aspects of the accessory principle see AJM Steven, 'Accessoriness and Security over Land' (2009) 13 Edinburgh Law Review 387, 410ff.

116 The MFC, art L313-23.

financing vehicle; and (ii) the receivables arise from a loan advanced to a debtor in relation to the debtor's business or professional activities. While the FCT qualifies as a French financing vehicle and can be used for a Dailly assignment,[117] important consumer receivables (like residential mortgages, auto loans, credit card loans, trade receivables, etc.) which do not relate to any business or professional activities of the debtors are excluded from the scope of the assignment.

7.5 ASSIGNMENT UNDER FRENCH SECURITISATION LAW (I.E. FCT ASSIGNMENT OR FRENCH *BORDEREAU*)

7.5.1 General overview of FCT assignments

This method of assignment was introduced by the French Securitisation Act of 1988 with the aim of simplifying the transfer of receivables in securitisation transactions.[118] The approach adopted by the 1988 Act in achieving this aim is substantially similar to that of the *Loi* Dailly.[119] The Act eliminated the need for *signification*, which existed under the former article 1690 of the FCC, and relies on the delivery of a signed document containing the list of receivables being assigned (i.e. the *bordereau*) to effect an assignment. The contents of the *bordereau* are specified by decree[120] and are similar to those of the Dailly assignment document.[121]

Once the *bordereau* is delivered to the assignee, the assignment of the receivables becomes enforceable between the assignee and the assignor, and against third parties (including the obligor), as of the date specified in the *bordereau* without any further formalities, regardless of the origination or the maturity date of the receivables and regardless of the law applicable to the receivables or the debtors.[122]

The delivery of the *bordereau* automatically passes to the assignee all the securities attached to each of the receivables assigned and their enforceability against third parties without any further formalities.[123]

117 The MFC, art L214-169-V(3-ii).
118 Its provisions are now contained in arts L214-166-1 to L214-190 of the MFC.
119 Leavy (n 12) 142.
120 The MFC, art L214-169-V(1).
121 The MFC, art D214-227. Except that the deed must be designated as an "act of assignment of receivables" and made subject to the provisions of arts L214-169 to L214-175 of the MFC.
122 The MFC, art L214-169-V(2).
123 The MFC, art L214-169-V(3).

Again, just as with the Dailly assignment, the debtors will continue to validly discharge their debt to the assignor and may continue to raise those defences that arise from their relationship with the assignor until they are notified of the assignment.[124]

7.5.2 *FCT assignments: advantages and disadvantages for securitisations*

The foregoing similarity with the Dailly assignment in relation to the purpose of notification and the application of the *accessorium* principle means that the advantages discussed in section 7.4.2 above apply to FCT assignments. Furthermore, the transfer of future receivables under the FCT assignment is insolvency proof. This is because the FCT assignment is effective as from the date of the transfer deed and not the date a relevant receivable arises.[125]

However, since an unnotified obligor may keep paying to the originator under an FCT assignment and remain entitled to raise defences arising from their relationship with the assignor, the double credit risks discussed in section 7.4.2 above and the subsequent argument on the discharge of the debts and the attached security interests without the concurrence of the FCT also applies to FCT assignments. Another consequence of the unnotified obligor's right to continue paying to the originator is that it makes the commingling risk present in FCT assignments. Again, however, the dedicated account arrangement can be used to mitigate the commingling risk.

The fundamental difference between the Dailly assignment and the FCT assignment is that there are no restrictions to the type of receivables that can be assigned under the FCT assignment. In other words, the FCT assignment not only covers receivables arising from professional or business relationship between the assignor and the debtor, it also extends to consumer receivables, like residential mortgages, personal car loans, consumer credits and trade receivables, that are typically used for securitisations. This feature gives the FCT assignment an edge over Dailly assignment and makes the FCT assignment the preferred solution in France.

7.6 Conclusion

The French law on assignment has been subject to significant reforms over the last four decades. These reforms are testament to the burdensome requirement, under the former article 1690 FCC, that notification should be done through a bailiff for an assignment to be valid against third parties and the obligor. In 1981, the Dailly assignment was introduced

124 The MFC, L214-172(i), (ii) and (iii).

125 For discussion see section 8.2.4.2(e).

to simplify assignments of receivables in professional or business funding arrangements by expunging this notification regime and downgrading the purpose of notification to that of an instruction to change the recipient of payments from the assigned receivables. However, the Dailly assignment is restricted to receivables arising from a business or professional relationship between the assignor and the obligor, and the assignee must be a French licensed (or an EU-passported) credit institution.

In 1988, the French securitisation law introduced another simplified form of assignment for securitisation transactions. This assignment operates like the Dailly assignment, except that there are no restrictions on the types of receivables it can apply to, and it is certain that FCT assignments are insolvency proof. In 2016, a new regime of assignment of rights was introduced to replace the regime under the former article 1690 FCC. The new regime removes the requirement for *signification* and allows an unnotified assignment to be enforceable against third parties (but not the obligor). This effectively downgrades notification to a requirement for enforceability against only the obligor.

This chapter has reviewed the above methods of assignment, as well as subrogation, with a view to identifying the most suitable method for transferring security rights in securitisation. The conclusion is that while the Dailly assignment and the FCT assignment are more suitable for securitisations (compared to the FCC assignment and subrogation), the wider applicability of the FCT assignment makes it the preferred solution under French law. The FCT assignment is referred to in the next chapter as the French *bordereau*.

8 LAW AND ECONOMICS ANALYSIS

Three solutions for the transfer of security rights have been recognised: (i) the Scottish trust, (ii) the English equitable assignment, and (iii) the French *bordereau*. The registration solution adopted under the Moveable Transactions (Scotland) Act 2023 (hereafter "the registration solution") has also been discussed. The registration solution is considered "revolutionary" and is expected to become fully effective in the second half of 2024 (see discussion in section 5.3.2.2). This chapter compares these solutions to determine the solution, or a model solution, that is most efficient for the transfer of security rights in securitisations. It does this in three sections. The first section revisits the property law principle of publicity and discusses how it is followed in the assignment and security laws of Scotland, England and France. Section 8.2 discusses the comparative analysis. It concludes that although the registration solution is the most efficient among the focus solutions, it is not Pareto optimal. Section 8.3 makes a case for a model solution. The model solution builds on the strengths of the registration solution and attempts to improve on its weaknesses. This section also considers the transferability of the model solution to English law and French law.

8.1 THE PUBLICITY PRINCIPLE

8.1.1 *Nature*

The publicity principle requires rights that are enforceable against third parties to be visible to third parties.[1] While the principle is a key aspect of property law, it is not absolute.[2] It is one of a number of other policies that are generally considered in the formulation of assignment laws.[3] One or more of these policies may come into conflict with each other and thus require a trade-off. For example, the need to make receivables easily transferable is one important policy that conflicts with and makes policymakers rethink the value of publicity. The mobility of rights incentivises mechanisms that simplify

---

1 W Gloag and J Irvine, *Law of Rights in Security, Heritable and Moveable: Including Cautionary Obligations* (W Green 1897) 8; GL Gretton and AJM Steven, *Property, Trusts and Succession* (4th edn, Bloomsbury Professional Scotland 2021) para 4.19ff. See also Joanna Benjamin, *Interests in Securities: A Proprietary Law Analysis of the International Securities Markets* (Oxford University Press 2000) 105f.

2 Scottish Law Commission, *Discussion Paper on Moveable Transactions* (DP 151, 2011) paras 11.4f.

3 See e.g. Andrew McAlpine, 'Raising Finance over Claims to Payment and Reform to the Law of Outright Assignation' (2015) 3 Juridical Review 275, 276 (identifying three policy objectives: (i) mobility of claims, (ii) debtor protection, and (iii) third-party protection).

the transfer of rights and ultimately facilitates commerce, while publicity creates formalities that may impede rights' mobility and adversely affects commerce.[4] The policy of mobility of rights and the consequent conflict with the publicity principle are discussed in detail below.[5] In summary, however, the trade-off between these two opposing policies will depend on the policy objective the relevant lawmaker sets out to achieve.

8.1.2 *Scots law*

Scots property law traditionally adheres to the publicity principle.[6] This is particularly true in relation to the creation and transfer of security rights, where publicity generally plays a constitutive role.[7] For example, the publicity act required to create and transfer a security over land (i.e. a standard security) is registration in the Land Register.[8] In the case of a security over corporeal moveable property (i.e. a pledge), delivery of possession is required.[9] With respect to security over incorporeal moveable property (i.e. an assignation in security), intimation to the debtor is required.[10] Some moveable assets have special

4 ibid 280.

5 See section 8.2.

6 See KGC Reid, *The Law of Property in Scotland* (Butterworths 1996) 602; RG Anderson and JWA Biemans, 'Reform of Assignation in Security: Lessons from the Netherlands' (2012) 16 Edinburgh Law Review 24, 34.

7 The following was said of the creation of security rights in Scotland: "[a]ll rights in security ... require for their constitution not only an agreement between the parties but some overt act." Gloag and Irvine, *Security* (n 1) 8.

8 Conveyancing and Feudal Reform (Scotland) Act 1970, ss 11(1) and 14 respectively. By virtue of art 3 of the Registers of Scotland (Voluntary Registration, Amendment of Fees, etc.) Order 2015 (SSI 2015/265), all registrations are now required to be in the Land Register rather than the Register of Sasines. For discussion see sections 5.1.2.3 and 5.2.2.1.

9 J Erskine of Carnock, *An Institute of the Law of Scotland* (Edinburgh Legal Education Trust 1773) II.i.19f; J Dalrymple, Viscount Stair, *The Institutions of the Law of Scotland* (DM Walker ed, Edinburgh University Press 1981) II.i.11. The statutory pledge would require registration in the Register of Statutory Pledges for its validity. See Moveable Transactions (Scotland) Act 2023, s 42(3). For discussion of the transfer of pledge see section 5.2.2.2.

10 See discussion in sections 5.1.2.2 and 5.2.2.5. The extent to which intimation (or notification) is equivalent to publicity is debatable. The Scottish Law Commission considers it as a "weak form of publicity" – Scottish Law Commission, *Report on Moveable Transactions* (Scot Law Com No 249, 2017) para 5.3. Intimation has also been considered as a "private publicity" – Bernard Rudden, 'Things as Thing and Things as Wealth' (1994) 14 Oxford Journal of Legal Studies 81, 92; and as an "external act rather than true publicity" – ADJ MacPherson, 'Registration of Company Charges Revisited: New and Familiar Problems' (2019) 23 Edinburgh Law Review 153, 156 at footnote 9. This can be compared to the Draft Common Frame of Reference (DCFR), which notes that "[n]otice to the debtor is not equivalent to public notice (for example, by registration), since it is visible only to the debtor" – Christian von Bar and others (eds), *Principles, Definitions and Model Rules of European Private Law: Draft Common Frame of Reference* (DCFR) (Sellier, European Law Publishers 2010) 1038 <https://www.law.kuleuven.be/personal/mstorme/european-private-law_en.pdf> accessed 28 May 2024. But the commentary may be challenged on the basis that informing the debtor means the assignation is verifiable by third parties through the debtor just as registration is through

registers in which security rights granted over them are required to be registered.[11] However, the floating charge is a rare exception, as publicity is not required for its creation and transfer.[12]

In addition to these special publicity schemes, another general publicity scheme exists under Part 25, Chapter A1 of the Companies Act 2006. This scheme requires securities[13] granted by UK-registered companies to be delivered for registration in the companies charges register within 21 days after the security's creation date.[14] A failure to register under section 859A, or to register out of time with leave of the court under section 859F(3) of the Act, renders the security void against the company's creditors, liquidators and administrators.[15] This therefore opens up the possibility of a security becoming subject to double publicity. For example, if a UK company grants a standard security, a double registration in the Land Register and the Companies Register will be required for the security to have an absolute third-party effect.[16] In the case of debts assigned in security, the assignation will have to be intimated to the debtor and registered in the Companies Register. This requirement for double publicity has been trenchantly criticised.[17]

---

the relevant register. Yet that itself may be contested on the basis that the notified debtor is under no obligation to inform the third party of the assignation or give accurate information about the assignation.

11 These include the register under Sch 1 of the Merchant Ship Act 1996 for registered ships, the register under the Mortgaging of Aircraft Order 1972 (SI 1972/1268), the register of patents under the Patents Act 1977, the register of trademarks under the Trade Marks Act 1994, and the register of designs under the Registered Designs Act 1949.

12 See discussion in sections 5.1.2.1(b) and 5.2.2.3. See also ADJ MacPherson, *The Floating Charge* (Edinburgh Legal Education Trust 2020) paras 3.16ff. The non-compliance with the publicity principle reflects the fact that the floating charge was transplanted from English law, a jurisdiction that is less keen on publicity. See discussion in section 8.1.3.

13 The Companies Act uses the term "charge", which also reflects the English security system – Companies Act 2006, s 859A(1) and (7). But the term "securities" will be used for present purposes to ensure coherence. For the avoidance of doubt, the term "securities" as used in this chapter means security rights, unless the context states otherwise.

14 Section 859E of the Companies Act 2006 sets out the creation dates of the various securities in the UK. For discussion of these dates in the context of Scottish security rights, see MacPherson, 'Registration of Company Charges Revisited' (n 10) 163ff.

15 Companies Act 2006, s 859(H)(3). Certain securities are expressly excluded from the registration scheme under s 859A (see Companies Act 2006, s 859A(6)) – these include securities that are excluded by or under other legislation, such as securities that fall within the Financial Collateral Arrangements (No 2) Regulations 2003 (SI 2003/3226) (see reg 4(4) of the 2003 Regulations). Possessory securities like pledges are excluded – Companies Act 2006, s 859A(7). Quasi-securities, such as hire purchase and retention of title clauses, are also excluded.

16 The company charges registration regime was introduced to Scots law by the Companies (Floating Charges) (Scotland) Act 1961. Scots law only needed the scheme for floating charges, as other forms of security had their own special publicity regimes. However, the adoption of the general publicity scheme extended beyond floating charges to other securities. See generally Scottish Law Commission (SLC), *Discussion Paper on Moveable Transactions* (n 2) paras 8.1ff.

17 See e.g. GL Gretton, 'Registration of Company Charges' (2002) 6 Edinburgh Law Review 146. The Scottish Law Commission recommended that company charges registration should be abolished and that a special register should instead be created for floating charges – Scottish Law Commission, *Report on Registration*

Publicity equally plays an important role in the Scottish law of assignation. There are two forms of assignation under Scots law: assignation in security and outright assignation. The dominant view is that both forms have the same proprietary effect (i.e. they transfer title from the assignor to the assignee)[18] and they are both governed by the general rules of assignation.[19] According to the Scottish Law Commission (SLC), what distinguishes the two forms of assignation is purpose.[20] While the purpose of one is to effect a permanent transfer, the purpose of the other is to provide security. Therefore, an absolute assignation of a claim, just as with an assignation in security, requires intimation to the debtor for it to be constituted.[21]

In addition to its constitutive role, publicity also plays a priority role in Scots law. Where there is a contest between two valid rights in security, the general rule is that the party who is first to complete their right ranks first.[22] First to complete generally means first to publicise, using the required step for the security in question.

In relation to the application of the *accessorium sequitur principale* principle (hereafter "the *accessorium* principle"), chapter 5 demonstrates that the publicity principle generally prevails over the *accessorium* principle, so that the transfer of a debt does not usually carry the related security.[23]

---

of Rights in Security by Companies (Scot Law Com No 197, 2004). The recommendation for the abolition of the company charges registration was not accepted by the Department of Trade and Industry (initially changed to the Department for Business, Energy and Industrial Strategy and now split to form the Department for Business and Trade, the Department for Energy Security and Net Zero and the Department for Science, Innovation and Technology). Regarding the recommendation for a new registration system for floating charges, this was implemented by Part 2 of the Bankruptcy and Diligence etc. (Scotland) Act 2007 but is yet to come into force and is now unlikely to ever be brought into force. On this, see section 5.1.2.1(b).

18 See e.g. AJ Sim, 'Rights in Security over Moveables' in *Stair Memorial Encyclopaedia* (1992) para 46; WM Gloag and R Candlish Henderson, *The Law of Scotland* (HL MacQueen and Lord Eassie eds, 14th edn, W Green 2017) para 36.28. Note the contrary view of Lord Bannatyne in *Edinburgh Schools Partnership Ltd v Galliford Try Construction (UK) Ltd* [2017] CSOH 133, [2017] 10 WLUK 545, at [120ff], where he suggested that there is a 'fundamental difference between an absolute assignation and an assignation in security' and held that a cedent (or assignor) with a financial interest in a property assigned in security has title to sue if the assignee fails to exercise their title to sue. The SLC also admits that the two assignations may be different in circumstances where the personal creditors of the assignee try to enforce diligence on a debtor who has been intimated of the assignation but is instructed to pay to the assignor, nevertheless. In this case, the SLC suggests that the claim may be protected from the personal creditors of an assignee in security. See SLC, *Report on Moveable Transactions* (n 10) para 5.60 (citing *Purnell v Shannon* (1894) 22 R 74).

19 See SLC, *Discussion Paper on Moveable Transactions* (n 2) para 7.6.

20 ibid.

21 See generally section 5.3.2.1.

22 This rule is also expressed as *prior tempore, potior jure*, which means "earlier by time, stronger by right". See Gretton and Steven, *Property, Trusts and Succession* (n 1) para 4.45.

23 See section 5.2.

8.1.3 *English law and French law*

8.1.3.1 General assignment law

Publicity is also recognised under English and French law. But its role is less important. Notification is not a constitutive requirement in the assignment laws of both systems.[24] Therefore, the conclusion of the contract of assignment is enough to effect a valid assignment. But notification is important in both systems for practical purposes. For example, an unnotified debtor can continue to validly discharge their debt to the assignor and may continue to raise defences that arise from their relationship with the assignor (such as the set-off of unconnected debts or the release of a debt) until they are notified of the assignment.[25] Notification is also essential in determining priority between two competing assignments in English law. The assignee who notifies first takes priority, provided that the assignee took the assignment for value and without knowledge of a prior assignment.[26] However, notification is not a priority point in French law.[27]

In relation to the transfer of the related securities, chapter 6 demonstrates that the application of the *accessorium* principle is uncertain under English law and advises that care should be taken to refer to both subjects of transfer expressly – i.e. the debts and security rights – in the assignment document.[28] Chapter 7 shows that the *accessorium* principle generally prevails over the publicity principle in relation to French law.[29]

8.1.3.2 Security law

Publicity is recognised under English and French security law. In French law, it plays an important role in relation to the creation of security rights over land. The two main immoveable securities in France (namely, mortgage and real estate pledge) have limited effect until they are registered at the land registry,[30] or until possession is delivered to the creditor in respect of the real estate pledge.[31] Similar publicity acts of registration and obtaining possession apply to moveable securities, such as the general possessory and non-possessory pledge,[32] and the special pledges over business, registered vehicles and

24 See sections 6.2.3 and 7.2.

25 See *Business Computers Ltd v Anglo African Leasing* [1977] 1 WLR 578 (Ch), per Templeman J at 582; the French Civil Code (FCC), art 1324.

26 *Dearle v Hall* (1828) 3 Russ 1 (Ch).

27 See e.g. art 1325 of the FCC: "[t]he competition between successive assignees of a debt is resolved in favour of the first to date; he has a remedy against the one to whom the debtor has made a payment". This English translation is based on Légifrance <https://www.legifrance.gouv.fr/codes/section_lc/LEGITEXT000006070721/LEGISCTA000032032398/#LEGISCTA000032032398> accessed 28 May 2024.

28 See section 6.1.2.

29 See section 7.2.2.2.

30 See art 2418 FCC.

31 The FCC, art 2379.

32 The FCC, arts 2337, 2338 and 2355.

intellectual property rights.[33] An example of a major exception to the foregoing is the pledge over receivables and the new assignment of receivables in security, which are enforceable against third parties merely on the conclusion of a written agreement.[34] However, notice is required for them to be enforceable against the debtor.[35]

The position under English security law is complex. This is mainly due to the distinction between legal and equitable rights.[36] Equity makes it possible for a security to attach to a property from the date the security agreement is concluded.[37] This attachment confers an equitable property right to the creditor, which is enforceable against the debtor and the debtor's unsecured non-insolvency creditors.[38] Therefore, if a debtor who has received an advance from a creditor signs an agreement with the creditor to create a present security interest over an identifiable property, equity considers such agreement to take effect as immediate security.[39]

The security may either be a charge or a mortgage.[40] All charges are equitable securities under English law.[41] Mortgages, on the other hand, can either be legal or equitable. Hence, in terms of non-possessory securities, a legal mortgage is currently the only means of acquiring a legal security in English law.[42] A legal mortgage will generally require publicity (i.e. registration, notification or obtaining possession) in order to be effective.[43]

---

33 For discussion see chapter 7 at section 7.2.2.1.

34 The FCC, arts 2361, 2362 and 2373.

35 Arts 2362 and 2373 FCC.

36 Unlike Scots law and French law, which have a unititular system of property law, English law has a divided system of property law that recognises two property rights: equitable rights and legal rights.

37 For discussion of when an equitable security takes effect see Louise Gullifer (ed), *Goode and Gullifer on Legal Problems of Credit and Security* (7th edn, Sweet & Maxwell 2022) paras 2.02ff.

38 ibid para 2.02; Ewan McKendrick (ed), *Goode and McKendrick on Commercial Law* (6th edn, Penguin Books 2020) para 23.20.

39 This is based on the principle that equity considers as done that which ought to be done. See e.g. *Tebb v Hodge* (1869) LR 5 CP 73 (Ex Ch); *Tailby v Official Receiver* (1888) 13 App Cas 523 (HL).

40 Both are non-possessory securities and can be taken over moveable and immoveable properties. For discussion of the forms of security see section 6.1.1.

41 One exception is the legal charge over land, which is a creation of statute. Yet it is "expressed to be by way of legal mortgage". See Law of Property Act 1925, s 85(1); Land Registration Act 2002, s 51.

42 Goode and Gullifer, *Legal Problems* (n 37) para 1.12.

43 E.g. a legal mortgage over a registered land requires registration in the Land Registry – Land Registration Act 2002. A legal mortgage over other assets that have special title registers (such as registered ships, registered aircraft and registrable intellectual property rights) requires registration in the relevant title register. A legal mortgage of debts or choses in action requires the debtor's notice (if effected by assignment – see s 136 of the Law of Property Act 1925) or consent (if effected by novation). In respect of certificated registered securities, an entry into the issuer's register is required, or into the CREST register for uncertificated registered securities – Goode and Gullifer, *Legal Problems* (n 37) paras 6.44ff. Where the legal mortgage is created on goods and by an individual, it will require registration under s 8 of the Bills of Sale Act (1878) Amendment Act 1882.

Therefore, publicity is not a constitutive requirement for creating securities in English security laws.[44] But publicity is important for two reasons. First, in a contest between an equitable security and a legal mortgage, priority is normally determined by reference to the date of publicity and not the date the security was created.[45] Hence, an equitable security may be displaced by a later legal mortgage if the legal mortgagee takes title for value and without notice of the earlier equitable security.[46] Secondly, publicity under the company charges registration scheme is a perfection requirement.[47] A failure to register makes the security void against the company's creditors,[48] liquidator and administrator.[49] This implies that the unregistered security will remain valid against other parties not included in that list, such as the company itself when not in insolvency, the outright purchaser of the security property and unsecured creditors of the non-insolvency company.[50]

In the company charges scheme, the priority between two competing securities is determined by reference to the date the charge is created rather than the date of registration. Therefore, a creditor who registers first will fall behind another creditor whose charge is created earlier but registered later, provided that the earlier charge is registered within the 21-day registration period.[51] For this reason, registration under section 859A is said to be a perfection requirement rather than a priority point. It is important to note here that

44 One exception to this is a pledge. A pledge is a common law security and is created by the delivery of possession and not merely by agreement. Also, a security bill of sale is void (even as between the creditor and the debtor) if not registered within the period of 7 days of its creation – s 8 of the Bills of Sale Act (1878) Amendment Act 1882.

45 Goode and Gullifer, *Legal Problems* (n 37) para 5.09.

46 ibid.

47 Registration as a perfection requirement under s 859A must be distinguished from registration as a priority point under the specialist registers scheme. Under the former, non-registration renders the security void on the debtor's insolvency. For the latter, an unregistered security is effective (even in the debtor's insolvency) as an equitable security but subject to a subsequent legal title acquired in the same property for value and without notice. See Goode and Gullifer, *Legal Problems* (n 37) para 2.21.

48 This has been held to mean secured creditors and execution creditors. See *Re Ashpurton Estates Ltd* [1983] Ch 110 (CA), per Lord Brightman at 123. See also Goode and Gullifer, *Legal Problems* (n 37) para 2.23; Goode and McKendrick, *Commercial Law* (n 38) para 24.51.

49 Companies Act 2006, s 859H(3).

50 Goode and McKendrick, *Commercial Law* (n 38) para 24.50. However, where the outright purchaser acquires the legal title for value and without notice, the purchaser will take the title free from the unregistered security. Goode and McKendrick, *Commercial Law* (n 38) para 24.52.

51 The position is different where the earlier charge is registered outside the 21-day period by leave of the court. In this case, the earlier charge will rank behind a later charge. This is because one of the conditions for granting leave to register out of time is that the leave will be without prejudice to interests acquired during the period between the creation and the registration of the charge. See Companies Act 2006, s 859F(3). See also *Watson v Duff, Morgan & Vermont (Holdings) Ltd* [1974] 1 WLR 450 (Ch).

there is no requirement to register outright sales of receivables under the company charges registration scheme, as an outright assignment is not considered to be a security.[52]

The priority rules and perfection rules under English security law are incoherent and complex.[53] For present purposes, it suffices to know that publicity is generally not required under English law for an equitable security to be effective against the debtor and third parties. But publicity is necessary for the security to be fully effective against third parties.[54]

8.1.4 *Concluding comments*

In an economy, the value of receivables financing structures like securitisation and the need to facilitate its growth is not in doubt. The Law Commission describes receivables financing as "enormously important".[55] The Scottish Law Commission describes the value of receivables as potential collateral as being "of great importance".[56] The facilitation of receivables financing is, therefore, important not just for businesses but for the wider economy.[57] However, the need to facilitate receivables financing will most often require non-publicity assignments,[58] which itself conflicts with the need to protect debtors and other third parties. Publicity can also help create legal certainty as to (i) the date an assignment becomes enforceable against third parties[59] and (ii) the priority ranking

52 There have been efforts to include outright assignments of receivables (particularly receivables financing arrangements) within the scope of the company charges registration scheme. See e.g. Law Commission, *Report on Companies Security Interests* (Law Com No 296, 2005) paras 4.18 and 4.25. See also City of London Law Society, 'Draft Secured Transactions Code' (2016) ss 26.2 and 26.4 <https://www.citysolicitors.org.uk/storage/2016/07/Draft-Secured-Transaction-Code-Commentary-July-2016.pdf> accessed 28 May 2024. But it appears that the proposal has now been abandoned, as the latest Code does not provide for it. See City of London Law Society, 'The Secured Transactions Code' (2020) <https://www.citysolicitors.org.uk/storage/2020/03/Secured-Transactions-Code-discussion-draft-March-2020-2.pdf> accessed 28 May 2024. The Secured Transactions Law Reform Project is also consulting on a similar proposal, which recommends that registration should be a priority point and a perfection requirement. See 'Discussion Paper Series: Sale of Receivables' (2017) ss 3 and 4 <https://securedtransactionslawreformproject.org/2017/01/03/january-2017-discussion-papers/> accessed 28 May 2024. For more discussion of these reforms see section 8.4.3.

53 See Goode and Gullifer, *Legal Problems* (n 37) ch 5, ss 2 and 4. See also Goode and McKendrick, *Commercial Law* (n 38) paras 24.69ff.

54 E.g. a third party who purchases the security property for value and without notice of the equitable security will take title free of the security. Goode and Gullifer, *Legal Problems* (n 37) para 5.36.

55 Law Commission (n 52) xii, para 14.

56 SLC, *Discussion Paper on Moveable Transactions* (n 2) para 3.

57 E.g. see chapter 3 for discussion of the economic function of securitisation.

58 The difficulties a strict adherence to the publicity principle poses to a securitisation transaction are highlighted in chapters five, six and seven.

59 This helps to avoid issues relating to fraudulent antedating. If assignments are completed secretly, parties may be tempted to falsify the date of the assignment. See SLC, *Discussion Paper on Moveable Transactions* (n 2) paras 14.8f.

between two competing assignments. Given the importance of these two policies and the conflict between them, there is a need for some trading-off.

8.2 Comparative analysis

8.2.1 *Initial comments*

This section analyses and compares how the Scottish trust, the registration solution, the English equitable assignment and the French *bordereau* address this conflict, to determine which solution is more efficient for securitisations. Both Pareto improvement and Kaldor-Hicks efficiency will be used as criteria for measuring efficiency.[60] To undertake the comparative analysis, it is necessary to make certain assumptions. First, it will be assumed that the Scottish assignation is the current state of affairs (or the status quo) for transferring receivables and related security rights for securitisations. The choice of the Scottish assignation as the status quo is due to its strict adherence to the publicity principle when compared with the English and French assignment laws. This choice is also informed by the fact that the publicity requirement is the main difficulty the legal solutions being compared are generally designed to address.

The Scottish trust, the registration solution, the English equitable assignment and the French *bordereau* will be considered the alternative states of affairs to which the Scottish assignation could be moved. The aim is to analyse the improvement made by each alternative state of affairs and the extent such improvement achieves a Pareto improvement outcome or a Kaldor-Hicks efficient outcome. An improvement that achieves a Pareto improvement will be considered the superior outcome. In contrast, an improvement that achieves a Kaldor-Hicks efficient outcome will be considered as the weaker outcome.

Secondly, it is assumed that the third parties that could be negatively affected by the transfers in securitisations are the debtors and the potential creditors and assignees of the originator. These are the most likely third parties to be affected by the securitisation transfer and limiting the scope of this research to this class of third parties is essential for a close-ended analysis to be achieved.[61]

Other third parties that could also be negatively affected are the existing unsecured creditors of the originator. This is because it can be argued that the transfer has the effect of redistributing the wealth of the originator from the unsecured creditors to the securitisation investors. This is especially the case where the transfer is effective against future receivables acquired after the originator enters insolvency. But this argument can be

60 See section 4.2.2.2.

61 See also chapter 4 at footnote 119 above.

countered on the basis that the originator receives actual money for the transfer of the debt receivables. In other words, through securitisation, the company is only substituting illiquid assets (such as mortgages, car loans and trade receivables) with a liquid asset (i.e. cash).[62] The money received becomes part of the originator's assets and can be used for further investments. Hence, the unsecured creditors are (at least) not worse off by the transfer.

An argument can be made that the transfer will make unsecured creditors better off. First, liquidity and credit risks are inversely related.[63] The higher the liquidity of the debtor, the lower their credit risk, and in turn, the higher the probability that the unsecured creditors (who are most vulnerable to the debtor's default risks) will get paid. Secondly, the assets sale transfers to the SPV both the rights to payment under the financial assets and the associated credit risks on a non-recourse basis.[64] This means that the originator is not only strengthening its liquidity by selling off the financial assets but also decreasing its credit-risk levels. This, in turn, increases the chances of the originator of paying its existing creditors and avoiding insolvency.[65] Hence, it can be said that the interests of the unsecured creditors and the originator are aligned: the ability of the originator to pay its debts depends on the success of the originator. Moreover, studies have shown that securitisation creates real value for the originator.[66]

The creditors/assignees of the SPV could also be affected by the transfer. However, SPVs are typically structured to be bankruptcy remote so that the issue of the transfer affecting the creditors/assignees will generally not arise.[67]

To determine the efficiency of the alternative states of affairs, it is necessary to measure each state of affairs against certain policy goals. From an analysis of the literature and policy documents, six policies can be recognised for this exercise. These are that:

1. debtors should be protected;

---

62 Solomon Deku and Alper Kara, *Securitization: Past, Present and Future* (Palgrave Macmillan 2017) 8.

63 Björn Imbierowicz and Christian Rauch, 'The Relationship between Liquidity Risk and Credit Risk in Banks' (2014) 40 Journal of Banking & Finance 242 (concluding that liquidity risks have a strong influence on bank's default risk – while the study relates to banks, same can be applied to businesses more generally).

64 See BG Buchanan, *Securitization and the Global Economy: History and Prospects for the Future* (Palgrave Macmillan 2017) 57. See also Philip Wood, *Title Finance, Derivatives, Securitisations, Set-off and Netting* (Sweet & Maxwell 1995) para 4.1.

65 See generally SL Schwarcz, 'Securitization and Structured Finance', *Encyclopedia of Financial Globalization* (2011) 10 (noting that the unsecured creditors "are not harmed", and may even be better off after the transaction, provided that the originator reinvests the proceeds of the sale wisely).

66 See e.g. Michael Lemmon and others, 'Securitization and Capital Structure in Nonfinancial Firms: An Empirical Investigation: Securitization and Capital Structure in Nonfinancial Firms' (2014) 69 The Journal of Finance 1787, 1815. For discussion see section 3.1.1.3.

67 The activities of the SPV will usually be limited to the securitisation transaction and the SPV will typically be restricted from incurring liabilities that are unrelated to the transaction. See JJ de Vries Robbé, *Securitization Law and Practice: In the Face of the Credit Crunch* (Kluwer Law International 2008) para 2.12.

2. third parties (particularly future creditors and assignees of the originator) should be protected;
3. future receivables transfers should be facilitated;
4. transfers without publicity should be facilitated;
5. transfers should be effective against all third parties, including the originator's liquidator or administrator; and
6. the *accessorium* principle should have a general application – this policy relates to security rights.

Policy one seeks to protect the interest of the underlying debtors. Policy two protects the interest of the third parties. Policies three to six protect the interests of the originator and/or the investors. The extent to which each state of affairs meets these policies is discussed below. But before then, it is necessary to provide one more clarification.

The analysis for each policy is followed by a table that scores each state of affairs according to the extent to which the state of affairs meets a relevant policy (see Tables 8.1 to 8.6 below). This is done in order to simplify the presentation of the results for each policy. It is therefore important to explain the scoring method adopted. It will be seen that the degree to which the states of affairs meet each policy varies. While one state of affairs may fully meet a policy, another may not do so at all. Also, a state of affairs may achieve aspects of a policy (either substantially or to a limited extent) but fall short of fully achieving the policy. The scores adopted range from 0 to 1. If a state of affairs fully achieves a relevant policy, it will score 1. If it does not achieve the relevant policy at all, it will score 0. However, where the state of affairs achieves the policy substantially (i.e. to a significant degree) but falls short in minor respects, it will score 0.75. If the state of affairs achieves the policy to a limited extent but falls short in other respects, it will receive 0.50. Where the state of affairs achieves the policy to a minimal (or very limited) extent, it will receive 0.25.

8.2.2 *Policy one: debtors should be protected*

8.2.2.1 General

This requires that the debtors in a securitisation transaction should not be prejudiced by the transfer of the receivables and related security rights. Five possible variants of this policy can be identified.

First, the policy requires that a debtor who is unaware of a transfer should be able to discharge to the creditor last known to them. According to the Scottish Law Commission, "where there has been an assignation of a claim, the debtor who performs in good faith to the person last known to the debtor to be the holder of the claim should be discharged."[68] Any rule to the contrary would expose the debtor to the risk of making double payments to the assignor and the assignee – since the debtor may mistakenly pay to the assignor and still need to pay to the assignee for the debt to be discharged. It would also impose potentially significant costs on debtors, who may, in a bid to avoid double payments, want to enquire from the original creditor about the status of the debt each time a payment is due.

A second variant requires a debtor who pays in good faith to the assignee who notifies first to be discharged. This requirement will apply where the original creditor fraudulently or negligently assigns the same debt to two assignees. This will be possible, for example, in systems where assignment occurs by agreement.[69] Therefore, suppose that D owes C £100. C sells their right to the debt to A1 on day one. On day two, C sells the same debt to A2. A2 notifies on day three, and A1 notifies on day four. D performs to A2. D should be discharged.

A third possible variant may arise where the debtor receives notifications from two assignees almost simultaneously. In this case, rules that do not prejudice the debtor should be adopted. For example, the debtor should be entitled to hold back payment and seek advice from the original creditor in such circumstances. And the debtor should be able to act on the basis of the advice. The aggrieved assignee can raise an action against the original creditor for breach of warranty. It is suggested that this solution offers a better protection than a multiplepoinding action solution (or interpleader, as it is referred to in England) since a multiplepoinding action may involve more expense and resources on the part of the debtor. A multiplepoinding action may be used as a last resort where the original creditor is uncooperative.

The fourth variant may arise where an assignee who does not have title to the debt notifies the debtor, and the debtor performs in good faith. This may arise where, for example, the assignee was acting in good faith, or bad faith – for instance, where the assignee forged the assignation document. If the debtor performs in good faith to the purported assignee, a strong policy of debtor protection will require that the debtor be discharged. The debtor should not be expected to always inquire from the original creditor about the validity or authenticity of an assignation/assignment each time they receive a notification, as that may prejudice their position. Having to always enquire with the creditor will most likely increase costs on the part of the debtor.

The last variant is the *assignatus utitur jure auctoris* rule. This stipulates that the assignee cannot acquire a better right than that which the assignor had. According to Stair: "all [defences] competent against the cedent before the assignation or intimation …

68 SLC, *Discussion Paper on Moveable Transactions* (n 2) para 12.4.
69 E.g. assignments under arts 1322 and 1323 of the FCC.

are relevant against the assignee."[70] Such defences may include a right to set-off, the grant of deferrals, to rescind due to material breach, or a defence of non-performance. Hence, suppose "S contracts to sell goods to B, delivery to be made in one month's time. S then assigns the seller's rights to A but fails to deliver the goods. B can refuse to pay the price to A."[71]

For present purposes, it is sufficient to focus on the first variant (debtor notification) and the last variant (the *assignatus utitur jure auctoris* rule). This is because issues relating to these variants are more relevant to securitisations. For securitisations, the difficulty in view is how to protect the large numbers of debtors who may or may not be notified of the transfer. Issues around double selling (as in variants 2 and 3) or notification without title (as in variant 4) are rare from the debtors' viewpoints.

8.2.2.2 Debtor notification

In Scottish assignation, the function of debtor notification is not just to inform the debtor of the assignation. Notification also plays a constitutive function, so that the transfer only takes effect when the debtor is informed of the assignation.[72] This gives the debtor extra protection. It may then be said that the debtor will always be aware of the transfer and the issues around the first variant highlighted above will not arise. But intimation may be formally made, yet the debtor is unaware of the transfer and pays to the assignor in good faith. Dr Anderson cites an example of a postal intimation that is delivered to the debtor after the debtor has paid to the assignor.[73] He suggests that the debtor should be discharged if the payment is made in good faith.[74]

Regarding the English equitable assignment, the French *bordereau*, the registration solution and the Scottish trust, notification to the debtor is not required for the transfer to occur.[75] But notification is required for the debtor to be obliged to pay directly to the SPV.[76] This works well for securitisation, since parties to the transaction do not generally disturb the payment system between the originator and the debtors.[77] Moreover, parties typically take steps to strengthen the SPV's position through other means. For example, in transactions under English or Scots law, the originator would typically undertake to effect

70 Stair (n 9) III.i.20.
71 von Bar and others (n 10) 1075.
72 For discussion see section 5.3.2.1.
73 RG Anderson, *Assignation* (Edinburgh Legal Education Trust 2008) para 7.10.
74 ibid.
75 See discussions in chapters 5, 6 and 7.
76 See respectively Law of Property Act 1925, s 136(1); the French Monetary and Financial Code (MFC) (as amended by Order 2017), art L214-172; Moveable Transactions (Scotland) Act 2023, s 10; Gretton and Steven, *Property, Trusts and Succession* (n 1) para 23.61 (noting that the beneficiary, i.e. the SPV, only gets a personal right against the trustee, i.e. the originator).
77 Louise Gullifer and Jennifer Payne, *Corporate Finance Law: Principles and Policy* (3rd edn, Hart 2020) 483.

a legal assignment (or a valid assignation) to the SPV following the occurrence of a perfection event.[78] The perfection events would be defined in the receivables sale agreement.[79] This precautionary measure is used to mitigate the risks associated with the equitable interest granted under the English equitable assignment and the beneficial interest granted under the Scottish trust, which are both vulnerable to a subsequent legal title in the same receivable(s) acquired for value and without notice.[80]

The usefulness of such a precautionary measure is significantly reduced under French law. This is because: (i) the delivery of the *bordereau* transfers a first ranking title to the SPV, which is enforceable against all third parties (including the debtors); and (ii) the dedicated account mechanism reduces the risk that collections from the debtors will be commingled, which would represent a particular problem in the originator's insolvency.[81] However, notification to the debtors will still be needed if the management company of the securitisation entity wants the receivables to be paid to a party other than the originator.[82]

The need for the precautionary measure is also reduced under the registration system. This is because the SPV acquires absolute title once the assignation is registered. If the SPV wishes the debtors to pay directly to it or its nominee, the SPV will simply notify the debtors of the transfer and instruct them accordingly.

The nature of the title transferred by each alternative solution is discussed below. For present purposes, it is enough to know that parties generally avoid giving debtors notices unless necessary. Hence, the alternative solutions help to facilitate non-notification transfers while still protecting the interest of the debtors.

8.2.2.3 The *assignatus utitur jure auctoris* rule

This rule applies under the current Scottish assignation law.[83] This is true to the extent that the defence is connected to the contract from which the assigned receivable arises.[84] If the defence is a right of set-off, the debtor will be able to plead both connected and unconnected cross-claims they have against the assignor.[85]

---

78 See e.g. Cardiff Auto Receivables Securitisation 2011-1 PLC (Prospectus, 7 February 2011) 76 <https://www.ise.ie/debt_documents/Prospectus%20-%20Standalone_2ce37b2a-18b8-4add-a220-f1a66fa89056.PDF> accessed 28 May 2024.

79 These will normally include the occurrence of an insolvency event on the part of the originator and the occurrence of a rating event. See ibid 76 and 184.

80 See section 8.2.6.2 for discussion.

81 For discussion about the dedicated account mechanism see section 7.2.3.

82 The MFC, art L214-172.

83 See e.g. *Johnstone-Beattie v Dalziel* (1868) 6 M (CSIH) 333; *Scottish Widows Fund v Buist* (1877) 4 R (CSOH) 1076.

84 For discussion see Anderson, *Assignation* (n 73) paras 8.12ff.

85 ibid para 8.15.

A related issue is when a defence must arise for it to be valid against the assignee. Different rules apply to set-off defences and non-set-off defences. In relation to non-set-off defences, there is no time limit – that is, the defences will continue to be available to the debtor even if they arise after intimation to the debtor. Where the defence is a set-off right (whether connected or unconnected to the contract under which the assigned receivable arises), the debtor can only plead against the assignee those set-off rights that arise before intimation is effected.[86] In other words, the time limit in respect of which a set-off defence can be pled is when the assignation is completed. Hence, using another example from the Draft Common Frame of Reference (DCFR),[87] if:

> C, who is owed [£100,000] by O for the cost of building works, assigns the rights under the building contract to A, who gives notice of the assignment to O. Subsequently O lends C [£40,000] under a loan agreement which is unconnected with the building contract. O cannot set off the right for repayment of the loan against the liability to A.
> [But if the £40,000 debt arose before the notice was given, O will be able to set off and reduce the £100,000 they owed C to £60,000.]

The debtor is similarly protected under the English equitable assignment and the Scottish registration system.[88] This also seems to apply to the French *bordereau*.[89] In relation to the Scottish trust, the rule presupposes that an assignation has occurred, but no such assignation takes place with the Scottish trust since the transfer is not intimated to the debtors. Therefore, the rule does not arise in the first place and the debtors will continue to be able to set up defences (including set-off defences) against the originator (i.e. the truster).

The time limit seems to only apply to unconnected set-offs in the English equitable assignment and the French *bordereau*. In respect to connected set-offs and other defences, it seems that there is no time limit – the defences will continue to be available to the debtor even if they arise after notification to the debtor.[90]

---

86 See ibid para 8.53; SLC, *Report on Moveable Transactions* (n 10) para 12.31.

87 von Bar and others (n 10) 1076.

88 See e.g. Goode and Gullifer, *Legal Problems* (n 37) paras 7.72f – for the English equitable assignment. For the registration solution see Moveable Transactions (Scotland) Act 2023 (hereafter "Moveable Transactions Act"), s 14(1) and (3).

89 See the FCC, art 1324.

90 Goode and Gullifer, *Legal Problems* (n 37) para 7.73. See also the FCC, art 1324 (providing that "[t]he debtor can set up against the assignee exceptions inherent to the debt, such as nullity, exception of non-performance, resolution or set-off of related debts. He may also set up exceptions arising from his relationship with the assignor before the assignment became enforceable against him, such as … the set-off of unrelated debts"). The English translation is as used on Légifrance, 'Civil Code' <https://www.legifrance.

The position is different under the registration system. Here, defences other than set-off rights do not have a time limit.[91] In relation to set-off defences (whether related or unrelated), it is mentioned above that under the current law the time limit in respect of which a set-off defence can be pled is the time the assignation is completed. This would suggest that under the registration system the time limit would be when the assignation is registered, since registration would be one of the two ways of completing assignations. The SLC considers that debtors may be prejudiced by such an outcome since they may not know about the registered assignation – they cannot be expected to check the register. The SLC therefore suggests in its Report on Moveable Transactions and the accompanying Draft Bill a time limit that is tied to the time when the debtor becomes aware of the assignation – i.e. that only those set-off rights which are available against the assignor "up to the time when the debtor would no longer have been in good faith had the debtor performed to the assignor" can be pled.[92] However, the resulting Moveable Transactions Act does not expressly include the quoted phrase. Instead, it provides in section 14(3) that "a debtor is not to be treated as receiving notice of the assignation of a claim only because an assignation document is registered in respect of the claim".

The foregoing analysis implies that the debtor's position is improved under the English equitable assignment and the French *bordereau*. This is because there is no time limit under both systems as to when the defence of a connected set-off right against the assignor can be pled against the assignee.

Nevertheless, since the debtors are allowed to plead those set-off rights which are available against the assignor up to the time they have actual notice of the assignment, it can be said that the effect of the difference between the Scottish registration approach and the approach in the English equitable assignment and the French *bordereau* is not prejudicial to the debtors. Moreover, allowing the debtor to continue to set off post-notification transactions with the assignor will enable the assignor to reduce the value of the assigned claim to the detriment of the assignee.[93]

8.2.2.4 Concluding comments on the debtor protection policy

The foregoing discussions demonstrate that the debtors will not be worse off as a result of a change from the status quo to any of the alternative solutions.

---

gouv.fr/codes/section_lc/LEGITEXT000006070721/LEGISCTA000032032400/#LEGISCTA000032032400> accessed 28 May 2024.

91 Moveable Transactions Act, s 14(1).

92 SLC, *Report on Moveable Transactions* (n 10) para 12.31ff; Scottish Law Commission, *Report on Moveable Transactions: Draft Bill* (Scot Law Com No 249, 2017) s 14(1)(b) and (2).

93 See Goode and Gullifer, *Legal Problems* (n 37) para 7.73.

Table 8.1 Debtor protection

Transfer solution	Score
Scottish assignation	1
Scottish trust	1
The registration solution	1
English equitable assignment	1
French *bordereau*	1

8.2.3 *Policy two: third-party protection*

8.2.3.1 General

The true sale requirement of securitisation means that the receivables will need to be removed from the originator's patrimony and transferred to that of the SPV so that the assets will no longer be available to the originator in its dealings with potential creditors and assignees. Therefore, future creditors and assignees of the originator will be interested in knowing in whose patrimony the receivables really are. If such transactions cannot be verified externally, third parties will be exposed to a potential double selling by the assignor. If they decide to verify title, they will have to incur significant costs in making inquiries all around. Even with these inquiries, the future assignees and creditors will still face uncertainty and will be left with no other option than hope that the assignor truly has title. This policy is the rationale behind the publicity principle, which requires that rights that affect third parties should be visible to third parties.

8.2.3.2 Analysis

The Scottish assignation requires intimation to the debtor for it to be constituted. It may then be said that intimation makes the assignation visible since third parties can verify title by contacting the debtor. But intimation as a form of publicity has its limitations. First, the notification is only made to the debtor and not necessarily the public.[94] Secondly, the extent to which the debtor is obligated to cooperate with the enquiries of the creditor or assignee is unclear.[95] Lastly, since assignation can occur before actual notice to the debtor, the debtor's information may not be reliable. Hence, to borrow from the SLC, "intimation is a very weak form of publicity".[96] Moreover, where multiple debtors are involved, it will be impracticable for the creditor or assignee to approach each and every debtor for verification.

94 See above at footnote 10.

95 Anderson, *Assignation* (n 73) para 6.06.

96 SLC, *Report on Moveable Transactions* (n 10) para 5.3.

The English equitable assignment, the Scottish trust and the French *bordereau* are constituted by mere agreement between the originator and the SPV.[97] This means that there is no protection for the third parties under these regimes.

On the other hand, assignation under the registration system requires registration in the Register of Assignations for its constitution.[98] This affords the future creditors and assignees stronger protection than intimation since information in the Register of Assignations would be publicly accessible and more reliable.[99]

There is, however, one issue with the registration system. The Moveable Transactions (Scotland) Act 2023 (hereafter "the Moveable Transactions Act") adopts a "combined system" of intimation and registration so that either registration or intimation can be used to complete an assignation.[100] This approach is problematic for at least three reasons. First, since title can be completed by intimation, the information in the new Register of Assignations would not be definitive.[101] Suppose a claim has been assigned twice. The first assignation is granted to Hamish and completed by registration on 1 November. The second assignation is granted by Hamish to Becky and completed by intimation on 5 November. The Register of Assignations would only reveal Hamish's title. A consultation with the debtor would be required to ascertain Becky's title. The preceding sentence leads to the second reason. If the debtor has to be consulted, third parties would be subject to the limitations associated with intimation in terms of costs and reliability (see discussion above). Thirdly, the need to consult both the register and the debtor means that the third party may incur additional costs on title verification.

Furthermore, the existence of two parallel means of completing title increases the possibility that the register would display false title. Suppose A completed an assignation to B with intimation on day 1, and A subsequently completed another assignation of the same claim to C by registration on day 2. A third party looking at the register would think that C held the claim, when in fact they never did.

---

97 Although an intimation to one of the beneficiaries is required for the Scottish trust, that cannot be said to be publicity since the beneficiary in this case (i.e. the SPV) is a party to the transaction rather than a third party.

98 Moveable Transactions Act, s 3(2)(b). See also SLC, *Report on Moveable Transactions* (n 10) paras 5.1ff.

99 In terms of cost, the SLC suggests a £0 to £4 fee per search. See Scottish Law Commission, *Business and Regulatory Impact Assessment: Draft Moveable Transactions (Scotland) Bill 2017* (Scot Law Com No 249, 2017) 43.

100 Moveable Transactions Act, s 3(1) and (2)(b). See also SLC, *Report on Moveable Transactions* (n 10) paras 5.9ff.

101 In its 2017 Discussion Paper, the Secured Transactions Law Reform Project criticises the combined system approach based on this reason, and notes that the system "defeat[s] the purpose of the register". See Secured Transactions Law Reform Project, 'Discussion Paper Series: Sale of Receivables' (2017) s 3.D.iii. See also Jonathan Hardman, 'Three Steps Forward, Two Steps Back: A View from Corporate Security Practice of the Moveable Transactions (Scotland) Bill' (2018) 22 Edinburgh Law Review 266, 271.

The SLC argues that the intimation/registration system offers flexibility since it allows assignation parties to choose from the two options according to their preference.[102] The SLC also suggests that the concern about the non-reliability of the register is exaggerated since it is expected that registration would be the preferred option for transactions involving multiple receivables and future receivables. Registration would be "much simpler and cheaper than intimation" for multiple receivables, and intimation would not be an option for future receivables.[103] Thus, the SLC expects the register to be definitive in such transactions. Nevertheless, the Scottish ministers would have the power to specify certain types of claim that would require only registration for their transfer.[104]

The SLC's argument is persuasive, especially in relation to future receivables. However, the argument is not conclusive for assignations of present receivables where intimation remains an option. There is a possibility that the register would not be definitive for such assignations. This possibility alone (even if in theory) would create uncertainty from the third party's point of view. Certainty is of crucial importance in commercial transactions.

Furthermore, it is not entirely unlikely for parties to prefer intimation over registration in securitisations. Some securitisation transactions involve fewer receivables. An example is a collateralised loan obligation, which could consist of as few as 20 commercial loans.[105] In this case, using intimation may not be too onerous. There may even be circumstances where intimation would be preferable for such transactions. It may be that the securitisation parties would need to contact the debtors anyway. Suppose that the relevant loans or receivables are subject to anti-assignation clauses. In that case, parties would have to contact the debtors for their consents (i.e. to agree to a waiver) and may choose to formally intimate to the debtors in the process.[106] Registration would be unnecessary in such circumstances. The same logic may be applied to factoring,[107] where the factor (the

102 SLC, *Report on Moveable Transactions* (n 10) paras 5.6ff.

103 ibid para 5.19. For discussion of the transfer of future receivables see section 8.2.4.2.

104 Moveable Transactions Act, s 3(8). SLC, *Report on Moveable Transactions* (n 10) paras 5.20ff. The SLC's preference for the registration/intimation approach may have been informed by the fact that its proposed scheme would apply to all kinds of assignments of claims, including assignments involving a single claim, multiple claims, financing and non-financing purposes. See SLC, *Report on Moveable Transactions* (n 10) para 5.20. This contrasts with schemes that are only targeted at receivables financing structures (such as securitisation, factoring and invoice discounting). An example of such a scheme is the Secured Transactions Law Reform Project's (STLRP) proposed scheme. See STLRP, 'Discussion Paper Series: Sale of Receivables' (n 101) s 5.B. For discussion of the STLRP's proposed scheme see section 8.4.3.

105 Frank J Fabozzi and Vinod Kothari, *Introduction to Securitization* (John Wiley & Sons 2008) 213–217.

106 Anti-assignation clauses are valid in Scotland since the provisions of the Business Contract Terms (Assignment of Receivables) Regulations 2018 (SI 2018/1254) do not apply to contracts governed by Scots law. See section 5.3.3.2 for discussion.

107 A factoring is a type of receivables financing transaction which involves the sale of receivables to a financier (i.e. the factor or lender) by statutory assignment (or assignation in Scotland). It is a notification-based transaction where the factor, unlike the SPV in securitisations, acquires (legal) title and receives payments directly from the debtors. For discussion see Gullifer and Payne, *Corporate Finance Law* (n 77) 346.

assignee) would want to be paid directly from the debtors. That would require intimation to the debtors under the Moveable Transactions Act regardless of how the title is completed.[108] In a registration-only system, registration would be compulsory in these cases. The preceding analysis shows that the register may not be definitive even in cases where multiple debtors are involved. (For further discussion, see section 8.3.5.)

8.2.3.3 Concluding comments

The above discussion demonstrates that a change from the status quo to either the English equitable assignment, the Scottish trust or the French *bordereau* will make future creditors and assignees of the originator worse off. But a change to the registration solution will make them better off in the sense that registration would be an easier and more efficient option (than intimation) for title verification. However, this is subject to the limitation that the register may not be definitive in certain respects.

Table 8.2 Third-party protection

Transfer solution	Score
Scottish assignation	0.25[109]
Scottish trust	0
The registration solution	0.50[110]
English equitable assignment	0
French *bordereau*	0

8.2.4 Policy three: facilitation of future receivables transfers

8.2.4.1 General

This policy serves the interest of the securitisation parties. It requires that future receivables transfers should be facilitated. Future receivables are receivables that are yet to be contracted for, rather than receivables arising under an existing contract but payable in the future.[111] Here, the focus is on the contract itself and not just the receivables arising from the contract: the contract, and hence the debtor and the receivable/security right, do not exist at the time of the transfer. This poses particular difficulties for national laws.

---

108 This is based on the policy of debtor protection. See Moveable Transactions Act, s 10. See also the discussion at section 8.2.2.2.

109 This reflects the weaknesses associated with notification as a form of publicity.

110 This reflects the limitation of the "combined system".

111 John Deacon, *Global Securitisation and CDOs* (Wiley 2004) 524; Tom Burns, 'The Transfer of Future Rights in Securitisations: A Comparative Study of the Law in England and Scotland' (2009) 24 Journal of International Banking Law and Regulation 35, 37.

First, the absence of debtors will make assignment impracticable in jurisdictions, such as Scotland, where debtor intimation is a constitutive requirement. This is because there will be no debtor to intimate to. The SLC termed this the "nobody to whom to intimate" problem.[112] The second problem relates to specificity. Specificity is a principle of property law which requires that the object of a transfer (i.e. the receivables and the related security rights) should be properly defined.[113] Achieving specificity will be difficult in securitisations involving future receivables, since the receivables and the related security rights are unknown at the time of the transaction. This specificity problem is similar to what the SLC called the "you can't transfer what doesn't exist" problem.[114] Lastly, even if a legal system allows the transfer of future receivables, there is the question of what happens to the future receivables that come into existence after the commencement of the assignor's insolvency proceedings. The risk that the transfer will become ineffective and thus leave investors as unsecured creditors during the said insolvency, is probable. This will be called the "insolvency problem".

8.2.4.2 Analysis

a) The Scottish assignation

The main difficulty in Scots law is the "nobody to whom to intimate" problem. Intimation is a prerequisite for completing an assignation in Scotland. In other words, the debtor must be present or identifiable at the time of the transaction and must be intimated to for the assignation to be valid. The relevant issues here are discussed in section 5.3.2.1. The analysis in that section divides the problem into two situations: (i) where the prospective obligor is identifiable and in fact intimated; and (ii) where the prospective obligor is not identifiable and so no intimation is possible. For the latter situation, it is stated that an assignation is not possible. For the former, it is stated that the law is unclear on whether accretion will operate to make the transfer valid once the receivables arise.[115] In *Gallemos*, it was suggested that future receivables may be assignable if the receivables are "clearly defined".[116] Unfortunately, the court did not elaborate on that subject.[117]

---

112 SLC, *Discussion Paper on Moveable Transactions* (n 2) paras 14.60f.

113 See Gretton and Steven, *Property, Trusts and Succession* (n 1) paras 4.14ff.

114 SLC, *Discussion Paper on Moveable Transactions* (n 2) para 14.60.

115 To make the law certain, s 3(3) of the Moveable Transactions Act would disapply the rules of accretion in relation to the assignation of future rights. See also SLC, *Report on Moveable Transactions* (n 10) para 5.100.

116 *Gallemos Ltd (In Receivership) v Barratt Falkirk Ltd* 1989 SC (IH) 239, per Lord Dunpark at 242. Cf McAlpine (n 3) 284ff.

117 McAlpine (n 3) 284.

The insolvency problem presupposes that a future receivables transfer is possible, at least at the time of transaction. Therefore, the problem does not arise under Scottish assignation since future transfers are impossible under the assignation.

b) The English equitable assignment

Notification is not a constitutive requirement for the English equitable assignment. This means that the "nobody to whom to intimate" problem does not arise. In *Tailby*, the House of Lords held that an assignment of future rights is enforceable at equity "[w]hen the consideration has been given, and the debt has been clearly identified as one of those in respect of which it was given".[118] The second limb of that dictum speaks to the specificity principle.

The future debts purportedly assigned in *Tailby* were described as "all the book debts … which may during the continuance of this security become due and owing to the said mortgagor." The Court of Appeal held that the description was too wide and comprehensive, and therefore "too vague", for the assignment to have any effect.[119] The House of Lords rejected this argument, holding that all that is required is for the book debt (on its coming into existence) to "answer the description in the assignment, or, in other words, that it shall be capable of being identified as the thing, or as one of the very things assigned."[120] The House of Lords added that "[w]hen there is no uncertainty as to its identification, the beneficial interest will immediately vest in the assignee."[121]

The court clearly adopted a liberal approach in relation to the extent of specification required. First, there is no need to identify each debt individually, as that would have made the assignment of future receivables impracticable. Secondly, the description of the relevant class of future debts can be wide-ranging, provided that the debts arising in the future are identifiable with the class being assigned.

There is also the insolvency problem. In *Tailby*, it was held that the transfer of a future debt takes effect from the date the debt comes into existence (and not from the date of the assignment). The question is whether the transfer of future receivables that arise after the commencement of the assignor's insolvency would be effective.

At first glance, it would seem that section 127 of the Insolvency Act 1986 renders such transfer unenforceable. That section provides that any "disposition of a company's property"[122] made after the commencement of a winding-up by the court is void, unless

118 *Tailby v Official Receiver* (1888) 13 App Cas 523 (HL), per Lord Watson at 536.

119 (1886) 18 QBD 25, per Lord Esher MR at 29.

120 (1888) 13 App Cas 523, per Lord Watson at 533.

121 ibid.

122 "Property" is also defined in wide terms, and it includes "every description of interest". Insolvency Act 1986, s 436.

the court otherwise orders.[123] "Disposition" is used here in a wide sense and has been interpreted to include "any act which in reducing or extinguishing the company's rights in an asset, transfers value to another person".[124]

The foregoing provisions of the Act imply that the "disposition" must have occurred following a positive step or decision taken by the insolvent company (either by itself or through an agent) after the commencement of the winding-up.[125] In *Tailby*, it was held that the acquisition of the equitable interest arises "as soon as [the receivable] comes into existence", and the assignee will take title "as if it had actually belonged to him, or had been within his disposition and control at the time when the assignment was made".[126] In other words, no further step, decision or act is required from any party (including the insolvent company) for the transfer to occur. It is therefore submitted that section 127 does not engage the assignment of future receivables.[127]

There is also another issue in relation to section 127. The assignment of future receivables is only effective in equity. That is, the assignee only gets the beneficial interest, while the legal interest remains with the assignor. The assignment needs to be completed (either by notification, registration or delivery of possession) for the assignee to acquire legal title. It is important that the assignee is able to convert to a legal title during the assignor's insolvency. That helps to avoid the limitations associated with equitable title[128] and enables the assignee to receive payments directly from the debtors. The issue then is whether the conversion of the equitable assignment to a legal assignment amounts to a "disposition" under the meaning of section 127.

Again, it would seem on first impression that the conversion would engage section 127, since it has the effect of transferring the legal interest from the insolvent assignor to the assignee.[129] This issue was addressed by the Court of Appeal in *Gorringe*.[130] In that case, D assigned to C (by way of security) a debt owed to it by X. Notice was not given to X until

123 The winding-up is deemed to commence at the time of the presentation of the petition for the winding-up. Where the presentation of the petition was made after a resolution has been passed by the company for voluntary winding-up, the court winding-up is deemed to commence at the time of the passing of the resolution. If the winding-up order is made on hearing an administration application, the winding-up is deemed to commence on the making of the order. See generally Insolvency Act 1986, s 129.

124 *Akers v Samba Financial Group* [2017] UKSC 6, [2017] AC 424, per Lord Neuberger at [67].

125 See MacPherson, *The Floating Charge* (n 12) para 6.41 (noting that "disposition" entails that the company is "taking an active step (whether or not in fulfilment of an existing obligation) to transfer proper").

126 *Tailby v Official Receiver* (1888) 13 App Cas 523 (HL), per Lord Watson at 533. This is of course subject to the condition that the receivable is identifiable with the class being assigned.

127 See K van Zwieten (ed), *Goode on Principles of Corporate Insolvency Law* (5th edn, Sweet & Maxwell 2018) para 13.123 (noting that "the vesting of a company's property in a secured creditor or other party under an after-acquired property clause in the security or other instrument is outside s.127").

128 For discussion of these limitations see section 8.2.6.2.

129 This is all more so given that s 436 of the Insolvency Act 1986 defines "property" broadly to include "every description of interest".

130 *Gorringe v Irwell India Rubber and Gutta Percha Works* (1886) 34 Ch D 128 (CA).

after the commencement of D's winding-up. It was held that the notice did not engage section 153 of the Companies Act 1862 (the predecessor of section 522 of the Companies Act 1985, and subsequently section 127 of the Insolvency Act 1986).[131] The court reasoned that an assignment without notice is effective as between the assignor and the assignee. Notice is not necessary for the assignment to be valid against the assignor.[132] Hence, since the debt had been transferred before the winding-up commenced, it was not part of D's property for section 153 (i.e. section 127) to apply.

The foregoing implies that the critical point at which a disposition is deemed to occur for the purposes of section 127 under English law is when the insolvent company loses its equitable (or beneficial) interest in the property.[133] If the company had already lost its equitable interest in the property before commencement of winding-up, section 127 will not apply.[134]

A related issue is whether the completion of the equitable assignment falls within the moratorium under paragraph 43(2) of Schedule B1 to the Insolvency Act 1986. That paragraph provides that "no step may be taken to enforce security" over the property of a company in administration unless the administrator's consent or the court's permission is obtained. Will the SPV's notification of the debtors or completion of the transfer of the related securities amount to a "step to enforce security" under paragraph 43(2)?

It should be noted that assignments in securitisation transactions operate as absolute transfers rather than security.[135] Paragraph 43(2) only applies to security. Section 248 of the Insolvency Act defines "security" as "any mortgage, charge, lien or other security". It therefore follows that a mortgagee of receivables who notifies and demands payment from the debtors will engage paragraph 43(2).[136] It also follows that where the assignment is an outright legal assignment (as against a security or an equitable assignment), the assignee can validly demand payment directly from the debtor without engaging paragraph 43(2).[137]

---

131 ibid 133 per Cotton LJ and 135 per Bowen LJ.

132 ibid at 132 and 135. See also *Holt v Heatherfield Trust Limited & Anor* [1942] 2 KB 1, per Atkinson J at 5 (noting that notice is only required for the protection of the debtor or subsequent assignees).

133 See *Re French's Wine Bar Ltd* (1987) 3 BCC 173 (Ch), per Vinelott J at 177 (noting that where a contract entered into before the commencement of the winding-up process was unconditional and enforceable, the completion of the contract after the commencement of the winding-up process did not amount to a disposition under s 522 of the Companies Act 1985 (the predecessor of s 127 of the Insolvency Act)).

134 See Goode and van Zwieten, *Corporate Insolvency Law* (n 127) para 13.121 (noting that "[s]ection 127 bites on beneficial ownership, not necessarily on legal title"); Andrew R Keay, *McPherson & Keay's Law of Company Liquidation* (5th edn, Sweet & Maxwell 2021) para 7.015. These texts are cited with approval in *Akers v Samba Financial Group* [2017] UKSC 6, [2017] AC 424, at [67] per Lord Neuberger.

135 See discussion in section 2.1.2.

136 See Goode and van Zwieten, *Corporate Insolvency Law* (n 127) para 11.62 (suggesting that such demands amount to "taking steps to enforce").

137 Legal assignments transfer absolute ownership rights to the assignee. See Law of Property Act 1925, s 136(1). See also Goode and van Zwieten, *Corporate Insolvency Law* (n 12) para 11.62.

What is not entirely clear is whether an equitable assignment, which is the focus here, can be conceived as creating a mere charge (since it does not transfer legal title) for paragraph 43(2) to apply. The dominant view is that an equitable assignment operates as an outright transfer of rights, at least as between the assignee and the assignor.[138] It was held in *Holt* that notice is only necessary to make the assignment binding against the debtor and subsequent assignees.[139] Hence, an equitable assignment also operates as an outright transfer of rights against unsecured creditors.[140] It is therefore submitted that an outright equitable assignment (as commonly used in a securitisation transaction) does not come within the provisions of paragraph 43(2) so that an outright equitable assignee can validly notify the debtor and demand to be paid directly without engaging paragraph 43(2).

Moreover, Professors Goode and van Zwieten note that the term "security" in the context of paragraph 43 "is used in its strict sense to denote a mortgage, pledge or consensual or non-consensual charge, lien or other right of detention or retention, and nothing beyond these".[141] Also, Totty, Moss and Segal, while explaining the meaning of the term "security" under paragraph 43(2), note that "a security is a right which is subject to an equity of redemption, or to release on payment if it can be characterised as a lien or 'quasi lien'".[142] An outright equitable assignment as used in a securitisation cannot be said to come under any of these definitions and so does not engage paragraph 43(2). The originator does not have any equity of redemption or a right to release on payment over the securitised assets. The securitisation transaction is structured to operate as a true sale rather than secured lending.[143]

c) The Scottish trust

In the Scottish trust, intimation to the debtor is not required for the trust to be effective. All that is required is for one beneficiary (i.e. the SPV) to be notified.[144] Therefore, the "nobody to whom to intimate" problem does not arise. The Inner House in *Tay Valley* held that a regular intimation to the beneficiary of the list of new assets that arises from time to

138 See e.g., *Gorringe v Irwell India Rubber and Gutta Percha Works* (1886) 34 Ch D 128 (CA), per Cotton LJ at 132 and per Bowen LJ at 135; *Holt v Heatherfield Trust Limited & Anor* [1942] 2 KB 1, per Atkinson J at 5. Cf J Edelman and S Elliot, 'Two Conceptions of Equitable Assignment' (2015) 131 Law Quarterly Review 228; Peter Walton, 'Assignments of Book Debts – Outright Transfers of Rights or Unregistered Securities?' (2018) 1 Wolverhampton Law Journal 1.

139 *Holt v Heatherfield Trust Limited & Anor* [1942] 2 KB 1.

140 It was held in *Holt* that a judgment creditor stands in the same position as the assignor in relation to the effectiveness of an equitable assignment. *Holt*, per Atkinson J at 5.

141 Goode and van Zwieten, *Corporate Insolvency Law* (n 12) para 11.60. See also the general definition of security under s 248 of the Insolvency Act 1986 (which is likewise restrictive).

142 P Totty, GS Moss and N Segal, *Insolvency* (Sweet & Maxwell 2021) C2.07.

143 See section 2.1.2.

144 *Allan's Trustees v Inland Revenue Commissioners* 1971 SLT (HL) 62.

time is sufficient to transfer those assets to the trust patrimony.[145] The regular intimation of new assets to the beneficiary indicates the relevance of the specificity principle in trust transactions. In *Cameron's Trustees*, Lord Kyllachy, while describing the requisite act needed for the valid delivery of trust property, notes that the act has to be "some overt extraneous and ostensible act [which] marks definitely the character of the trustee's possession".[146] That may suggest that the trust property will have to be individually described. It is not entirely clear whether a description by reference to an identifiable class would be valid in this regard.[147]

Regarding the insolvency problem, the position with the Scottish trust is different from that of the English equitable assignment. This is because the disposition of the future trust property does not occur automatically under the Scottish trust. As discussed above, the truster must undertake further acts of delivery for it to be divested.[148] In *Tay Valley*, a regular intimation to the beneficiary of the list of new assets that arise from time to time was held to be a sufficient act of delivery for the truster to be divested.[149] It therefore seems that such further acts of delivery would constitute a disposal under section 127 of the Insolvency Act, so that any transfer of the beneficial interests of future receivables arising after commencement of the winding-up would be void.

The crucial element in the previous paragraph (i.e. in relation to the declaration of trust over future receivables) is that the final step required for the transfer to occur has to be carried out by the company itself (as the truster). But consider a different transaction where the company had done all that was required of it before the commencement of the winding-up, and the transferee carried out the final step required to complete the transfer after the commencement of winding-up. This issue may arise in a conveyancing transaction where the first two stages of the transaction (i.e. the missives and the delivery of the transfer deed) require the active participation of the transferor and the last stage (i.e. registration in the Land Register) can be completed by the transferee alone. Professor McKenzie Skene states that the critical time in this case is the time at which the "disposition" within the meaning of section 127 is deemed to occur.[150] In English law, such critical time is the time the beneficial interest transfers to the transferee (see above discussion). But this is unlikely the case in Scots law, given the unititular nature of Scots property law[151] and the rejection of the beneficial interest concept in *Burnett's Tr v Grainger*.[152] Dr Alisdair

145 *Tay Valley Joinery Ltd v CF Financial Services Ltd* 1987 SLT (CSIH) 207, per Lord Dunpark at 216.

146 *Cameron's Trustees v Cameron* (1907) 14 SLT (CSIH) 720 at 724.

147 See discussion in section 5.3.3.2.

148 *Clark Taylor & Co Ltd v Quality Site Development (Edinburgh) Ltd* 1981 SC (IH) 111, per Lord President Emslie at 118.

149 *Tay Valley Joinery Ltd v CF Financial Services Ltd* 1987 SLT (CSIH) 207, per Lord Dunpark at 216.

150 Donna W McKenzie Skene, *Insolvency Law in Scotland* (2nd edn, Tottel 2007) 175.

151 That is, there is no division between equitable title and legal title under Scots property law.

152 [2004] UKHL 8, 2004 SC 19.

MacPherson suggests that there is not a "disposition" if the company has already completed all that is required of it in relation to the transfer, even if the transferee needs to carry out a step to complete the transfer.[153] He notes that there would be no race to the register if registration by the transferee was considered a disposal. This argument is forceful. However, the position is not entirely clear, especially because, under Scots law, property transfers generally occur when the transferor and the transferee have completed all the necessary formalities.[154]

Nevertheless, the focus here is the transfer of future receivables through the Scottish trust. As concluded above, the subsequent supplemental trust over receivables arising after the commencement of winding-up will likely constitute a "disposition" under section 127.

The other issue is whether the subsequent supplemental trust engages the moratorium under paragraph 43(2) of Schedule B1 to the Insolvency Act 1986. Section 248(ii) of the Insolvency Act 1986 defines "security" in relation to Scotland as "any security (whether heritable or moveable), any floating charge and any right of lien or preference and any right of retention (other than a right of compensation or set off)". Again, as discussed above for the equitable assignment, the Scottish trust as used in a securitisation does not operate as a security and so does not engage paragraph 43(2).

d) The registration solution

Under the registration solution, transfers would be completed through registration rather than intimation. Hence, the "nobody to whom to intimate" problem would not arise. And since the debtor's information is not required for the purposes of the registration,[155] the "nobody to register" problem does not arise either. This clears the way for the assignability of future receivables under the registration system.[156] Under the Moveable Transactions Act, the transfer of a future receivable would become effective when the receivable comes into existence and is held by the assignor.[157] In respect of the specificity principle, the Act adopts a liberal approach that allows identification to be made by reference to an identifiable class of receivables.[158]

---

153 Using the conveyancing transaction, this would be the stage where the seller delivers the transfer deed to the buyer. See MacPherson, *The Floating Charge* (n 12) para 6.41.

154 See e.g. *Gibson v Hunter Home Designs Limited* 1976 SC (CSIH) 23, where Lord Emslie made the following statement at page 27 in relation to heritable property "[o]n delivery of the disposition the purchaser becomes vested in a personal right … and his acquisition of a real right … is dependent upon recording the disposition in the appropriate Register of Sasines.

155 SLC, *Report on Moveable Transactions* (n 10) para 5.93.

156 ibid paras 5.93ff.

157 Moveable Transactions Act, s 3(1) and (2). See also SLC, *Report on Moveable Transactions* (n 10) paras 5.97 and 7.27.

158 Moveable Transactions Act, s 1(3). See also SLC, *Report on Moveable Transactions* (n 10) paras 4.25ff.

Regarding the insolvency problem, the SLC considered the DCFR approach in its report.[159] The DCFR provides that the transfer of a future right takes effect at the time of the act of assignment rather than the time the right comes into existence.[160] In other words, if the act of assignment of a future receivable is concluded on 1 January and the receivable comes into existence on 15 January, the assignment will be deemed to have taken place on 1 January. This would effectively protect assignments of future rights from the effects of the assignor's insolvency, provided that the assignment agreement has been concluded prior to the insolvency. The DCFR notes that the policy reason behind its approach is that the assignee "will very often have paid for the rights" and so "should be preferred to the creditors of the assignor".[161]

The SLC, however, considered the DCFR approach to be "unsatisfactory".[162] According to the SLC, the approach "seems to involve re-writing the past".[163] The SLC instead came up with a different approach that is subsequently adopted under the Moveable Transactions Act. As a general rule, the Act provides that the assignation of future claims that arise after the assignor's insolvency would be ineffective.[164] This also indicates that the transfer would occur when the claims come into existence (that is, on 15 January in the example above).[165]

The Moveable Transactions Act also provides for a special rule for transfers involving a claim in respect of income from property in so far as that claim:

i. is not attributable to anything agreed to by, or done by, the assignor after the assignor became insolvent; and
ii. relates to the use of property in existence at the time the assignor became insolvent.[166]

For this category of claims, the transfer would continue to be effective even if the "claims arise" after the assignor's insolvency.

The extent to which the special rule would be commercially helpful in the present context is unclear. The special rule excludes all claims attributable to any agreement or act done by the assignor after the insolvency. In other words, the special rule would not apply to receivables created by the assignor after the assignor becomes insolvent. As noted above, there is a difference between a claim that is yet to come into existence and one in

159 SLC, *Report on Moveable Transactions* (n 10) paras 5.105ff.
160 von Bar and others (n 10) s III.–5:114(2). This is an exception to the general rule. The general rule is that transfers take effect from the date the rights come into existence – ibid s III.–5:114(1).
161 The Commentary to the DCFR, s III.–5:114(2) at 1071.
162 SLC, *Discussion Paper on Moveable Transactions* (n 2) para 14.65. See also SLC, *Report on Moveable Transactions* (n 10) para 5.105.
163 SLC, *Report on Moveable Transactions* (n 10) para 5.105.
164 Moveable Transactions Act, s 4(2).
165 ibid s 3(1) and (2).
166 ibid s 4(3).

existence but payable in the future. The focus here is on the former – that is, the effect of insolvency on receivables created after the commencement of the assignor's insolvency. The value of the DCFR approach is that it allows the transfer of the claims created after insolvency to remain effective. This is achieved because the transfer is deemed to have occurred before the insolvency occurred.

The two examples cited in the explanatory note to section 4(3) of the Moveable Transactions Act do not address the difficulty of envisaging how the special rule would be helpful in practice. The examples appear to relate to claims that are created before the insolvency. If the claims were created after the assignor's insolvency (that is, if the use of the licence was granted after the insolvency or the rent was increased by the assignor, or a new tenancy was agreed to by the assignor, after the insolvency), the claims would most likely fall into the insolvency estate since they would not meet the first limb of the above conditions required for the special rule to apply.

e) The French bordereau

Under the French *bordereau*, the debtor's notification is not required for the assignment to be valid.[167] Therefore, the "nobody to whom to intimate" problem does not arise, and future receivables are assignable under the French *bordereau*. In respect of the specificity problem, the French MFC allows the receivables to be described generically.[168] The insolvency problem also does not arise in the French *bordereau*. The MFC provides that the acquisition or assignment of receivables takes effect between the parties, and becomes enforceable against third parties, on the date affixed on the transfer document, "regardless of the date of birth, or due date of the [receivables], without the need for any other formality".[169] In other words, the transfer of the future receivables becomes effective not from the date the receivables come into existence but from the date of the assignment, provided that the receivables are identifiable with those to which the assignment relates.[170] Ordinarily, this should be enough to protect the future receivables from the insolvency problem. The transfer is backdated to the date of the transaction and, thus, protected from the effects of the proceedings under the French insolvency law. The MFC, however, expressly exempts such transfers from the effects of the insolvency proceedings under Book VI of the Commercial Code.[171] This statutory backing provides certainty in respect of transfers under the French *bordereau* being insolvency proof.

167 The MFC, art L 214-169-V(1).
168 The MFC, art D214-227(4).
169 The MFC, art L214-169-V(2). The English translation is as used on Légifrance.
170 This approach is similar to that of the DCFR, see von Bar and others (n 10) s III.–5:114. The FCC recently adopted the same approach under art 1323.
171 The MFC, art L214-169-V(4).

8.2.4.3 Concluding comments

The foregoing discussion shows that a change from the status quo to any of the alternative states of affair will make the securitisation parties better off. This is because the transfer of future receivables, which is otherwise impossible under the Scots assignation law, is possible under all the alternative solutions.

Table 8.3 Facilitation of future receivables

Transfer solution	Score
Scottish assignation	0
Scottish trust	0.50[172]
The registration solution	0.75[173]
English equitable assignment	1
French *bordereau*	1

8.2.5 Policy four: facilitation of non-publicity transfer

8.2.5.1 General

This policy aims to keep the cost of transfer low. Hence, it serves the interest of the originator. The policy requires that the transfer of receivables and the security rights in a securitisation should be completed without publicity (i.e. registration, transfer of possession or notification).

8.2.5.2 Analysis

Intimation is a constitutive requirement under the current Scottish assignation law. It was noted in chapter 5 that the three formal methods of intimation[174] are the only legally safe ways of carrying out intimation.[175] The postal method is the least onerous of the three methods since it does not involve a notary.[176] It involves the delivery of a certified copy of the assignation to the debtor by post and requires a written acknowledgement of receipt to be obtained from the obligor.[177] Sending a certified copy of the assignation to every debtor through the post will be costly for securitisations involving multiple debtors. Also, obtaining the acknowledgements may be burdensome and require chasing up the debtors

172 This reflects the additional formality of regular intimation of newly created receivables to the beneficiary and the likelihood that such formality will engage s 127 of the Insolvency Act 1986.

173 This reflects the limitation of the special rule.

174 That is, the common law notarial method, the 1862 Act notarial method and the 1862 Act postal method.

175 See section 5.3.2.1.

176 See Anderson, *Assignation* (n 73) paras 6.23 and 6.35.

177 GJ Bell, *Principles of the Law of Scotland* (10th edn, T&T Clark 1899) para 1464.

and recording the acknowledgements received. Furthermore, as shown above, intimation makes future receivables securitisation impracticable.

The French *bordereau*, the English equitable assignment and the Scottish trust do not require any form of publicity for their creation.[178] However, the position is different for the registration solution, where registration would be a constitutive requirement for assignations.[179] Two issues are normally associated with registration. The first is cost. Registration means that the originator will necessarily incur additional transaction costs. Hence, the cost of registration would be crucial.[180] It is expected that the Scottish registration system will be easy and less expensive compared with intimation.[181] This is especially so given that the registration would be completed directly online, with minimum human involvement by registry staff.[182] Furthermore, registering a single transfer document online should be easier than having to post multiple copies of the certified assignation to each debtor.

The Scottish ministers would fix the registration fees.[183] The registration system is expected to be self-financing so that the cost would not be passed on to taxpayers.[184] The SLC believes that a fee range of £10 to £60 would be enough to recoup within three years the initial cost of setting up the system.[185] It is unclear if the suggested fee is intended to be flat rate or *ad valorem*. It is equally unclear how the fee will work in terms of a single transfer document containing multiple claims – whether it would apply for each individual claim or for the whole assignation. Currently, a flat-rate fee structure is adopted to register the assignation of standard securities (i.e. £60 for an electronic-based registration and £80 for a paper-based registration), and the rate applies to each title deed affected.[186]

Adopting a similar approach for the Register of Assignations (i.e. applying the fee to each individual claim) will be costly for securitisation, given the multiple claims typically involved in such transactions. Such an approach will also not be suitable for securitisations

---

178 As noted earlier, the Scottish trust requirement for intimation to the beneficiary cannot be said to be publicity since the beneficiary (i.e. the SPV) is a party in the transaction.

179 See the Moveable Transactions Act, s 3(2)(b)(ii). See also SLC, *Report on Moveable Transactions* (n 10) para 5.22.

180 The registration cost includes the hard cost (i.e. the registration fee) and the soft cost (i.e. the staff time required to complete registration).

181 The SLC notes that the "[r]egistration … should be easy and inexpensive". SLC, *Report on Moveable Transactions* (n 10) para 5.10.

182 ibid paras 6.33ff.

183 The Scottish ministers are required to do this in consultation with the Keeper of Scottish Registers. Land Registration etc. (Scotland) Act 2012, s 110. See also SLC, *Business and Regulatory Impact Assessment* (n 99) 42.

184 The SLC notes that Registers of Scotland estimated the cost of setting up the two new registers (i.e. the Register of Assignations and the Register of Statutory Pledges) to be between £500,000 and £1 million. See SLC, *Report on Moveable Transactions* (n 10) para 6.11.

185 SLC, *Business and Regulatory Impact Assessment* (n 99) 42 and 43.

186 Registers of Scotland (Fees) Amendment Order 2021 (SSI 2021/139), art 2(5).

that involve future receivables since the contracts from which the receivables will arise are non-existent at the time of registration and would be described generically in the assignation document. A more likely approach intended by the SLC would be for the suggested fee to be a flat-rate fee and apply to the assignation document registered rather than each claim. This approach is used in comparator systems like New Zealand, where registration fees are flat rates and are attributed to the financing document.[187]

The second issue associated with registration is confidentiality. The originator may wish to keep the sales confidential for genuine commercial reasons. For example, the originator may fear that publicising the transfer may send incorrect signals to its customers and creditors that it is facing financial difficulties. These issues are, however, trivial in relation to securitisations. First, securitisations are already subject to strict transparency and publicity requirements under current laws.[188] So, if the registration system is in any way a confidentiality problem, it would not create a greater problem than already exists. Secondly, unlike intimation, which involves direct notice to customers, registration requires a search in the relevant register for it to be visible. Few customers conduct such searches before dealing with businesses.[189] Moreover, creditors are more concerned about the overall financial capacity of the debtor and not whether the debtor engages in receivables finance. The SLC notes that the Asset Based Finance Association (ABFA) "viewed the desire for confidentiality as not being strong".[190]

---

187 In New Zealand, a one-off fee of NZ$16.10 (i.e. around £8.5) is charged for registering any financing statement on the Personal Property Securities Register. See New Zealand Companies Office, 'Personal Property Securities Register: Schedule of Fees' <https://ppsr.companiesoffice.govt.nz/help-centre/paying-ppsr-fees/schedule-of-fees/> accessed 24 May 2024.

188 E.g. originators in the EU are obligated to make detailed information of securitisations (including asset level information) available by means of a securitisation repository or a specified website (where a securitisation repository is not available), which will "provide direct and immediate access free of charge" to investors and relevant authorities. See Council Regulation (EU) 2017/2402 of 12 December 2017 laying down a general framework for securitisation and creating a specific framework for simple, transparent and standardised securitisation, and amending Directives 2009/65/EC, 2009/138/EC and 2011/61/EU and Regulations (EC) No 1060/2009 and (EU) No 648/2012 [2017] OJ L347/35, arts 7 and 17. This transparency requirement is retained in the UK under arts 14–23 of the Securitisation Regulations 2024 (SI 2024/102). Also, originators or issuers are required to publicise a prospectus relating to securities they intend to offer to the public or trade in a regulated market. See Financial Services and Markets Act 2000, s 85(1) and (2). See also art 3 of Council Directive 2003/71/EC of 4 November 2003 on the prospectus to be published when securities are offered to the public or admitted to trading and amending Directive 2001/34/EC [2003] OJ L345/64.

189 See STLRP, 'Discussion Paper Series: Sale of Receivables' (n 101) s 3.D.ii.

190 SLC, *Report on Moveable Transactions* (n 10) para 5.13. The ABFA formerly represented the receivables finance and asset-based lending industry in the UK. It has now been integrated into a new association called UK Finance.

8.2.5.3 Concluding comments

The foregoing shows that a change from the status quo to the English equitable assignment, the Scottish trust or the French *bordereau* will make the originator better off. This is because the costs associated with publicity are avoided under any of the alternative solutions mentioned above. In respect of the registration solution, while some costs would be incurred for registration, it is expected that registration costs would be much cheaper and easier than intimation. Therefore, a change from the status quo to the registration solution would make the originator better off.

Table 8.4 Facilitation of non-publicity transfer

Transfer solution	Score
Scottish assignation	0
Scottish trust	1
The registration solution	0.75[191]
English equitable assignment	1
French *bordereau*	1

8.2.6 *Policy five: validity of transfer*

8.2.6.1 General

This policy primarily serves the interests of the SPV and the investors. The policy also serves the interest of the originator since any risk accompanying the transfer will be reflected in the cost of funding. This policy will be measured based on the validity of the transfer against (i) subsequent assignments and (ii) the assignor's/originator's insolvency.

8.2.6.2 Analysis

A valid transfer completed under the Scottish assignation confers absolute title to the assignee.[192] This means that the transfer is valid against subsequent assignments and also against the assignor in insolvency.[193]

a) Validity against subsequent assignments

The registration solution and the French *bordereau* also confer absolute title on the assignee, which is enforceable against all third parties.[194] The fact that transfers under both

191 This reflects the registration costs that would be incurred, which is expected to be cheaper and easier than intimation costs. See section 8.3.4 for more discussion on registration fees.

192 Reid, *The Law of Property* (n 6) para 656.

193 ibid.

194 Moveable Transactions Act, s 3(1) and (2)(b)(ii); the MFC, art L214-169-V(2).

systems have not been notified to the debtors does not affect their third-party effect. This is because notification is not a priority point in both systems.[195] Notification is only required if the assignee wants the debtor to pay directly to them.[196] Hence, the function of notification in both systems is to protect the debtor who pays to the assignor in good faith.[197]

The position is different in respect of the English equitable assignment and the Scottish trust. In these systems, notification does not just serve to protect the debtor, it is also a priority point.[198] To borrow the words of the Scottish Law Commission, "[t]he first assignee to intimate prevails".[199] Therefore, the interest of an equitable assignee or a beneficiary of the Scottish trust can be defeated by a subsequent legal title that is acquired for value and without notice of the equitable or beneficial interest.[200]

b) Validity against the originator's insolvency

As noted in section 8.2.2 above, the unnotified debtor is protected under the four alternative states of affairs, so that the debtor will be able to discharge by paying the assignor until they are notified of the transfer. This usually does not pose any problem in securitisation since payments are normally made to the originator. But issues may arise where the originator becomes subject to insolvency proceedings. The French *bordereau* is protected from the effects of insolvency.[201] Therefore, the management company of the SPV will be able to validly instruct the debtors to pay directly to it or to any other nominee even during the originator's insolvency.

---

195 In both systems, priority is determined by date of completion of title. For the French *bordereau*, title is completed (or transferred) from the date affixed on the transfer document once the document is delivered to the assignee. See the MFC, art L214-169-V(2). The date of completion for the registration solution would be the date of registration. See Moveable Transactions Act, s 3(1) and (2). See also SLC, *Report on Moveable Transactions* (n 10) paras 5.67ff.

196 The MFC, art L214-172. For the Scottish registration solution, see Moveable Transactions Act, ss 10 and 11; SLC, *Report on Moveable Transactions* (n 10) paras 12.1ff.

197 See SLC, *Report on Moveable Transactions* (n 10) paras 12.1ff. Although the purpose of notification is not explicitly stated to be debtor protection under the MFC, art L214-172, it can be inferred from the provision.

198 *Dearle v Hall* (1828) 3 Russ 1 (Ch), for the English equitable assignment. For Scottish assignation see A McDouall, Lord Bankton, *An Institute of the Law of Scotland in Civil Rights: With Observations upon the Agreement or Diversity between them and the Laws of England* (1751–53, reprinted by Stair Society, vols 41–42, 1993–95) III, i, 6.

199 SLC, *Report on Moveable Transactions* (n 10) para 5.26.

200 See *Dearle v Hall* (1828) 3 Russ 1 (Ch), for the English equitable assignment. For the Scottish trust, see Scottish Law Commission, *Discussion Paper on the Nature and the Constitution of Trusts* (DP 133, 2006) para 2.9. Note, however, that a subsequent assignee who acquires trust property in bad faith may get a good title in certain circumstances. See Trusts (Scotland) Act 1961, s 2(1).

201 Art L 214-169(v-4) of the MFC exempts assignments completed through the French *bordereau* from the effects of the stay of enforcement proceedings under Book VI of the French Commercial Code.

In relation to the registration solution, a similar outcome for registered assignations seems to apply.[202] The registration solution's approach appears to be based on the distinction between title completion (which would be achieved through registration) and debtor protection (which would be achieved through notification).[203] So that where title has been completed through registration, the registered assignation would be protected from the originator's insolvency proceedings. The SPV will, therefore, be able to notify the debtors during the originator's insolvency validly.

However, the case is different in relation to the English equitable assignment, where notification not only serves to protect the debtor but also determines the priority of competing interests.[204] In other words, notification has the effect of transferring (legal) title from the insolvent assignor to the assignee.[205] But, as discussed above, such notification would not amount to "disposition" under section 127 of the Insolvency Act 1986 and the assignment does not constitute a security within the meaning of paragraph 43(2) of Schedule B1 to the Insolvency Act. Hence, an equitable assignment is protected from the effects of the moratorium regimes.

In relation to the Scottish trust, while the sale of Scottish receivables in a securitisation is given effect by a declaration of trust, the receivables sale agreement would typically contain words of assignation.[206] But the completion of the assignation (i.e. notification of debtors) will be deferred until some specified perfection events occur.[207] Therefore, the title to the receivables remains with the originator/truster while the SPV gets a beneficial interest by virtue of the trust.[208] A subsequent intimation of the assignation to the debtor has the effect of transferring title from the originator/truster-trustee to the SPV/beneficiary.

202 SLC, *Report on Moveable Transactions* (n 10) paras 5.27f.

203 ibid.

204 This is based on the rule in *Dearle v Hall* (1828) 3 Russ 1 (Ch), which provides that where there are competing assignments of a claim, the assignee who notifies first will prevail, provided that the assignee takes the assignment with value and without notice of the other assignment.

205 See Law of Property Act 1925, s 136(1). See also *Bexhill UK Ltd v Abdul Razzaq* [2012] EWCA Civ 1376, [2012] 10 WLUK 745, per Aikens LJ at [34].

206 See e.g. Towd Point Mortgage Funding 2020 – AUBURN 14 PLC (Prospectus, February 2020) 115f <https://www.chlmortgages.co.uk/wp-content/uploads/2020/03/Auburn-14-Black-Prospectus-dated-13-February-2020.pdf> accessed 24 January 2024.

207 ibid. See also 'Cardiff Auto Receivables Securitisation 2011-1 PLC (Prospectus)' (n 78) 68f and 76.

208 The beneficiary's right is a personal right against the trustee. Gretton and Steven, *Property, Trusts and Succession* (n 1) para 23.61. But the right can be analogous to a real right in some respects. For instance, the right will prevail over the claims of the trustee's personal creditors in the event of the trustee's insolvency. See *Heritable Reversionary Co v Millar* (1892) 19 R (HL), per Lord Watson at 49f. This insolvency effect of the beneficiary's right has been explained in terms of the dual patrimony theory. See GL Gretton, 'Trust and Patrimony' in HL MacQueen (ed), *Scots Law into the 21st Century: Essays in Honour of W. A. Wilson* (W Green 1996); GL Gretton, 'Trusts Without Equity' (2000) 49 International and Comparative Law Quarterly 599; KGC Reid, 'Patrimony Not Equity: The Trust in Scotland' in Remus Valsan (ed), *Trusts and Patrimonies* (Edinburgh University Press 2017).

As noted above, the time at which "disposition" under section 127 is deemed to occur under Scots law is not entirely clear. Dr Alisdair MacPherson suggests that the "disposition" is deemed to involve an active step taken by the company, so that there is no disposition if another party carries out a step to complete the transfer once the transaction is out of the company's hands (i.e. it has already completed everything it needs to do to transfer the property).[209] If this approach is taken, the question will then be whether the assignee can give notification. Under general Scots property law, transfer transactions typically go out of the transferor's hands when the transferor delivers the executed transfer deed. After that, the transferee will be able to independently carry out the final steps necessary to transfer property (e.g. registration for conveyancing or intimation for assignation). Based on the foregoing, it seems that notification by the SPV will not constitute "disposition" under section 127.

In relation to the moratorium under paragraph 43(2), it is noted in section 8.2.4.2(c) above that assignation as used in securitisation does not constitute a security and hence does not engage the paragraph. In any case, as noted above in section 5.1.2.1.c, trust property falls outside the insolvency process of the trustee's private estate.

8.2.6.3 Concluding comment

The foregoing discussions show that a change from the status quo to the French *bordereau* or the registration solution will not make any party worse off. However, a change from the status quo to the English equitable assignment or the Scottish trust will make the investors (and, in turn, the originator) worse off. This is because transfers effected by the English equitable title and the Scottish trust can be defeated by a subsequent statutory assignment or a completed assignation taken with value and without notice of the equitable assignment or the trust.

Table 8.5 Validity of transfer

Transfer solution	Score
Scottish assignation	1
Scottish trust	0.50
The registration solution	1
English equitable assignment	0.50
French *bordereau*	1

209 MacPherson, *The Floating Charge* (n 12) para 6.41.

8.2.7 *Policy six: the accessorium principle*

8.2.7.1 General

The *accessorium* principle states that when a principal right (e.g. the right to receive payment of a debt) is transferred, any related accessory rights (e.g. a security right) automatically go with it.[210] In other words, the transfer of the accessory right does not need to be either (i) expressed or referred to in the transfer document, or (ii) publicised.[211] This policy particularly serves the originator's interest: the easier it is to transfer the security rights, the cheaper the transaction. It is also beneficial to the SPV and the investors, who will have greater certainty with respect to the rights transferred.

8.2.7.2 Analysis

In relation to the Scottish assignation, the prevalence of the publicity principle in Scots property law means that the rule will most often be excluded.[212] For example, the assignation of a standard security will need to be expressly stated and duly registered for the assignation to be valid.[213]

The position on the application of the rule to the French *bordereau* is unambiguous. The French Monetary and Financial Code provides that upon delivery of the transfer document to the assignee, all securities attached to each of the receivables described in the transfer document will automatically pass to the assignee without any formalities.[214] In other words, the provision achieves the first and the second limbs of the rule as identified above. However, the position on the application of the principle is not clear in relation to the English equitable assignment, the Scottish trust, and the Scottish registration solution.

The difficulty in likening the transfer arising from the English equitable assignment to that of the *accessorium* principle is that the transfer in the latter arises by operation of law and does not need to be referred to in the transfer document. So, where the debt is assigned without a mention of the related security, does the security automatically pass to the assignee? This question is discussed in section 6.1.2, where it is concluded that the law is inconclusive. In any case, whether or not the rule applies is of little practical effect since the English equitable assignment achieves the second limb of the rule (i.e. publicity of the transfer is not required). This is achieved based on the principle that equity considers as done that which ought to be done.[215] So, suppose the originator who has received a

210 See e.g. AJM Steven, 'Accessoriness and Security over Land' (2009) 13 Edinburgh Law Review 387, 403.

211 See e.g. *Edinburgh Entertainments Ltd v Stevenson* 1926 SC (IH) 363, per Lord Anderson at [386]; Anderson, *Assignation* (n 73) paras 2.01ff.

212 The floating charge seems to be the only instance where the rule applies. For discussion see section 5.2.2.

213 Conveyancing and Feudal Reform (Scotland) Act 1970, s 14(1). For discussion of the application of the rule in Scots security laws see section 5.2.2.

214 The MFC, art L214-169-V(3).

215 *Walsh v Lonsdale* (1882) 9 Ch D 9 (CA); *Tebb v Hodge* (1869) LR 5 CP 73 (Ex Ch).

payment from the SPV signs an agreement with the SPV to transfer the relevant security rights. In that case, equity treats the SPV as the owner of the security rights from the moment the agreement is signed.[216] Moreover, the transfer of security rights in most securitisations is dealt with expressly. Hence, the formality of referring to the relevant security rights in the transfer document is not a burden for parties.

Regarding the Scottish trust, the truster-as-trustee structure does not necessarily involve an assignation of title since the truster who also acts as the trustee already has title to the trust property. As discussed above, the assets meant for the trust purpose are required to be specifically described for the trust to be constituted.[217] That suggests that the first limb of the *accessorium* principle does not apply to the Scottish trust. The second limb also does not apply since the truster needs to intimate to the beneficiary for the truster-as-trustee trust to be constituted.[218] Nevertheless, the non-application of the *accessorium* principle to the Scottish trust is of little practical effect since references are typically made to the related securities in securitisation transactions and intimating to the SPV would not be a burden to parties.

The position in relation to the registration solution is discussed in section 5.3.2.2. Section 16(2) of the Moveable Transactions Act provides that the *accessorium* principle applies as a default rule,[219] even where the claim and the related security right are subject to conflicting transfer rules.[220] But section 16(2) would be subject to section 16(3) of the Act. Section 16(3) excludes the application of the *accessorium* principle where the claim and the related security are subject to conflicting transfer rules.[221] So, to take the standard security as an example, the assignor would have to comply with the additional formality of assigning the standard security in accordance with section 14 of the Conveyancing and Feudal Reform (Scotland) Act 1970 "as soon as reasonably practicable" for the assignation to be effective.[222] This additional formality will be prohibitively costly in a securitisation transaction.[223] Hence, section 16(3) could make the registration system less helpful.

216 See also *Lysaght v Edwards* (1876) 2 Ch D 499 (Ch), per Jessel MR at 506 (on the effect of a valid contract of sale).

217 *Cameron's Trustees v Cameron* (1907) 14 SLT (CSIH) 720, per Lord Kyllachy at 724; *Clark Taylor & Co Ltd v Quality Site Development (Edinburgh) Ltd* 1981 SC (IH) 111, per Lord President Emslie at 118.

218 *Allan's Trustees v Inland Revenue Commissioners* 1971 SLT (HL) 62.

219 The two exceptions to the default rule are where the security is not restricted to the assigned claim and where the claim is partially assigned. In both exceptions, the security right would remain with the assignor unless parties expressly agree otherwise. Moveable Transactions Act, s 16(1) and (2).

220 This is contrary to the current law, which excludes the application of the rule where the claim and the related security right are subject to conflicting transfer rules. For discussion see SLC, *Report on Moveable Transactions* (n 10) paras 13.26ff.

221 See Moveable Transactions Act, s 16(3).

222 See the notes accompanying s 16(3) of the Act.

223 This is all more so considering that the current law is not clear on the issue of whether multiple standard securities can be assigned in a single assignation document. The SLC in its ongoing consultation proposes

The SLC seems to cite the need to maintain the "publicity value" of the land register as the policy behind section 16(3). According to the SLC:

> It would be possible to go further, and provide that an assignation of the secured claim automatically gives to the assignee a completed title to the security. This is perhaps the most logical solution. But it would be a radical reform and would affect the law of standard securities. It would reduce the "publicity" value of registration as the register would not state the holder of the standard security.[224]

Based on the above quotation, it may seem that section 16(3) would only apply to standard securities. But that is not the case.[225] Also, the SLC's policy appears to overstate the value of publicity in the context of assignation of security rights. Third parties are more concerned with whether a security exists over the property of the person being searched against than with who the holder of the security right is.[226] Interestingly, the SLC validates the proposition in the last sentence for the assignation of the statutory pledge that will be introduced under the Moveable Transactions Act and suggests that the assignation would be valid without registration.[227] According to the SLC, "[t]he third party can ascertain whether there has been an assignation by contacting the party named as the secured creditor."[228] The SLC also notes that the registered secured creditor should be under a duty to provide information about the holder of the pledge when requested by certain third parties.[229] Unfortunately, the SLC did not go further than the quotation above on the reason why a similar approach should not apply to other security rights.[230]

---

that it should be made clear that the same deed can assign multiple standard securities. See Scottish Law Commission, *Discussion Paper on Heritable Securities: Pre-Default* (DP 168, 2019) paras 10.36ff.

224 SLC, *Report on Moveable Transactions* (n 10) para 13.28.

225 The SLC indicates that the section would also apply to possessory pledges. SLC, *Report on Moveable Transactions* (n 10) para 13.32. In respect of the transfer of an assignation in security, it is unclear whether intimation to the obligor will be required. For discussion see section 5.2.2.5.

226 See e.g. Anderson, *Assignation* (n 73) para 2.14.

227 See SLC, *Report on Moveable Transactions* (n 10) para 23.45.

228 ibid.

229 SLC, *Report on Moveable Transactions* (n 10) paras 35.3ff. This has been legislated for in s 107(1)(b) of the Moveable Transactions Act.

230 In terms of the standard security, s 16(3) may have been informed by the policy agenda on transparency of ownership and use of land in Scotland. See Scottish Land Rights and Responsibilities Statement (2017) principle 5. But this is not clear, as the SLC's Report does not make any reference to the Statement nor any related document. Moreover, this would not have explained why the section has a general application. The SLC has revisited this matter in its ongoing heritable securities project and has re-consulted on the applicability of the *accessorium* principle to standard securities. See SLC, *Discussion Paper on Heritable Securities* (n 223) paras 10.23ff.

8.2.7.3 Concluding comment

The foregoing discussions on the *accessorium* principle show that a change from the status quo to the French *bordereau*, the English equitable assignment or the Scottish trust will make the originator better off. However, a change from the status quo to the registration solution would make the originator better off only in terms of securities that would be excluded from the effect of section 16(3) of the Moveable Transactions Act.

Table 8.6 The *accessorium* principle

Transfer solution	Score
Scottish assignation	0
Scottish trust	1
The registration solution	0.50[231]
English equitable assignment	1
French *bordereau*	1

8.2.8 *Efficiency analysis*

This section compares the extent to which the alternative states of affairs achieve a Pareto improvement outcome or Kaldor-Hicks efficient outcome. This is done by measuring each state of affairs against the six policy goals. Four policy goals are identified for the securitisation parties: (i) facilitation of future receivables securitisation; (ii) facilitation of non-publication transfer; (iii) validity of transfer; and (iv) the application of the *accessorium* principle. One policy goal is identified for the debtors, i.e. debtor protection. The policy goal identified for the prospective creditors and assignees is third-party protection. The result of the comparison has been summarised in figures in Table 8.7 below.

231 This reflects the fact that the registration solution would make the rule a default rule in relation to the statutory pledge (which is expected to have a significant impact on securitisations in Scotland in relation to security rights over moveable assets) and other security rights that do not require additional formality for their transfer to be valid (e.g. the floating charge). But the score also reflects the limitations of the registration solution in that the default rule would not apply to other security rights that require additional formality for their transfer to be valid (like the standard security, the possessory pledge and, probably, the assignation in security).

Table 8.7 Efficiency Analysis

	Scottish Assignation (Status Quo)	Scottish Trust	Registration Solution	English Equitable Assignment	French *Bordereau*
Securitisation Parties	1	3	3	3.5	4
Debtors	1	1	1	1	1
Originator's Prospective Creditors/Assignees	0.25	0	0.50	0	0

It can be seen from Table 8.7 that a change from the status quo to the Scottish trust will make the securitisation parties better off without making the debtors worse off. However, such a change will make the prospective creditors and assignees worse off. A change from the status quo to the English equitable assignment or the French *bordereau* also produces a similar outcome: the securitisation parties will be better off, the debtors will not be worse off, but the prospective creditors and assignees will be worse off.

However, a change from the status quo to the registration solution will make the securitisation parties and the prospective creditors and assignees better off without making the debtors worse off. Therefore, the improvement caused by the registration solution is the closest to a Pareto improvement. This makes the registration solution the most efficient solution, based on the Pareto criterion.

The analysis above and the figures in Table 8.7 also suggest that the registration solution is not Pareto optimal. A solution is said to be Pareto optimal (or Pareto efficient) if no further improvements can be made without making at least one party worse off. But it seems that the registration solution could still accommodate a further Pareto improvement. This is discussed in section 8.3.

The French *bordereau* produces an interesting outcome. Though it does not achieve a Pareto improvement outcome, it achieves the best outcome for the securitisation parties. In other words, although a change to the solution will make the prospective creditors and assignees worse off, the change will make the securitisation parties best off. Hence, its outcome is the closest to a Kaldor-Hicks efficient outcome.[232] It would be considered Kaldor-Hicks efficient if it generated cost reductions for the securitisation parties that exceeded the cost increases it caused to the future assignees and creditors. Unfortunately, this will be difficult to measure since the calculation requires empirical data, which requires further research beyond the scope of this book. But given that future creditors and assignees may be able to mitigate their costs by charging higher interest rates (in the

232 The registration solution achieves a Pareto improvement change rather than a Kaldor-Hicks improvement change, hence it is not considered in this context.

case of creditors) or buying at a discount (in the case of assignees), it seems very likely that the French *bordereau* achieves a Kaldor-Hicks efficient outcome.

8.3 A case for a model solution

8.3.1 *Initial comments*

A model solution that achieves a Pareto optimal outcome can be conceived from the discussion above. The registration solution achieves a Pareto improvement outcome but could be made better to achieve a Pareto optimal outcome. The model solution builds on the strength of the registration solution and will attempt to improve on some of its weaknesses as identified above. These weaknesses are those relating to (i) the application of the *accessorium* principle and (ii) the validity of the transfer of future receivables during the assignor's insolvency. The third issue that will be addressed is that of registration cost. Registration cost is crucial to the attainment of efficiency and, therefore, deserves a closer analysis. Lastly, a case will be made for a registration-only system to apply to securitisations. These issues are discussed in turn below.

8.3.2 *The accessorium principle revisited*

Suppose that the registration solution applied the *accessorium* principle to all security rights. The position of the securitisation parties would be enhanced since the relevant security rights would be transferable at no cost. The present research submits that the affected third parties (i.e. the debtor and the originator's future creditors and assignees) would also not be made worse off by such an outcome. In relation to the debtor, the outcome does not disturb the two debtor protection requirements[233] discussed in sections 8.2.2.2 and 8.2.2.3 above.

It may be argued that the outcome would make the future creditors and assignees worse off on two grounds: (i) the outcome would make the transfer of security rights invisible to third parties; and (ii) it would undermine the reliability of the Land Register. But these arguments can be refuted.

Regarding (i), if the security automatically passes with the debt, then the registration of the debt should suffice as publicity for the security right. A third party that finds that a debt has been assigned can safely conclude that the accompanying security right has passed with the debt. This also addresses related arguments about legal certainty. The

233 That is, the ability of the debtors to keep paying to the originator and the application of the *assignatus utitur jure auctoris* rule.

certainty of the date of the debt transfer[234] means that the date of the security transfer is certain. In addition, since the date would be externally verifiable (i.e. through the new Register of Assignations), issues relating to fraudulent antedating would not arise. The foregoing may be criticised on the basis that the Register of Assignations would not be definitive on the transfer of the security right since parties can disapply the default rule by agreement.[235] So a searcher of the register may still need to enquire from the originator as to whether the default rule was disapplied or not. One way to address this would be to make such disapplication visible in the Register of Assignations simply by way of a tick box.[236]

Applying the *accessorium* principle generally may potentially make the future creditors and assignees better off for two reasons. First, it would eliminate any doubt arising from the interaction of section 16(2) and (3) of the Moveable Transactions Act as to whether the rule applies to a particular security or not (see discussion above at sections 5.3.2.2 and 8.2.7.2). This, in turn, ensures that there is no split between the debt and the security[237] and, therefore, avoids the problems that may arise from such a split.[238] Secondly, where the security automatically passes with the debt, the future creditor or assignee would only need to search a single register (i.e. the Register of Assignations) to confirm the holder of the debt and the security right, rather than conducting an additional search for the security right.

Regarding (ii) – that the *accessorium* principle would undermine the reliability of the Land Register – it is noted above that third parties are more concerned with whether a security exists than with who the holder of the security is. Also, the position of the future assignees and creditors can be strengthened by adopting a solution that mirrors the secured creditor's duty to provide information in respect of the statutory pledge.[239] That is, the registered secured creditor (or the originator) who has transferred a security right by virtue of the default rule will have a duty to provide the details of the assignee (or any subsequent assignee if known) to the future assignees and creditors upon request. The registered secured creditor will also have the option to register the assignation of the security right if they consider registration most convenient.

234 Section 3(2) of the Moveable Transactions Act regulates when transfer occurs.

235 See s 16(1)(b) Moveable Transactions Act.

236 In any case, it is expected that parties would apply the rule in a securitisation transaction in order to achieve a true sale. This is because leaving out the security rights from the transfer may warrant having recourse to the originator in the future in the event of defaults.

237 Dr Anderson calls this the "unity principle", which requires the debt and the security to be held by the same person. See Anderson, *Assignation* (n 73) para 2.11.

238 One such problem arises where an assignor fraudulently assigns the same debt twice; one assignee intimates first to complete the debt transfer, while the other registers or takes possession first to complete the related security transfer. See Anderson, *Assignation* (n 73) paras 2.11f.

239 See Moveable Transactions Act, s 107(1)(b). See also SLC, *Report on Moveable Transactions* (n 10) paras 35.2ff.

Moreover, the information in the Land Register is currently not conclusive. For example, the presence of a standard security in the register does not guarantee that a debt exists.[240] It may be that the debtor has been fully discharged of the debt but has not recorded the discharge in the Land Register.[241] A registered standard security without a debt is worthless.[242] Even section 16(3) has the potential to throw the register into a further state of inconclusiveness. Section 16(3) provides that the assignation of relevant security rights must be completed "as soon as reasonably practicable". That appears to create an uncertain "invisibility period" within which the transfer of the standard security may either be deemed to have occurred without registration or be delayed until registration. This would effectively make the information in the register unreliable during the "invisibility period". This also means that the prospective creditors/assignees cannot rely on the information in the register and will need to make further inquiries to ascertain the true holder of the relevant security right.

8.3.3 *Effect of the assignor's insolvency on assignments of future receivables*

It was noted in section 8.2.4.2 above that the approach adopted under the Moveable Transactions Act on this subject is unsatisfactory, and that it is not clear how the special rule would be commercially helpful for securitisations. This contrasts with the DCFR approach and the French *bordereau*, which protect assignments of future receivables from the effects of the assignor's insolvency. The Moveable Transactions Act's approach does not achieve this.

The SLC's difficulty in adopting the DCFR approach seems to be that the approach deems the assignment to take place before the claim arises (which, according to the SLC, involves "re-writing the past").[243] While the SLC's difficulty is understandable,[244] it seems overstated. The SLC could have given more weight to the policy behind the DCFR approach, which is that "the assignee, who will very often have paid for the rights, should be preferred to the creditors of the assignor." This policy seems fair and would make the

240 Anderson, *Assignation* (n 73) para 2.14.
241 See Conveyancing and Feudal Reform (Scotland) Act 1970, s 17.
242 Roderick RM Paisley, *Land Law* (Green 2000) para 11.24. The fact that the standard security is unenforceable without a debt makes the argument for the general application of the *accessorium* principle more forceful.
243 SLC, *Report on Moveable Transactions* (n 10) para 5.105.
244 Section 3(2)(a) of the Moveable Transactions Act provides that the assignation would be effective from the date the assignor becomes the holder of the claim and not the date the assignation is registered. And if such effective date falls within the period of the assignor's insolvency, the assignment would be subject to the insolvency proceedings.

law more attractive to financiers than one that renders the assignment ineffective during insolvency. Moreover, property rights with deeming effects are recognised in Scots law.[245]

Also, for the special rule to be commercially valuable, it is necessary that transfers of future claims which the assignor acquires after the assignor's insolvency are protected from the effects of the insolvency. This can be achieved not necessarily through the DCFR's "deeming" approach but also through the French approach, where assignments of future receivables are statutorily exempt from the effects of insolvency proceedings.[246]

One last point should be made in respect of the unsecured creditors of the originators. It is contended in section 8.2.1 that the transfer of receivables and the related security rights in a securitisation does not negatively affect the originator's unsecured creditors. That argument may not be forceful if the transfer is protected from the originator's insolvency. Granting such preference to the SPV may significantly reduce the assets available for the unsecured creditors during the originator's insolvency. If that is true, then such a change will not be Pareto efficient.

The author's view is that the argument made in section 8.2.1 sufficiently addresses this concern. The assignment exchanges illiquid assets with cash and transfers the credit risks associated with the assets to the SPV's investors. This helps to keep the originator further away from insolvency, which in turn benefits the unsecured creditors. Moreover, the unsecured creditors may not be better off in a world where assignments are not insolvency proof. This is because assignees/investors will be unwilling to buy future receivables in such a world.[247] Not only will that increase the credit and liquidity risks of the originator, it will also impede the originator's access to funds which would have been used to acquire assets that could increase the originator's value during its insolvency.

In any case, even if it is possible that unsecured creditors will lose out, the change would be a significant Kaldor-Hicks improvement.

8.3.4 *Registration costs*

It is crucial that the total cost of registering a transfer document under the registration solution is as low as possible. This includes both the hard cost (i.e. the registration fee) and

245 For example, s 14 of the Conveyancing and Feudal Reform (Scotland) Act 1970 deems an assigned standard security to have been granted to the assignee from the date the security was created and not from the date the assignation is registered. On the effect of such deemed right in relation to an all-sums standard security see GL Gretton, 'Assignation of All Sums Standard Securities' [1994] Scots Law Times (News) 207; RG Anderson, 'Assignations of All Sums Securities' in Frankie McCarthy, James Chalmers and Stephen Bogle (eds), *Essays in Conveyancing and Property Law in Honour of Professor Robert Rennie* (Open Book Publishers 2015) 73, 89.

246 See the MFC, art L214-169-V(4).

247 Where they accept to buy, the receivables will be significantly priced down in order to account for the insolvency risk.

the soft cost (i.e. staff time and expertise required). The SLC recommends a wholly electronic-based registration system.[248] Electronic registrations are generally considered to be easier, quicker and cheaper compared to paper-based registrations.[249] Therefore, it is expected that the cost of the Scottish registration system would be reduced. The SLC's suggestion of £10 to £60 is modest, provided it would be a flat-rate fee and would be attributed to the transfer document and not individual claims. Yet the responsibility of fixing the fees ultimately falls on the Scottish ministers, and it is uncertain what the cost might be. The proposed model solution would adopt a flat-rate fee that has an upper limit of £60. The fee would also be attributed to the transfer document rather than each receivable being transferred.

8.3.5 Registration-only approach for securitisations

It is noted in section 8.2.3.2 that the combined system of registration and intimation would make the register inconclusive for assignations of present receivables. This creates uncertainty and possibly more costs for third parties. A preferable option would be to make registration compulsory for assignations involving securitisations. In other words, the combined system would continue to apply in other assignations, while registration would be the sole option for completing title for securitisations. One way of achieving this is to apply a registration-only approach to bulk assignations intended for financing purposes, such as securitisations, factoring and invoice discounting. Alternatively, the registration-only approach could be applied solely to securitisations. This would make the new Register of Assignations definitive for securitisations and remove the uncertainty.

The registration-only approach is also necessary for other features of the model solution to work effectively. For example, the argument in section 8.3.2 above on the *accessorium* principle depends on the existence of a definitive registration system. If the publicity of security rights transfers is to be tied to that of the related debts in the Register of Assignations, it is essential that the register is definitive.

Applying two sets of rules for assignations (e.g. the combined system and the registration-only system) is not a new concept. It has worked in other jurisdictions, notably in the United States of America (US). Under the US's Uniform Commercial Code (UCC), registration is required for an assignment of receivables to achieve priority over third parties.[250] However, assignments that do not "transfer a significant part of the

248 SLC, *Report on Moveable Transactions* (n 10) paras 6.33ff.

249 See e.g. UNCITRAL Guide on the Implementation of a Security Rights Registry (2013) paras 83ff; STLRP, 'Discussion Paper Series: Sale of Receivables' (n 101) ss 3.A–3.B.

250 Registration is only required for priority purposes under the UCC system (compare with the registration solution, which requires registration (or intimation) for both constitutive and priority purposes). Intimation

assignor's outstanding accounts or payment intangibles" are exempt from registration.[251] In other words, two sets of rules exist: registration only for large-scale assignments and no registration for low-scale assignments. The Secured Transactions Law Reform Project also adopts a two-rule approach (see discussion at section 8.4.3).

Therefore, the rules for the model solution would be: (i) a registration-only system, which would apply to securitisations (or, more broadly, bulk assignations intended for financing purposes); and (ii) the combined-system approach, which would apply to other assignations.

8.3.6 *Concluding comments*

Therefore, the features of the model solution are outlined below.

i. Debtor protection – the model solution would guarantee the protection of the debtors by: (a) allowing debtors to continue to pay to the person last known to them to be the holder of the claim, and (b) applying the *assignatus utitur jure auctoris* rule.

ii. Third-party protection – registration would be the sole constitutive requirement for assignations in securitisation transactions. This would make title verification easier, cheaper and more reliable for third parties.[252] They would be able to consult an online public register that would provide conclusive information for securitisations.

iii. Facilitation of transfers of future receivables – since title would be completed by registration and the particulars of the debtor would not be required for registration, the "nobody to whom to intimate" problem would not arise under the model solution. Also, since the receivables can be described generically, the "you can't transfer what doesn't exist" problem would not arise. In terms of the insolvency effect, the model solution excludes the transfer of future receivables from the effects of insolvency proceedings, so that the transfer would continue to be effective even if the receivables arise after the assignor's insolvency.

iv. Facilitation of non-publicity transfer – while the model solution would require registration to complete title, the model guarantees that the cost of registration is low and attractive for the originator (i.e. a fee range of £10 to £60, which would be a flat-rate fee and would apply to the transfer document as a whole).

---

or notification is not an alternative option under the UCC system. See arts 9-202 and 9-310(a) of the Uniform Commercial Code.

251 Uniform Commercial Code of the USA, art 9-309(2).

252 The SLC predicts a £0 to £4 fee per search. See SLC, *Business and Regulatory Impact Assessment* (n 99) 43.

v. Validity of transfer – the model solution would confer absolute title to the assignee (i.e. the SPV) upon registration, which would be enforceable against all third parties, including the assignor in insolvency.

vi. The *accessorium* principle – the model solution would apply the relevant rule to all security rights.

8.4 Transferability of the model solution

8.4.1 *Initial comments*

This section considers the extent to which the model solution, which builds from the Scottish registration solution, can be transplanted to English law and French law.[253]

There are two reasons why a legal transplant may not be difficult to achieve in this case, with reference specifically to legal coherence matters. First, the focus regimes are already familiar with a registration system, particularly in relation to their security laws.[254] For example, under current English law, registration in the Register of Charges is necessary to make a security granted by a company fully effective.[255] In 2005, the Law Commission recommended that the securities registration scheme should be extended to assignments of receivables, so that registration should serve as a priority point and a perfection requirement for assignments of receivables.[256] The calls for bringing assignments of receivables within a registration system have persisted ever since.[257] Under French law, a similar registration scheme is used for moveable securities,[258] and the special pledges over business, registered vehicles and intellectual property rights.[259]

Secondly, the Scottish legal system is sufficiently related to the English and French legal systems to justify a legal transplant between the systems. Scots law is a mixed legal system containing civil law and common law components.[260] The Scottish civil law heritage

253 For discussion of the concept of legal transplant see section 4.3.

254 See section 8.1.3.2.

255 Companies Act 2006, ss 859A and 859H. See also section 8.1 hereof.

256 Law Commission (n 52) paras 4.18 and 4.25, although this aspect of the Law Commission's recommendation was not implemented.

257 See e.g. City of London Law Society, *Discussion Paper: Secured Transactions Reform* (2012) paras 7.25f <https://www.citysolicitors.org.uk/storage/2013/09/20121120-Secured-Transactions-Reform-discussion-paper.pdf>; STLRP, 'Discussion Paper Series: Sale of Receivables' (n 52) ss 3 and 4.

258 Arts 2337 and 2338 FCC. Regarding incorporeal moveables, see art 2355 FCC, which indicates in its last paragraph that the pledge over incorporeal moveables (excluding receivables) is subject to the same publicity rules applicable to the pledge over corporeal moveables.

259 See chapter 7 at sections 7.2.2.1 and 7.2.2.2.

260 HL MacQueen, 'Scots Law' in JM Smits (ed), *Elgar Encyclopedia of Comparative Law* (2nd edn, Edward Elgar 2012) 789.

was facilitated by the early connection Scotland had with France. This dated to 1295 when both kingdoms (as they then were) formed the "Auld (Old) Alliance", which was built to address England's invasion threats.[261] Though initially a military alliance, the Auld Alliance later extended into other spheres of the Scottish and French systems, including legal education. Before Scottish universities were founded in the fifteenth century, many Scotsmen received a legal education in French universities and brought knowledge of Roman law to Scotland.[262] The influence of Roman law continued over the following centuries. The effect of this is particularly apparent in the highly influential work of James Dalrymple, Viscount Stair, whose *Institutions of the Law of Scotland* – first published in 1681 and still regarded as the foundation of modern Scots law – relies substantially on Roman law sources.[263] The connection with France has also resulted in legal borrowings.[264] It has been suggested, for example, that the formality of intimation may have been inspired by the practice of *signification* in French law.[265]

Scotland equally shares a long history with England. This, indeed, is expected, given that the two nations share a land border. But the influence of English law only became strong in the later part of the eighteenth century, after the ratification of the Treaty of Union in 1707, by which the two kingdoms were united.[266] This led to the English common law having a rising influence over Scots law.[267] The influence was apparent in the Scottish institutional works that were published (after the Union) by David Hume (on criminal law, first published in 1797) and George Joseph Bell (on mercantile law, first published in 1800), in which English precedents and sources were extensively referred to.[268] The Union subsequently brought the Scottish legal system into closer contact with the English legal system. However, it must be noted that the Treaty preserved the Scottish court system and

261 William Gordon, 'Scotland and France. The Legal Connection' in *Roman Law, Scots Law and Legal History: Selected Essays* (Edinburgh University Press 2007) 299.

262 David Baird Smith, 'Roman Law' in *An Introductory Survey of the Sources and Literature of Scots Law*, vol 1 (Stair Society 1936) 171, 176. See also TB Smith, 'The Influence of the "Auld Alliance" with France on the Law of Scotland' in *Studies Critical and Comparative* (Green 1962) 28ff.

263 See Alan Watson, *Legal Transplants: An Approach to Comparative Law* (2nd edn, University of Georgia Press 1993) 48.

264 See e.g. Gordon (n 261) 304f.

265 See discussion in Anderson, *Assignation* (n 73) paras 5.30ff.

266 This was mainly due to strained relationships and long years of warfare which took place before and after the Union until the mid- to late eighteenth century. For discussion see e.g. TB Smith, 'English Influences on the Law of Scotland' (1954) 3 The American Journal of Comparative Law 522, 523ff.

267 ibid 525ff (discussing the influence English law had on Scots law after the Treaty of Union, both directly, through the acts of the newly formed UK parliament and the judgments of the House of Lords in Scottish appeals, and indirectly, through the citation of English precedents in Scottish courts, the citation of English law literature and the use of common language).

268 William Gordon, 'Scotland as a Mixed Jurisdiction' in *Roman Law, Scots Law and Legal History: Selected Essays* (Edinburgh University Press 2007) 343, 349.

Scots private law (and, by implication, its civilian heritage).[269] This laid the foundation for the continuance of Scots law as a legal system separate from the English legal system. Yet there are instances where English law has influenced aspects of Scots private law. Notable examples include the reception of an adapted form of the English floating charge in Scotland and the influence the English trust had on the development of the Scottish trust.[270]

The above discussion of Scottish legal history is extremely brief and selective. Much more could be written on the subject, but that is beyond the scope of the present work. The purpose here has been to show that the Scottish legal system is sufficiently related to the English and French legal systems to enable a legal transplant.

Some may question the practicability of a transplant from Scotland to England and/or France for at least two reasons. First, law reform in the area of secured transactions is itself difficult to achieve. For example, the Law Commission of England and Wales recommended a reform that assignments of receivables should be registrable, but this was not implemented.[271] In France, the rules governing assignments under the old article 1690 of the Civil Code were unchanged from 1804 until 2016, even though the rules were generally considered unsuitable for modern commerce.[272] The difficulty is also demonstrated in Scotland by the fact that it took more than 150 years to present a generally acceptable reform of the Scottish assignation law (that is, the registration solution) despite the widespread dissatisfaction with the current law.[273]

One reason for the difficulty is that while the law of secured transactions exists in the commercial domain, it is conceptually property law. Any proposed reform will generally need to be coherent with the local property law for it to be acceptable.[274] Professor Michael Bridge notes the following about a wholesale transplant of the US secured transactions law model:

> [a] free-standing version of Article 9 cannot be transplanted into another legal system without considerable thought being given to all features of the legal

---

269 A notable consequence of the preservation of Scots private law is that the law/equity duality that exists in English law does not exist in Scots law.

270 See respectively MacPherson, *The Floating Charge* (n 12) para 10.07 and Gretton, 'Trusts without Equity' (n 208) 620.

271 Law Commission (n 52) paras 4.18 and 4.25.

272 See discussion at sections 7.1.1 and 7.2.1.

273 The last substantial reform occurred in 1862, through the Transmission of Moveable Property (Scotland) Act 1862. The SLC appreciates this difficulty and had to take a conservative approach in its reform proposals to gain the support of stakeholders. See SLC, *Report on Moveable Transactions* (n 10) paras 18.50ff.

274 See e.g. Hamish Patrick and AJM Steven, 'Moveable transactions law reform coming in Scotland?' (2018) Butterworths Journal of International Banking and Financial Law 71, 72.

terrain, especially the property law of the receiving jurisdiction, into which it is being transplanted.[275]

The above statement is also true of the transplant of the model solution to England and France. Sections 8.4.3 and 8.4.4 discuss some of the practical difficulties that may arise and suggest ways to deal with the difficulties to make the model solution more easily receivable in England and France.

The second ground on which the practicability of a transplant from Scotland to England and/or France may be questioned is that it seems unlikely that English and French law and lawyers will agree to emulate a solution from a much smaller jurisdiction like Scotland with a low volume of securitisation transactions. However, the author believes this challenge is limited since both English and French laws are already familiar with a registration system in their secured transaction laws.[276] Moreover, a reform similar to the model solution is currently being proposed in England by the Secured Transactions Law Reform Project and the City of London Law Society.[277] In addition, it is possible (at least to some extent) to view the solution and its appealing features on their own merits, without focusing specifically on its Scottish origins.

The subsequent discussion considers the difficulties that may arise and suggests ways to deal with the difficulties to make the model solution more easily receivable in England and France. But before then, it is important to consider first the main point of divergence between the model solution and the alternative states of affairs. Specifically, what distinguishes the model solution and makes it more desirable in terms of efficiency?

8.4.2 *The divergence*

The main point of divergence between the model solution and the other alternative solutions is how the title is completed. The model solution requires completion by registration and ensures that the cost of registration is low. This, in turn, enables the transfer to be cheaply registered by the originator and easily verifiable by the originator's future creditors and assignees. It also ensures that the transfer to the SPV is good against any subsequent transfers of the same receivables. The French *bordereau*, for its part, is completed by the delivery of the transfer document to the SPV. No publicity is required, making it difficult for the future creditors and assignees of the originator to verify title. The

275 Michael Bridge, 'Secured Credit Legislation: Functional or Transactional Co-Existence' in Spyridon V Bazinas and N Orkun Akseli (eds), *International and Comparative Secured Transactions Law: Essays in honour of Roderick A Macdonald* (Hart 2020) 1, 16.

276 See respectively footnote 43 above and chapter 7 at section 7.2.2.1.

277 For discussion see section 8.4.3.

same limitation applies to the English equitable assignment, where assignment is completed by mere agreement between the originator and the SPV.[278]

8.4.3 *Applicability in English law*

Under the model solution, registration serves two purposes: it is a constitutive requirement and a priority point. In other words, an assignment under the model solution is ineffective (even as between the assignor and the assignee) until it is registered. In English law, assignments can be either equitable or legal.[279] An equitable assignment can be constituted by a simple agreement, without notification. This is based on the principle that equity "looks on as done that which ought to be done".[280] So, if B agrees to assign an existing claim to L for value, L will acquire an equitable interest in the claim immediately upon the agreement being concluded.

On the other hand, notification is a constitutive requirement for a legal assignment.[281] The proprietary effect of an equitable assignment is substantially the same as that of a legal assignment, provided that the assignor does not subsequently assign the same receivable to a second assignee who notifies first.[282] This is because notice is a priority point – the second assignee would get priority if they notified first and had no notice of the first equitable assignment.[283] Hence, notice is optional: it is only required for priority purposes and is not constitutive.

Therefore, the constitutive function of registration under the model solution conflicts with a principle of equity. Making registration a constitutive requirement would mean disregarding that principle of equity. This will be considered radical and difficult to achieve, given the importance of equity in the English property law. Hence, it is necessary to refine the registration system to make it compatible with English law. This can be done by making registration a priority requirement and not a constitutive requirement. This will preserve the effectiveness of the equitable assignment, so that a mere agreement to assign a receivable will remain effective as between the assignor and the assignee, and against unsecured creditors of the assignor. Registration would be voluntary but would have the advantage of improving the priority position of the registered assignee against competing equitable assignments and subsequent legal assignments.

---

278 Although the Scottish trust requires intimation to the beneficiary for it to be effective, this cannot be said to be true of publicity, since the beneficiary in this case (i.e. the SPV) is not a third party.

279 A legal assignment is, properly speaking, a statutory assignment which complies with requirements under s 136(1) of the Law of Property Act 1925.

280 See e.g. *Tebb v Hodge* (1869) LR 5 CP 73 (Ex Ch); *Tailby v Official Receiver* (1888) 13 App Cas 523 (HL).

281 For discussion of other requirements for constituting a statutory assignment, see section 6.2.3.2.

282 Goode and van Zwieten, *Corporate Insolvency Law* (n 127) para 2.55.

283 *Dearle v Hall* (1828) 3 Russ 1 (Ch).

A similar voluntary registration scheme was originally considered in the discussion paper on Secured Transactions Reform published in 2012 by the City of London Law Society's Financial Law Committee (CLLS).[284] The discussion paper considered the establishment of a register of outright transfers of receivables.[285] But the Draft Secured Transactions Code that was subsequently issued in 2016 seemed to have replaced the proposal for a new register with a proposal to include the relevant registration in the company charges registration scheme.[286]

The 2016 Draft Code provided for the registration of assignments of "receivables financing agreements" for priority purposes.[287] A receivables financing agreement was defined as "an agreement by which one person (the receivables financier) agrees to purchase receivables owing to a UK business (the customer) and the purpose, or one of the purposes, of the arrangement is to provide finance to the customer".[288] It appears that the Committee has now abandoned the receivables transfer registration proposal, as the latest Draft Code that was issued in 2020 does not make any provision to that effect.[289] The reason for this is unclear.[290]

The Secured Transactions Law Reform Project (STLRP) proposes a similar registration scheme for outright assignments.[291] The proposed scheme would only apply to assignments of receivables that have a financing purpose.[292] However, unlike the CLLS proposal, where registration was required only for priority purposes, the STLRP recommends that registration be a priority point and a "perfection" requirement.[293]

The STLRP also considered whether to adopt a "combined system", where either notification or registration would determine priority. The STLRP rejects the "combined system" option on the basis that it would make information in the register unreliable. And third parties would have to consult both the register and the debtor, which "would defeat

284 City of London Law Society, *Discussion Paper: Secured Transactions Reform* (n 257) paras 7.25f.
285 ibid para 7.26.
286 City of London Law Society, 'Draft Secured Transactions Code' (n 52) ss 26.2 and 26.4.
287 ibid ss 35.4 and 38.5.
288 The Code provided that a receivables financing agreement "includes securitisation, factoring and invoice discounting agreements" – at s 35.1.
289 See City of London Law Society, 'The Secured Transactions Code' (n 52).
290 It seems that the responses received on the 2016 Draft Code did not support the proposal, as the Committee noted in the Cover Note to the 2020 Draft Code that "[b]ased on the discussions we have had with a wide-cross section of interested people, we believe that this latest draft of the Code has a broad consensus of support". The Cover Note, which was previously available on the Society's website, is unfortunately no longer accessible online as of the time of this book's publication.
291 STLRP, 'Discussion Paper Series: Sale of Receivables' (n 101). The policy of third-party protection seems to be the main policy behind the STLRP's proposed scheme. See pages 5–6 of the discussion paper; see also para 3.D.iii, where the STLRP indicates the "purpose of the register".
292 ibid. The priority point of other forms of assignments will continue to be determined by the order of notification and subject to the rule in *Dearle v Hall* (1828) 3 Russ 1 (Ch).
293 The perfection requirement means that registration is required for the assignment to be effective in the assignor's insolvency. See STLRP, 'Discussion Paper Series: Sale of Receivables' (n 101) ss 3 and 4.

the purpose of the register".[294] Hence, registration would be the only priority point for assignments of receivables financing structures. The STLRP also recommends a new register of secured transactions for the registration scheme, which would be wholly electronic based.[295] It notes that such a system makes registration "easy, quick and cheap".[296]

The foregoing discussion of the registration schemes proposed by the CLLS and the STLRP further indicates that the refined model solution (i.e. making the registration voluntary and a priority point) would be workable in the English legal system.

It may be argued that making registration voluntary instead of constitutive would defeat its purpose since securitisers may still prefer to use the equitable assignment, given that it does not require registration costs. But it is expected that the benefit of registration would outweigh its costs, such that registration would be attractive to financiers. Unlike the equitable assignment, the registered assignment would confer absolute title to the SPV, which would be enforceable against all third parties, including the assignor's liquidator and administrator. This protection would increase the investor's chances of getting paid and, in turn, reduce the overall funding cost. Moreover, the registration cost would be modest (i.e. a fee range of £10 to £60, which would be a flat-rate fee and would apply to the transfer document as a whole).[297] The cost of establishing the registration scheme may be reduced by including the registration scheme in the existing company charges registration system as initially proposed by the Law Commission and the CLLS.

8.4.4 *Applicability in French law*

France has special legislation that governs securitisations.[298] This was introduced in 1988 to address the difficulties posed by French law in enabling the transactions.[299] One such difficulty was the rigid nature of completing an assignment under the former article 1690 of the French Civil Code.[300] Article 1690 required notice for the validity of assignments and required an enforcement officer to deliver the notice. The securitisation law introduced a simpler transfer mechanism, which only required for its completion the delivery of a transfer slip that listed the receivables to be assigned.[301] This was a radical approach, given

294 ibid para 3.D.iii. See discussion at section 8.2.3.2.

295 Secured Transactions Law Reform Project, 'Discussion Paper Series: Registration' (2017) ss 3.A and 7.B.v <https://stlrp.files.wordpress.com/2017/01/gullifer-registration.pdf> accessed 28 May 2024.

296 ibid s 3.B.

297 For example, the fee for filing a security right online at the Companies House is £15, see <https://www.gov.uk/guidance/registering-a-charge-mortgage-for-a-company> accessed 28 May 2024.

298 The law is currently set out under arts L214-166-1 to L214-190 of the MFC.

299 For discussion see section 7.1.1.

300 A recently modified provision is now contained in arts 1321 to 1326 of the FCC, which was implemented pursuant to Order No 2021-1192 of 15 September 2021.

301 This provision is now contained in arts L214-166-1 to L214-190 of the MFC.

the rigid nature of the French assignment law under article 1690. But since the reform only applied to securitisation transactions rather than the general assignment law, concerns about the integration of the new transfer mechanism into the French legal system was conceivably minimal. The same would be true for the introduction of the registration scheme under the model solution. Moreover, the registration system is not alien to French law. A similar registration scheme applies to moveable securities, such as the general non-possessory pledge,[302] and the special pledges over business, registered vehicles and intellectual property rights.[303]

Also, given that equity is not recognised in French law, the model solution would not require any refining, as it would for English law. In other words, registration would be required for constitutive and priority purposes. This is particularly important as securitisers will not be incentivised to register if the scheme is voluntary, since the existing system of completing by delivery is cheap and grants absolute title.

302 The FCC, arts 2337, 2338 and 2355.

303 See chapter 7 at section 7.2.2.1.

9 CONCLUSION

This book has established a number of important points about the preferred solutions in Scotland, England and France for transferring money claims and related security rights in securitisation, and the extent to which the solutions are efficient. It has confirmed that the preferred solutions under current law are the Scottish trust, the English equitable assignment and the French *bordereau*. In doing so, the book explains why these solutions are thus preferred in their respective jurisdictions.

The book has shown that a move from the status quo (i.e. the Scottish assignation) to either of the Scottish trust, the English equitable assignment or the French *bordereau* does not achieve a Pareto improvement outcome. It does, however, demonstrate that the French *bordereau* achieves the best outcome for the securitisation parties and considers the French *bordereau* to be the closest to achieving a Kaldor-Hicks efficient outcome.

The book has also shown that a move to the registration solution is the closest to a Pareto improvement. And it is on this basis that the book has considered the registration solution to be the most efficient solution among the other alternative solutions. Yet the book demonstrates that the registration solution is not Pareto optimal. It proposes a model solution that achieves a Pareto optimal outcome, or at the very least a significant Kaldor-Hicks outcome.

In achieving its optimal outcome, the model solution builds on the strength of the registration solution and borrows some of the superior aspects of the French *bordereau*.

The following is a brief outline of the features of the model solution:

i. it would guarantee the protection of the debtors by (a) allowing debtors to continue to pay to the person last known to them to be the holder of the claim, and (b) applying the *assignatus utitur jure auctoris* rule;
ii. it would protect third parties by having a low-cost registration system and making registration compulsory for transfer purposes;
iii. it would facilitate the transfer of future receivables both during and after the solvency of the originator;
iv. it would grant absolute title to the assignee (i.e. the SPV) upon registration; and
v. it would apply the *accessorium* principle to all security rights.

Furthermore, this book has shown that the model solution could be applied relatively straightforwardly and trouble-free in Scotland and France. It has also shown that the solution could be used in England, but would need some refinements for it to be received in a manner that coheres acceptably with wider law. The constitutive function of registration under the model solution conflicts with the principle of English equity, which "looks on as done that which ought to be done". Making registration a constitutive requirement would mean disregarding that principle. This may be considered radical and difficult to achieve, given the importance of equity in the English legal system. The book has, however, proposed the nature and extent of the refinement required.

BIBLIOGRAPHY

Legislation

England and Wales[1]

Air Navigation Order 2016 (SI 2016/765)
Business Contract Terms (Assignment of Receivables) Regulations 2018 (SI 2018/1254)
Companies Act 1985
Companies Act 2006
Consumer Credit Act 1974
Co-operative and Community Benefit Societies Act 2014
European Economic Interest Grouping Regulations 1989 (SI 1989/638)
Finance Act 2020
Financial Collateral Arrangements (No 2) Regulations 2003 (SI 2003/3226)
Financial Services (Banking Reform) Act 2013 (Commencement (No 8) and Consequential Provisions) Order 2015 (SI 2015/428)
Hire Purchase Act 1964
Insolvency Act 1986
International Interests in Aircraft Equipment (Cape Town Convention) Regulations 2015 (SI 2015/912)
Land Registration Act 2002
Law Commissions Act 1965
Law of Property Act 1925
Limited Partnerships Act 1907
Merchant Shipping Act 1995
Merchant Shipping (Registration of Ships) Regulations 1993 (SI 1993/3138)
Mortgaging of Aircraft Order 1972 (SI 1972/1268)
Patents Act 1977
Registered Designs Act 1949
Sale of Goods Act 1893
Securitisation Regulations 2024 (SI 2024/102)
Supreme Court of Judicature Act 1873
Trade Marks Act 1994

1 This legislation applies to constitute parts of the UK (other than Scotland) or to the UK as a whole.

France

Banking Act 1984
Civil Code
Commercial Code
Intellectual Property Code
Law No. 88-2001 dated 23 December 1988, implemented by Decree No. 89-158 of 9 March 1989
Loi Dailly (Law No 81-1 of 2 January 1981)
Monetary and Financial Code

Scotland[2]

Agricultural Credits (Scotland) Act 1929
Bankruptcy and Diligence etc. (Scotland) Act 2007
Conveyancing and Feudal Reform (Scotland) Act 1970
Housing (Scotland) Act 2006
Land Registration etc. (Scotland) Act 2012
Leases Act 1449
Limited Liability Partnerships (Scotland) Regulations 2001 (SSI 2001/128)
Moveable Transactions (Scotland) Act 2023
Registers of Scotland (Fees) Amendment Order 2021 (SSI 2021/139)
Registers of Scotland (Voluntary Registration, Amendment of Fees, etc.) Order 2015 (SSI 2015/265)
Registration of Leases (Scotland) Act 1857
Requirements of Writing (Scotland) Act 1995
Scotland Act 1998
Succession (Scotland) Act 1964
Transmission of Moveable Property (Scotland) Act 1862
Trusts (Scotland) Act 1961

2 This legislation applies to Scotland, whether passed by the pre-union Parliament of Scotland, the present Scottish Parliament or by the UK Parliament.

European Union

Council Directive 2000/12/EC of 20 March 2000 relating to the taking up and pursuit of the business of credit institutions [2000] OJ L126/1

Council Directive 2003/71/EC of 4 November 2003 on the prospectus to be published when securities are offered to the public or admitted to trading and amending Directive 2001/34/EC [2003] OJ L345/64

Council Directive 2011/61/EU of 8 June 2011 on Alternative Investment Fund Managers and amending Directives 2003/41/EC and 2009/65/EC and Regulations (EC) No 1060/2009 and (EU) No 1095/2010 [2011] OJ L174/1

Council Directive 2013/36/EU of 26 June 2013 on access to the activity of credit institutions and the prudential supervision of credit institutions and investment firms [2013] OJ L176/338

Council Regulation (EC) 575/2013 on prudential requirements for credit institutions and investment firms and amending Regulation (EU) No 648/2012 [2013] OJ L176/1

Council Regulation (EU) 2015/760 of 29 April 2015 on European long-term investment funds [2015] OJ L123/98

Council Regulation (EU) 2017/2401 of 12 December 2017 amending Regulation (EU) No 575/2013 on prudential requirements for credit institutions and investment firms [2017] OJ L347/1

Council Regulation (EU) 2017/2402 of 12 December 2017 laying down a general framework for securitisation and creating a specific framework for simple, transparent and standardised securitisation, and amending Directives 2009/65/EC, 2009/138/EC and 2011/61/EU and Regulations (EC) No 1060/2009 and (EU) No 648/2012 [2017] OJ L347/35

Council Regulation (EU) 2021/557 of 31 March 2021 amending Regulation (EU) 2017/2402 laying down a general framework for securitisation and creating a specific framework for simple, transparent and standardised securitisation to help the recovery from the COVID-19 crisis [2021] OJ L116/1

Council Regulation (EU) 575/2013 of 26 June 2013 on prudential requirements for credit institutions and investment firms and amending Regulation (EU) No 648/2012 (Text with EEA relevance) [2013] OJ L176/1

International

UNCITRAL Guide on the Implementation of a Security Rights Registry (2013)

Other Jurisdictions

Housing and Urban Development Act 1968
Justice (NI) Act 2002
National Housing Act 1934
Servicemen's Readjustment Act 1944
Uniform Commercial Code of the USA

Cases

England and Wales

Akers v Samba Financial Group [2017] UKSC 6, [2017] AC 424
Aluminium Industrie Vaassen BV v Romalpa Aluminium Ltd [1976] 1 WLR 676 (CA)
Barbados Trust Co Ltd v Bank of Zambia & Anor [2007] EWCA Civ 148, [2007] 2 WLUK 645
Bexhill UK Ltd v Abdul Razzaq [2012] EWCA Civ 1376, [2012] 10 WLUK 745
Bibby Factors Northwest Ltd v HFD Ltd [2015] EWCA Civ 1908, [2016] 1 Lloyd's Rep
Business Computers Ltd v Anglo-African Leasing Ltd [1977] 1 WLR 578 (Ch)
Central Insurance Co Ltd v Seacalf Shipping Corp (The Aiolos) [1983] 2 Lloyd's Rep 25 (CA)
Charnesh Kapoor v National Westminster Bank Plc [2011] EWCA Civ 1083, [2012] 1 All ER 1201
Compaq Computer Ltd v Abercorn Group Ltd [1991] BCC 484 (Ch)
Dearle v Hall (1828) 3 Russ 1 (Ch)
Denney v Conklin [1913] 3 KB 177 (KB)
Don King (Productions) Inc v Warren [2000] Ch 291 (CA)
Durham Brothers v Robertson [1898] 1 QB 765 (CA)
First Abu Dhabi Bank PJSC v BP Oil International Limited [2018] EWCA Civ 14, [2018] 1 WLUK 203
Fitzroy v Cave [1905] 2 KB 364 (CA)
Gorringe v Irwell India Rubber and Gutta Percha Works (1886) 34 Ch D 128 (CA)
Harmer v Armstrong [1934] Ch 65 (CA)
Hayim v Citibank NA [1987] AC 730 (PC)
Hendy Lennox (Industrial Engines) Ltd v Grahame Puttick Ltd [1984] 1 WLR 485 (QB)

Hockley and Papworth v Goldstein (1920) 90 LJKB 111
Holt v Heatherfield Trust Limited & Anor [1942] 2 KB 1 (KB)
Independent Trustee Services Ltd v GP Noble Trustees Ltd [2012] EWCA Civ 195, [2012] 3 WLR 597
Jones v Gibbons (1804) 9 Ves Jr 407 (Ch)
Knight v Knight (1840) 3 Beav 148 (Ch)
Linden Gardens Trust Ltd v Lenesta Sludge Disposals Ltd [1994] 1 AC 85 (HL)
Lyle (BS) v Rosher [1959] 1 WLR 8 (HL)
Lysaght v Edwards (1876) 2 Ch D 499 (Ch)
MBNA Europe Bank Limited v The Commissioners of HM Revenue and Customs [2006] EWHC 2326 (Ch)
Milroy v Lord (1862) 45 ER 1185 (QB)
Morley v Morley (1858) 53 ER 633 (Ch)
Nokes v Doncaster Amalgamated Collieries Ltd [1940] AC 1014 (HL)
Paul v Constance [1977] 1 WLR 527 (CA)
Re Ashpurton Estates Ltd [1983] Ch 110 (CA)
Re Bowden [1936] Ch 71 (Ch)
Re Cosslett (Contractors) Ltd [1998] Ch 495 (CA)
Re French's Wine Bar Ltd (1987) 3 BCC 173 (Ch)
Re Spectrum Plus Ltd [2005] UKHL 41, [2005] 2 AC 680
Tailby v Official Receiver (1888) 13 App Cas 523 (HL)
Tebb v Hodge (1869) LR 5 CP 73 (Ex Ch)
Tolhurst v Associated Portland Cement Manufacturers Ltd [1902] 2 KB 660 (CA)
Vandepitte v Preferred Accident Insurance Corp of New York [1933] AC 70 (PC)
Van Lynn Developments Ltd v Pelias Construction Co Ltd [1969] 1 QB 607 (CA)
Walsh v Lonsdale (1882) 9 Ch D 9 (CA)
Watson v Duff, Morgan & Vermont (Holdings) Ltd [1974] 1 WLR 450 (Ch)
William Brandt's Sons & Co v Dunlop Rubber Company, Limited [1905] AC 454 (HL)
Wright v Atkyns (1823) Turn & R 143 (Ch)

France

Cour de Cassation, 15 March 1988, JCP G 1989, II 21348
Cour de Cassation, 5 July 1994, RTD com 1995, 172
Cour de Cassation, 3 January 1996, JCP G 1996, II 22682
Cour de Cassation, 13 February 1996, Banque 1996, No 569, 91
Cour de Cassation, 19 December 2006, *N° de pourvoi* 05-16.395

Scotland

Allan's Trustees v Inland Revenue Commissioners 1971 SLT (HL) 62
Archivent Sales & Development Ltd v Strathclyde Regional Council 1985 SLT (CSOH) 154
Armour v Thyssen Edelstahlwerke AG 1990 SLT (HL) 891
Ballachulish Slate Quarries Co v Bruce (1908) 16 SLT (CSIH) 48
Bank of Scotland Cashflow Finance v Heritage International Transport Ltd 2003 SLT (Sh Ct) 107
Bedwells and Yates v Tod 2 December 1819 FC (CS) 50
Brownlee v Robb 1907 SC (IH) 1302
Buchanan v Alba Diagnostics Ltd 2004 SC (HL) 9
Burnett's Tr v Grainger [2004] UKHL 8, 2004 SC 19
Cameron's Trustees v Cameron (1907) 14 SLT (CSIH) 720
Carter v McIntosh (1862) 24 D (CSIH) 925
Christie Owen and Davies Plc v Campbell [2009] CSIH 26, 2009 SC 436
Clark v West Calder Oil Co (1882) 9 R (CSIH) 1017
Clark Taylor & Co Ltd v Quality Site Development (Edinburgh) Ltd 1981 SC (IH) 111
Edinburgh Entertainments Ltd v Stevenson 1926 SC (IH) 363
Edinburgh Schools Partnership Ltd v Galliford Try Construction (UK) Ltd [2017] CSOH 133, [2017] 10 WLUK 545
Enviroco Ltd v Farstad Supply A/S [2011] UKSC 16, [2011] 1 WLR 921
Gallemos Ltd (In Receivership) v Barratt Falkirk Ltd 1989 SC (IH) 239
Gibson v Hunter Home Designs Limited 1976 SC (CSIH) 23
Guidi v Promontoria (Chestnut) Ltd 2021 SLT (Sh Ct) 441
Guidi v Promontoria (Chestnut) Ltd [2023] CSIH 4, 2023 SCLR 417
Hamilton v Western Bank (1856) 19 D (CSIH) 152
Heritable Reversionary Co v Millar (1892) 19 R (HL) 43
Johnstone-Beattie v Dalziel (1868) 6 M (CSIH) 333
Joint Administrators of Rangers Football Club Plc, Noters [2012] CSOH 55, 2012 SLT 599
Libertas-Kommerz GmbH v Johnson 1977 SC (OH) 191
MacMillan v T Leith Developments Ltd (In Receivership and Liquidation) [2017] CSIH 23, 2017 SC 642
North Western Bank Limited v John Poynter Son & Macdonalds (1894) 22 R (HL) 1
OneSavings Bank Plc v Burns 2017 SLT (Sh Ct) 129
Promontoria (Ram) Ltd v Moore [2017] CSOH 88, 2018 SCLR 299
Scottish Widows Fund v Buist (1877) 4 R (CSOH) 1076
Shear v Clipper Holding II SARL (26 May 2017) (CSOH) [unreported]
Tay Valley Joinery Ltd v CF Financial Services Ltd 1987 SLT (CSIH) 207
UK Acorn Finance Ltd v Smith 2014 Hous LR (Sh Ct) 50

Watson v Bogue (No 1) 2000 SLT (Sh Ct) 125

Books

Anderson, R.G., *Assignation* (Edinburgh Legal Education Trust, 2008).
Armour, J., and others, *Principles of Financial Regulation* (1st ed., Oxford University Press, 2016).
Bankton, A.M., *An Institute of the Law of Scotland in Civil Rights* (1751–53) [reprinted 1993–95].
Beale, H.G., and others, *The Law of Security and Title-Based Financing* (3rd ed., Oxford University Press, 2018).
Beccaria, C., *On Crimes and Punishments* (Henry Paolucci translation, Bobbs Merrill, 1963).
Bell, G.J., *Principles of the Law of Scotland* (10th ed., T&T Clark, 1899).
Benjamin, J., *Interests in Securities: A Proprietary Law Analysis of the International Securities Markets* (Oxford University Press, 2000).
Bentham, J., *An Introduction to the Principles of Morals and Legislation* (John Bowring ed., W. Tait, 1843).
Blackstone, W., *Commentaries on the Laws of England* (1st ed., Clarendon Press, 1766).
Buchanan, B.G., *Securitization and the Global Economy: History and Prospects for the Future* (Palgrave Macmillan, 2017).
Calabresi, G., *The Costs of Accidents: A Legal and Economic Analysis* (Yale University Press, 1970).
Cannon, J. and Crowcroft, R. (eds.), *The Oxford Companion to British History* (2nd ed., Oxford University Press, 2015).
Cashin-Ritaine, E., *Contractual Assignments of Claims for Sums of Money in Franco-German Civil and Commercial Relations* (LGDJ, 2001).
Cranston, R., and others, *Principles of Banking Law* (3rd ed., Oxford University Press, 2017).
Dalrymple, J., *Institutions of the Law of Scotland* (D.M. Walker ed, Edinburgh University Press, 1981).
Davidson, A., and others, *Securitization: Structuring and Investment Analysis* (Wiley, 2003).
Deacon, J., *Global Securitisation and CDOs* (Wiley, 2004).
Deku, S.Y. and Kara, A., *Securitization: Past, Present and Future* (Palgrave Macmillan, 2017).
Erskine, J., *An Institute of the Law of Scotland* (Edinburgh Legal Education Trust, 1773).
Fabozzi, F.J. and Kothari, V., *Introduction to Securitization* (John Wiley & Sons, 2008).

Furst, S., and others, *Keating on Construction Contracts* (11th ed., Sweet & Maxwell, 2016).
Gloag, W. and Irvine, J., *Law of Rights in Security, Heritable and Moveable: Including Cautionary Obligations* (W. Green, 1897).
Gloag, W.M. and Henderson, R.C., *The Law of Scotland* (H.L. MacQueen and Lord Eassie (eds.), 14th ed., W. Green, 2017).
Goodman, L.S., *Subprime Mortgage Credit Derivatives* (John Wiley & Sons, 2011).
Gordon, W.M. and Wortley, S., *Scottish Land Law*, vol. 2 (3rd ed., W. Green, 2020).
Gretton, G.L. and Reid, K.G.C., *Conveyancing* (5th ed., W. Green, 2018).
Gretton, G.L. and Steven, A.J.M., *Property, Trusts and Succession* (4th ed., Bloomsbury Professional Scotland, 2020).
Gullifer, L. (ed.), *Goode and Gullifer on Legal Problems of Credit and Security* (7th ed., Sweet & Maxwell, 2022).
Gullifer, L. and Payne, J., *Corporate Finance Law: Principles and Policy* (3rd ed., Hart, 2020).
Halliday, J.M., *The Conveyancing and Feudal Reform (Scotland) Act 1970* (W. Green, 1970).
Halliday, J.M., *Conveyancing Law and Practice in Scotland*, vol. II (Iain J.S. Talman (ed.), 2nd ed., W. Green, 1997).
Hardman, J., *A Practical Guide to Granting Corporate Security in Scotland* (W. Green, 2018).
Hudson, A., *The Law of Finance* (2nd ed., Sweet & Maxwell, 2013).
Hyland, R., *Gifts: A Study in Comparative Law* (Oxford University Press, 2009).
Keay, A.R., *McPherson & Keay's Law of Company Liquidation* (5th ed., Sweet & Maxwell, 2021).
Lawson, F.H. and Rudden, B., *The Law of Property* (3rd ed., Oxford University Press, 2002).
Liew, Y.K. (ed.), *Guest on the Law of Assignment* (4th ed., Sweet & Maxwell, 2021).
Macgregor, L., and others, *Commercial Law in Scotland* (6th ed., W. Green, 2020).
MacPherson, A.D.J., *The Floating Charge* (Edinburgh Legal Education Trust, 2020).
McBryde, W.W., *The Law of Contract in Scotland* (3rd ed., Thomson/W. Green, 2007).
McKendrick, E. (ed.), *Goode and McKendrick on Commercial Law* (6th ed., Penguin Books, 2020).
McKenzie Skene, D.W., *Insolvency Law in Scotland* (2nd ed., Tottel, 2007).
Örücü, E., *The Enigma of Comparative Law* (Springer, 2004).
Paisley, R.R.M., *Land Law* (W. Green/Sweet & Maxwell, 2000).
Pareto, V., *Manual of Political Economy* (Ann S. Schwier and Alfred N. Page (eds.), AM Kelley Publishers, 1971).
Peel, E. and Treitel, G.H., *The Law of Contract* (14th ed., Sweet & Maxwell/Thomson Reuters, 2015).
Pettit, P.H., *Equity and the Law of Trusts* (12th ed., Oxford University Press, 2012).

Pigou, A.C., *The Economics of Welfare* (4th ed., Macmillan, 1932).
Posner, R.A., *Economic Analysis of Law* (7th ed., Aspen Publishers, 2007).
Reid, K.G.C., *The Law of Property in Scotland* (Butterworths, 1996).
Schäfer, H.-B. and Ott, C., *The Economic Analysis of Civil Law* (Edward Elgar, 2004).
Siems, M., *Comparative Law* (2nd ed., Cambridge University Press, 2018).
Smith, A., *An Inquiry into the Nature and Causes of the Wealth of Nations* (W. Strahan and T. Cadell, 1776).
Sparkes, P., *European Land Law* (Hart, 2007).
Steiner, E., *French Law: A Comparative Approach*, vol. 1 (2nd ed., Oxford University Press, 2018).
Steven, A.J.M., *Pledge and Lien* (Edinburgh Legal Education Trust, 2008).
Stewart, J.G., *A Treatise on the Law of Diligence* (W. Green, 1898).
Sweeney, A., *The Landlord's Hypothec* (Edinburgh Legal Education Trust, 2021).
Tolhurst, G., *The Assignment of Contractual Rights* (2nd ed., Hart, 2016).
Totty, P., Moss, G. and Segal, N., *Insolvency* (Sweet & Maxwell, 2021).
Tucker, L., Le Poidevin, N. and Brightwell, J., *Lewin on Trusts*, vol. 2 (20th ed., Sweet & Maxwell, 2020).
Virgo, G., *The Principles of Equity & Trusts* (5th ed., Oxford University Press, 2023).
Vries Robbé, J.J. de, *Securitization Law and Practice: In the Face of the Credit Crunch* (Kluwer Law International, 2008).
Wallison, P.J., *Bad History, Worse Policy: How a False Narrative about the Financial Crisis Led to the Dodd-Frank Act* (AIE, 2013).
Watson, A., *Legal Transplants: An Approach to Comparative Law* (2nd ed., University of Georgia Press, 1993).
Wilson, W.A., Duncan, A.G.M. and Elliott, W.A., *Trusts, Trustees and Executors* (2nd ed., W. Green, 1995).
Wood, P., *Title Finance, Derivatives, Securitisations, Set-off and Netting* (Sweet & Maxwell, 1995).
Wood, P., *Law and Practice of International Finance* (University Edition, Sweet & Maxwell, 2008).
Worthington, S., *Equity* (2nd ed., Oxford University Press, 2006).
Zweigert, K. and Kötz, H., *Introduction to Comparative Law* (3rd ed., Oxford University Press, 1998).
Zwieten, K. van (ed.), *Goode on Principles of Corporate Insolvency Law* (5th ed., Sweet & Maxwell/Thomson Reuters, 2018).

Chapters from Edited Books

Anderson, R.G., 'Assignations of All Sums Securities', in: Frankie McCarthy, James Chalmers and Stephen Bogle (eds.), *Essays in Conveyancing and Property Law in Honour of Professor Robert Rennie* (Open Book Publishers, 2015).

Bridge, M., 'Secured Credit Legislation: Functional or Transactional Co-Existence', in: Spyridon V. Bazinas and N. Orkun Akseli (eds.), *International and Comparative Secured Transactions Law: Essays in honour of Roderick A Macdonald* (Hart, 2020).

Drobnig, U., 'Basic Issues of European Rules on Security in Movables', in: John De Lacy (ed.), *The Reform of UK Personal Property Security Law: Comparative Perspectives* (Routledge Cavendish, 2010).

Gdanski, M., 'Taking Security in France', in: M.G. Bridge and Robert H. Stevens (eds.), *Cross-border Security and Insolvency* (Oxford University Press, 2001).

Gordon, W., 'Roman Law in Scotland', in: R. Evans-Jones, *The Civil Law Tradition in Scotland* [The Stair Society, supplementary series, vol. 2] (Stair Society, 1995).

Gordon, W., 'Scotland and France. The Legal Connection', in: *Roman Law, Scots Law and Legal History: Selected Essays* (Edinburgh University Press, 2007).

Gordon, W., 'Scotland as a Mixed Jurisdiction', in: *Roman Law, Scots Law and Legal History: Selected Essays* (Edinburgh University Press, 2007).

Graziadei, M., 'The Functionalist Heritage', in: Pierre Legrand and Roderick Munday (eds.), *Comparative Legal Studies: Traditions and Transitions* (1st ed., Cambridge University Press, 2003).

Gretton, G.L., 'The Concept of Security', in: D.J. Cuisine (ed.), *A Scots Conveyancing Miscellany: Essays in Honour of Professor J. M. Halliday* (W. Green, 1987).

Gretton, G.L., 'Trust and Patrimony', in: H.L. MacQueen (ed.), *Scots Law into the 21st Century: Essays in Honour of W. A. Wilson* (W. Green, 1996).

Hyland, R., 'Comparative Law' in: Dennis Patterson (ed.), *A Companion to Philosophy of Law and Legal Theory* (1st ed., Blackwell, 1996).

Kendall, L.T., 'Securitization: A New Era in American Finance', in: Michael J. Fishman and Leon T. Kendall (eds.), *A Primer on Securitization* (The MIT Press, 1996).

Leavy, J., 'France', in: Harry C. Sigman and Eva-Maria Kieninger (eds.), *Cross-border Security over Receivables* (Sellier European Law Publishers, 2009).

MacLeod, J., 'Non-Judicial Real Security', in: Iain MacNeil (ed.), *Scots Commercial Law* (Avizandum Publishing Ltd, 2014).

MacQueen, H., 'Scots Law', in: J.M. Smits (ed.), *Elgar Encyclopedia of Comparative Law* (2nd ed., Edward Elgar, 2012).

McFarlane, B., 'Assignment and Novation', in: H.G. Beale (ed.), *Chitty on Contracts* (35th ed., Sweet & Maxwell, 2023).

Major, W.T., 'The Assignment of Things in Action', in: *Basic English Law. Macmillan Professional Master* (Palgrave Macmillan, 1990).

Michaels, R., 'The Functional Method of Comparative Law', in: Mathias Reimann and Reinhard Zimmermann (eds.), *The Oxford Handbook of Comparative Law* (2nd ed., Oxford University Press, 2019).

Rabel, E., 'Some Major Problems of Applied Comparative Law, Especially in the Conflict of Law (Summary)', in: Association of American Law Schools (ed.), *Summarized Proceedings of the Institute in the Teaching of International and Comparative Law* ([Publisher not identified] New York 1948).

Reid, K.G.C., 'Patrimony Not Equity: The Trust in Scotland', in: Remus Valsan (ed.), *Trusts and Patrimonies* (Edinburgh University Press, 2017).

Reid, K.G.C., 'Unintimated Assignations' [1989] Scots Law Times (News) 267.

Riffard, J.-F., 'The Still Uncompleted Evolution of the French Law on Secured Transactions Towards Modernity', in: L. Gullifer and N. Orkun Akseli (eds.), *Secured Transactions Law Reform: Principles, Policies and Practice* (Hart, 2016).

Schwarcz, S., 'Securitization and Structured Finance', in: *Encyclopedia of Financial Globalization* (Elsevier, 2011).

Sim, A., 'Rights in Security over Moveables', in: *Stair Memorial Encyclopaedia* (1992).

Smith, D.B., 'Roman Law', in: *An Introductory Survey of the Sources and Literature of Scots Law*, vol. 1 (Stair Society, 1936).

Smith, L., 'Security', in: Andrew Burrows (ed.), *English Private Law* (Oxford University Press, 2013).

Smith, T., 'The Influence of the "Auld Alliance" with France on the Law of Scotland', in: *Studies Critical and Comparative* (Green, 1962).

Steven, A.J.M., 'Reform of Security over Moveables: Still a Longstanding Reform Agenda in: Scots Law', in: D. Bain, and others (eds.), *Northern Lights: Essays in Private Law in Memory of Professor David Carey Miller* (Aberdeen University Press 2018).

Swadling, W., 'Property: General Principles', in: Andrew Burrows (ed.), *English Private Law* (3rd ed., Oxford University Press, 2013).

Whitman, J.Q., 'The Neo-Romantic Turn', in: Pierre Legrand and R.J.C. Munday (eds.), *Comparative Legal Studies: Traditions and Transitions* (Cambridge University Press, 2003).

Whittaker, S., 'Contract Law and Other Legal Categories', in: H.G. Beale (ed.), *Chitty on Contracts* (35th ed., Sweet & Maxwell, 2023).

Journal Articles

Anderson, R.G., 'Buchanan v Alba Diagnostics: Accretion of Title and Assignation of Future Patents' (2005) 9, Edinburgh Law Review, 457.

Anderson, R.G., 'A Strange Notice' (2009) 13, Edinburgh Law Review, 484.

Anderson, R.G. and Biemans J.W.A., 'Reform of Assignation in Security: Lessons from the Netherlands' (2012) 16, Edinburgh Law Review, 24.

Bailey, S., 'Assignment of Debts in England from the Twelfth to the Twentieth Century' (1932) 48, Law Quarterly Review, 547.

Beau, E., and others, 'Bank Funding Costs: What Are They, What Determines Them and Why Do They Matter?' (2014), Bank of England Quarterly Bulletin, 370.

Benmelech, E., Dlugosz, J. and Ivashina, V., 'Securitization without Adverse Selection: The Case of CLOs' (2012) 106, Journal of Financial Economics, 91.

Bord, V.M. and Santos, J.A.C., 'The Rise of the Originate-to-Distribute Model and the Role of Banks in Financial Intermediation' (2012), F.R.B.N.Y. Economic Policy Review, 21.

Brand, O., 'Conceptual Comparisons: Towards a Coherent Methodology of Comparative Legal Studies' (2007) 32, Brooklyn Journal of International Law, 405.

Brunnermeier, M.K., 'Deciphering the Liquidity and Credit Crunch 2007–2008' (2009) 23, Journal of Economic Perspectives, 77.

Buchanan, B., 'Back to the Future: 900 Years of Securitization' (2014) 15, The Journal of Risk Finance, 316.

Burns, T., 'The Transfer of Future Rights in Securitisations: A Comparative Study of the Law in England and Scotland' (2009) 24, Journal of International Banking Law and Regulation, 35.

Burrows, A., 'We Do This at Common Law but That in Equity' (2002) 22, Oxford Journal of Legal Studies, 1.

Button, R., Pezzini, S. and Rossiter, N., 'Understanding the Price of New Lending to Households' (2010), Bank of England Quarterly Bulletin, 172.

Calabresi, G., 'Some Thoughts on Risk Distribution and the Law of Torts' (1961) 70, The Yale Law Journal, 499.

Calabresi, G., 'The Decision for Accidents: An Approach to Nonfault Allocation of Costs' (1965) 78, Harvard Law Review, 713.

Calabresi, G., 'An Exchange: About Law and Economics: A Letter to Ronald Dworkin' (1980) 8, Hofstra Law Review, 553.

Calabresi, G., 'The Pointlessness of Pareto: Carrying Coase Further' (1991) 100, The Yale Law Journal, 1211.

Calabresi, G. and Hirschoff J.T., 'Toward a Test for Strict Liability in Torts' (1972) 81, The Yale Law Journal, 1055.

Calomiris, C.W., 'The Subprime Turmoil: What's Old, What's New, and What's Next' (2009) 15, The Journal of Structured Finance, 6.

Carey Miller, D.L. and Combe, M.M., 'The Boundaries of Property Rights in Scots Law: Report to the XVIIth Congress of Comparative Law' (2006) 10, Electronic Journal of Comparative Law, 1.

Coase, R., 'The Problem of Social Cost' (1960) 3, The Journal of Law & Economics, 1.

Coase, R., 'The Nature of the Firm: Influence' (1988) 4, The Journal of Law, Economics and Organization, 33.

Coase, R., 'Law and Economics and A.W. Brian Simpson' (1996) 25, The Journal of Legal Studies, 103.

Cohn, M., 'Asset Securitization: How Remote Is Bankruptcy Remote?' (1998) 26, Hofstra Law Review, 929.

Coleman, J., 'The Normative Basis of the Economic Analysis of Law' (1982) 34, Stanford Law Review, 1105.

Coleman, J.L., 'Economics and the Law: A Critical Review of the Foundations of the Economic Approach to Law' (1984) 94, Ethics, 649.

David, R., 'A Civil Code for Ethiopia: Considerations on the Codification of the Civil Law in African Countries' (1962–1963) 37, Tulane Law Review, 187.

De Coninck, J., 'The Functional Method of Comparative Law: Quo Vadis?' (2010) 74, Rabels Zeitschrift, 318.

Dvorak, Y.A, 'Transplanting Asset Securitization: Is the Grass Green Enough on the Other Side?' (2001) 38, Houston Law Review, 541.

Edelman, J. and Elliot, S., 'Two Conceptions of Equitable Assignment' (2015) 131, Law Quarterly Review, 228.

Emedosi, C.J., 'The 2007/2008 Global Financial Crisis: A Further Reassessment of the Originate-to-Distribute Narrative' (2020) 35, Banking and Finance Law Review, 279

Goode, R.M., 'Contractual Prohibitions against Assignment' (2009) 3, Lloyd's Maritime and Commercial Law Quarterly, 300.

Gretton, G.L., 'Trusts Without Equity' (2000) 49, International and Comparative Law Quarterly, 599.

Gretton, G.L., 'Registration of Company Charges' (2002) 6, Edinburgh Law Review, 146.

Gretton, G.L., 'Ownership and its Objects' (2007) 71, Rabels Zeitschrift, 802.

Gretton, G.L., 'Assignation of All Sums Standard Securities' [1994] Scots Law Times (News), 207.

Gropp, R., and others, 'Banks Response to Higher Capital Requirements: Evidence from a Quasi-Natural Experiment' (2019) 32, The Review of Financial Studies, 266.

Hackney, J., 'Guido Calabresi and the Construction of Contemporary American Legal Theory' (2014) 77, Law and Contemporary Problems, 45.

Hardman, J., 'Some Legal Determinants of External Finance in Scotland: A Response to Lord Hodge' (2017) 21, Edinburgh Law Review, 30.

Hardman, J., 'Three Steps Forward, Two Steps Back: A View from Corporate Security Practice of the Moveable Transactions (Scotland) Bill' (2018) 22, Edinburgh Law Review, 266.

Hardman, J., 'Clarificatory Evolutionary Reform – The Importance of the Scottish Law Commission's Discussion Paper on Heritable Securities: Pre-Default' (2020) 2, Juridical Review, 96.

Hicks, J.R., 'The Foundations of Welfare Economics' (1939) 49, The Economic Journal, 696.

Hirsch, W.Z. and Osborne, E., 'Law and Economics – Valuable but Controversial' (1992) 17, Law & Social Inquiry, 521.

Husa, J., 'Farewell to Functionalism or Methodological Tolerance?' (2003) 67, Rabels Zeitschrift, 419.

Husa, J., 'Metamorphosis of Functionalism – or Back to Basics?' (2011) 18, Maastricht Journal of European and Comparative Law, 548.

Imbierowicz, B. and Rauch, C., 'The Relationship between Liquidity Risk and Credit Risk in Banks' (2014) 40, Journal of Banking & Finance, 242.

Jackson, T.H. and Kronman, A.T., 'Secured Financing and Priorities among Creditors' (1979) 88, The Yale Law Journal, 1143.

Kaldor, N., 'Welfare Propositions of Economics and Interpersonal Comparisons of Utility' (1939) 49, The Economic Journal, 549.

Keys, B.J., and others, 'Did Securitization Lead to Lax Screening? Evidence from Subprime Loans' (2010) 125, Quarterly Journal of Economics, 307.

Kraus, A. and Litzenberger, R.H., 'A State-Preference Model of Optimal Financial Leverage' (1973) 28, The Journal of Finance, 911.

Langfield, S. and Pagano, M., 'Bank Bias in Europe: Effects on Systemic Risk and Growth' (2016) 31, Economic Policy, 51.

Legrand, P., 'The Impossibility of "Legal Transplants"' (1997) 4, Maastricht Journal of European and Comparative Law, 111.

Lemmon, M., and others, 'Securitization and Capital Structure in Nonfinancial Firms: An Empirical Investigation: Securitization and Capital Structure in Nonfinancial Firms' (2014) 69, The Journal of Finance, 1787.

Lucas, W., 'The Assignation of Floating Charges' [1996] Scots Law Times (News), 203.

MacMahon, P., 'Rethinking Assignability' (2020) 79, The Cambridge Law Journal, 288.

MacPherson, A.D.J., 'The Future of Moveable Security in Scots Law? Comments on the Scottish Law Commission's Report on Moveable Transactions' (2018) 2, Juridical Review, 98.

MacPherson, A.D.J., 'Registration of Company Charges Revisited: New and Familiar Problems' (2019) 23, Edinburgh Law Review, 153.

MacPherson, A.D.J., 'The Circle Squared? Floating Charges and Diligence after *MacMillan v T Leith Developments Ltd*' (2018) 4, Juridical Review, 230.

Marciano, A., 'Guido Calabresi's Economic Analysis of Law, Coase and the Coase Theorem' (2012) 32, International Review of Law and Economics, 110.

Mayer, C., Pence K. and Sherlund, S.M., 'The Rise in Mortgage Defaults' (2009) 23, Journal of Economic Perspectives, 27.

McAlpine, A., 'Raising Finance over Claims to Payment and Reform to the Law of Outright Assignation' (2015) 3, Juridical Review, 275.

Mésonnier, J.-S. and Monks, A., 'Did the EBA Capital Exercise Cause a Credit Crunch in the Euro Area?' (2015) 11, International Journal of Central Banking, 75.

Modigliani, F. and Miller, M., 'The Cost of Capital, Corporation Finance and the Theory of Investment' (1958) 48, The American Economic Review, 261.

Modigliani, F. and Miller, M., 'Corporate Income Taxes and the Cost of Capital: A Correction' (1963) 53, The American Economic Review, 433.

Mousourakis, G., 'Legal Transplants and Legal Development: A Jurisprudential and Comparative Law Approach' (2013) 54, Acta Juridica Hungarica, 219.

Ogus, A., 'Competition Between National Legal Systems: A Contribution of Economic Analysis to Comparative Law' (1999) 48, International and Comparative Law Quarterly, 405.

Örücü, E., 'Law as Transposition' (2002) 51, International and Comparative Law Quarterly, 205.

Patrick, H. and Steven, A., 'Moveable transactions law reform coming in Scotland?' (2018) Butterworths Journal of International Banking and Financial Law, 71.

Penn, G. and Papadogiannis T., 'Regulating Securitisation in the Aftermath of the Global Financial Crisis: Lessons from Europe' (2021) 36, Journal of International Banking Law and Regulation, 225.

Posner, R.A., 'Book Review (Reviewing Guido Calabresi, The Cost of Accidents: A Legal and Economic Analysis (1970))' (1970) 37, University of Chicago Law Review, 636.

Posner, R.A., 'Some Uses and Abuses of Economics in Law' (1979) 46, The University of Chicago Law Review, 281.

Raines, M., 'Cutting Edge Close-up: Sumitomo's Aurora CLO' (1998) 17, International Financial Law Review, 6.

Raines, M., 'UK Regulation of Term Securitization Following a Hard Brexit' (2018) 13, Capital Markets Law Journal, 534.

Rudden, B., 'Things as Thing and Things as Wealth' (1994) 14 Oxford Journal of Legal Studies, 81.

Schwarcz S.L., 'The Alchemy of Asset Securitization' (1994) 1, Stanford Journal of Law, Business & Finance 133.

Scitovszky, T.D., 'A Note on Welfare Propositions in Economics' (1941) 9, The Review of Economic Studies, 77.

Scott, J.H., 'A Theory of Optimal Capital Structure' (1976) 7, The Bell Journal of Economics, 33.

Smith, T.B., 'English Influences on the Law of Scotland' (1954) 3, The American Journal of Comparative Law, 522.

Steven, A.J.M., 'Accessoriness and Security over Land' (2009) 13, Edinburgh Law Review, 387.

Teubner, G., 'Legal Irritants: Good Faith in British Law or How Unifying Law Ends Up in New Divergencies' (2003) 61, The Modern Law Review, 11.

Tolhurst, G.J. and Carter, J.W., 'Prohibitions on Assignment: A Choice to be Made' (2014) 73, The Cambridge Law Journal, 405.

Turner, P., 'Prohibitions on Assignment: Intellectualism v. Law' (2018) 134, Law Quarterly Review, 532.

Van den Bergh, R., 'Introduction: The Impact of Guido Calabresi on Law and Economics Scholarship' (2008) 1, Erasmus Law Review, 1.

Vinokurova, N., 'How Mortgage-Backed Securities Became Bonds: The Emergence, Evolution, and Acceptance of Mortgage-Backed Securities in the United States, 1960–1987' (2018) 19, Enterprise & Society, 610.

Walker, G., 'Credit Crisis-Regulatory and Financial Systems Reform' (2007) 22, Butterworths Journal of International Banking & Financial Law, 567.

Walker, G., 'Sub-Prime Loans, Inter-Bank Markets and Financial Support' (2008) 29, Company Lawyer, 22.

Walton, P., 'Assignments of Book Debts – Outright Transfers of Rights or Unregistered Securities?' (2018) 1, Wolverhampton Law Journal, 1.

Watson, A., 'Legal Transplants and European Private Law' (2000) 4, Electronic Journal of Comparative Law.

Willen, P., 'Mandated Risk Retention in Mortgage Securitization: An Economist's View' (2014) 104, American Economic Review, 82.

Wonnell, C., 'Efficiency and Conservatism' (2001) 80, Nebraska Law Review, 643.

Commission Reports and Related Publications

Law Commission, *Report on Companies Security Interests* (2005).

Scottish Law Commission, *Examination of the Companies (Floating Charges) (Scotland) Act 1961* (Memorandum No 10, 1969).

Scottish Law Commission, *Report on the Companies (Floating Charges) (Scotland) Act 1961* (No 14 (Cmnd 4336), 1970).

Scottish Law Commission, *Corporeal Moveables: Some Problems of Classification* (Consultative Memorandum No 26, 1976).

Scottish Law Commission, *Discussion Paper on the Nature and the Constitution of Trusts* (DP 133, 2006).

Scottish Law Commission, *Report on Sharp v Thomson* (Scot Law Com No 208, 2008).

Scottish Law Commission, *Discussion Paper on Moveable Transactions* (DP 151, 2011).

Scottish Law Commission, *Business and Regulatory Impact Assessment: Draft Moveable Transactions (Scotland) Bill 2017* (Scot Law Com No 249, 2017).

Scottish Law Commission, *Report on Moveable Transactions* (Scot Law Com No 249, 2017).

Scottish Law Commission, *Report on Moveable Transactions: Draft Bill* (Scot Law Com No 249, 2017).

Scottish Law Commission, 'Improving Access to Finance in Scotland: Report on Moveable Transactions' (News Release, 19 December 2017).

Scottish Law Commission, *Discussion Paper on Heritable Securities: Pre-Default* (DP 168, 2019).

Others

Association for Financial Markets in Europe, 'Securitisation Data Report – Q4 2009' (AFME, 2010).

Association for Financial Markets in Europe, 'The Economic Benefits of High Quality Securitisation to the EU Economy' (AFME, 2013).

Association for Financial Markets in Europe, 'Securitisation Data Report – Q4 2014' (AFME, 2015).

Association for Financial Markets in Europe, 'Securitisation Data Report – Q2 2019' (AFME, 2019).

Association for Financial Markets in Europe, 'Securitisation Data Report – Q4 2023 & 2023 Full Year' (AFME, 2024).

Bank of England and European Central Bank, 'The Case for a Better Functioning Securitisation Market in the European Union' (May 2014).

Bar, C. von, and others (eds.), *Principles, Definitions and Model Rules of European Private Law: Draft Common Frame of Reference (DCFR)* (Sellier, European Law Publishers, 2010).

Basel Committee on Banking Supervision, *International Convergence of Capital Measurement and Capital Standards: A Revised Framework* (Comprehensive version, Bank for International Settlements, 2006).

Basel Committee on Banking Supervision, *Basel III: A Global Regulatory Framework for More Resilient Banks and Banking Systems* (Bank for International Settlements, 2011).

Basel Committee on Banking Supervision, *Basel III: The Liquidity Coverage Ratio and Liquidity Risk Monitoring Tools* (Bank for International Settlements, 2013).

Basel Committee on Banking Supervision, *Basel III: The Net Stable Funding Ratio* (Bank for International Settlements, 2014).

Basel Committee on Banking Supervision, *Revisions to the Securitisation Framework: Amended to Include the Alternative Capital Treatment for "Simple, Transparent and Comparable" Securitisations* (Bank for International Settlements, 2016).

Basel Committee on Banking Supervision, *Finalising Post-Crisis Reforms* (Bank for International Settlements, 2017).

Basel Committee on Banking Supervision and Board of the International Organization of Securities Commissions, *Criteria for Identifying Simple, Transparent and Comparable Securitisations* (Consultative Paper, Bank for International Settlements, 2014).

Blanc-Jouvan, H., 'Direct Lending: A Matured Market?' (February 2018).

Board of Governors of the Federal Reserve System, 'An Introduction to Asset Securitisation' (The Federal Reserve Board, 1989).

Bremner, A., 'Moveable Transactions Summary of Evidence' (SPICe, 2020).

Brown, R. and Lee, N., 'Funding Issues Confronting High Growth SMEs in the UK' (ICAS, 2014).

Cardiff Auto Receivables Securitisation 2011-1 PLC (Prospectus, 7 February 2011).

Cars Alliance Auto Loans France V 2018-1 (Prospectus, 29 March 2018).

Cartwright, J., Fauvarque-Cosson, B. and Whittaker, S., *French Civil Code 2016* (Trans-Lex.org: Law Research).

Church & Dwight Co. Inc., '2011 Annual Report to the Securities and Exchange Commission' (SEC, 2012).

City of London Law Society, *Discussion Paper: Secured Transactions Reform* (2012).

City of London Law Society, 'Draft Secured Transactions Code' (2016).

City of London Law Society, 'The Secured Transactions Code' (2020).

Cœuré, B., 'SME Financing: A Euro Area Perspective' (www.ecb.europa.eu, 13 December 2012).

Elland RMBS 2018 Plc (Prospectus, 13 December 2018).

European Banking Authority, 'Recommendation on the Creation and Supervisory Oversight of Temporary Capital Buffers to Restore Market Confidence' (EBA BS No 173, 2011).

European Banking Authority, 'EBA Report on Qualifying Securitisation' (EBA, 2015).

European Banking Authority, 'Final Report on the Implementation of Capital Plans Following the EBA's 2011 Recommendation on the Creation of Temporary Capital Buffers to Restore Market Confidence' (EBA BS No 188, 2012).

European Central Bank, 'ECB Announces Measures to Support Bank Lending and Money Market Activity' (www.ecb.europa.eu, 8 December 2011).

European Central Bank and Bank of England, 'The Impaired EU Securitisation Market: Causes, Roadblocks and How to Deal with Them' (April 2014).

European Commission, 'Action Plan on Building a Capital Markets Union' COM (2015) 468 final.

European Savings and Retail Banking Group, 'Financial Systems in Europe and the United States: Structural Differences Where Banks Remain the Main Source of Finance for Companies' (ESBG, May 2016).

Financial Crisis Inquiry Commission, *Final Report of the National Commission on the Causes of the Financial and Economic Crisis in the United States* (2011).

Finsbury Square 2019-1 Plc 8 (Prospectus, 26 March 2019).

Ford Credit Auto Owner Trust 2016-C (Prospectus, 2016).

Gorton, G., 'Slapped by the Panic of 2007' (The Federal Reserve Bank of Kansas City, Jackson Hole Conference, 2008).

Greenspan, A., 'Federal Reserve Board's Semi-Annual Monetary Policy Report to the Congress' (The Federal Reserve Board, 2002).

Greenspan, A., 'Understanding Household Debt Obligations' (The Federal Reserve Board, 2004).

Hamilton, J., 'Business Finance and Security over Moveable Property' (Scottish Executive Central Research Unit, 2002).

Helbling, T., 'Externalities: Prices Do Not Capture All Costs' (www.imf.org, December 2018).

International Monetary Fund, 'Global Financial Stability Report: Navigating the Financial Challenges Ahead' (IMF, 2009).

Jackson, P., and others, 'Capital Requirement and Bank Behaviour: The Impact of the Basel Accord' (Bank for International Settlements, April 1999).

Jenkins, P., Atkins, R. and Spiegel, P., 'Europe's Banks Face 9% Capital Rule', *Financial Times* (London, 11 October 2011).

Levitin, A.J., Pavlov, A.D. and Wachter, S.M., 'Securitization: Cause or Remedy of the Financial Crisis?', (2009) Georgetown Law and Economics Research Paper Series, No. 1462895 <https://papers.ssrn.com/sol3/papers.cfm?abstract_id=1462895> accessed 06 May 2024.

MacInnes, M., Stephen, B. and Brading, P., 'Scotland: Securitisation Laws and Regulations 2020' (ICLG, 2020).

MacPherson, A., McKenzie Skene, D. and West, E., 'Moveable Transactions – Written Submissions' (University of Aberdeen, April 2020).

Moody's, 'Rating Action: Moody's Upgrades Ford and Ford Credit Long-Term Ratings to Baa2 from Baa3; Outlook Is Stable' (2016).

Organisation for Economic Co-operation and Development, *Mobilising Bond Markets for a Low-Carbon Transition* (OECD, 2017).

Pinto, E., 'Memorandum: Sizing Total Federal Government and Federal Agency Contributions to Subprime and Alt-A Loans in US First Mortgage Market as of 6.30.08' (Financial Crisis Inquiry Commission, November 2010).

Salomons, A.F., 'Deformalisation of Assignment Law and the Position of the Debtor in European Property Law' (2007) Centre for the Study of European Contract Law Working Paper Series No. 2007/01 <http://www.ssrn.com/abstract=968654> accessed 28 May 2024.

Salzberger, E.M., 'The Economic Analysis of Law – The Dominant Methodology for Legal Research?!' (2007) University of Haifa Faculty of Law Legal Studies Research Paper No. 1044382 <http://www.ssrn.com/abstract=1044382> accessed 28 May 2024.

Saltmarsh, M., 'Paris Financial Center Wins Respite from Creditors', The New York Times (8 March 2011).

Scottish Government, 'Protecting Scotland, Renewing Scotland' (September 2020).

Secured Transactions Law Reform Project, 'Discussion Paper Series: Sale of Receivables' (2017).

Standard & Poor's, 'General Criteria: Principles of Credit Ratings' (16 February 2011).

Turner, J.A., *The Turner Review: A Regulatory Response to the Global Banking Crisis* (FSA, March 2009).

Towd Point Mortgage Funding 2020 – AUBURN 14 PLC (Prospectus, February 2020).

US Department of Housing and Urban Development, 'The National Homeownership Strategy: Partners in the American Dream' (US Department of Housing and Urban Development, May 1995).

US Government Accountability Office, 'Fannie Mae and Freddie Mac: Analysis of Options for Revising the Housing Enterprises' Long-Term Structures' (GAO-09-782, 2009).

US Securities and Exchange, 'Enhancing Disclosure in the Mortgage-Backed Securities Markets' (www.sec.gov, January 2003).

Wilson, J., 'ECB Cuts Interest Rates to Historic Low', *Financial Times* (5 July 2012).